DYNAMITE®

Online at www.DYNAMITE.com
On Facebook /Dynamitecomics
On Instagram /Dynamitecomics
On Tumblr dynamitecomics.tumblr.com
On Twitter @dynamitecomics
On YouTube /Dynamitecomics

Nick Barrucci, CEO / Publisher
Juan Collado, President / COO

Joe Rybandt, Executive Editor
Matt Idelson, Senior Editor
Anthony Marques, Associate Editor
Kevin Ketner, Assistant Editor

Jason Ullmeyer, Art Director
Geoff Harkins, Senior Graphic Designer
Cathleen Heard, Graphic Designer
Alexis Persson, Graphic Designer

Chris Caniano, Digital Associate
Rachel Kilbury, Digital Multimedia Ass

Brandon Dante Primavera, V.P. of IT and O
Rich Young, Director of Business Develo

Alan Payne, V.P. of Sales and Marke
Pat O'Connell, Sales Manager

FOREWORD

So here we are at Volume Two of THE SECRET DIARY OF BETTIE PAGE. Colonel McKnight instructs me to tell you that I made all this stuff up. So sure. That's what I did. None of this happened.

But it should have.

Seriously though… Volume Two wasn't part of the original plan. The four issues in Volume One did well enough to justify extending the series, which was an honor and a delight. I chose to spend the rest of the run continuing what I did in the first volume: paying tribute to all my favorite 1950s culture, through the eyes of a kickass real-life icon. So inside this book you will find radioactive monsters and movie stars and supervillains and spies. And where to buy the best apple pie in Los Angeles.

I dedicated the first volume to my wife Augusta, aka Penny Starr, Jr.: burlesque dancer, filmmaker, costume designer (her "Space Commie" costumes come back in chapter 8), and like Bettie, entirely her own woman. Like so many, Bettie was one of the inspirations for how she looks and dresses and lives her life: with strength and style and sass. Without shame. So this one is dedicated to all the Bettie Page fans… all the strong, shameless, sassy, stylish sisters (and brothers) out there, kicking ass and taking names and doing it their own way.

Bettie would be proud of you. Hope you enjoy the book.

DAVID AVALLONE
HOLLYWOOD, CALIFORNIA

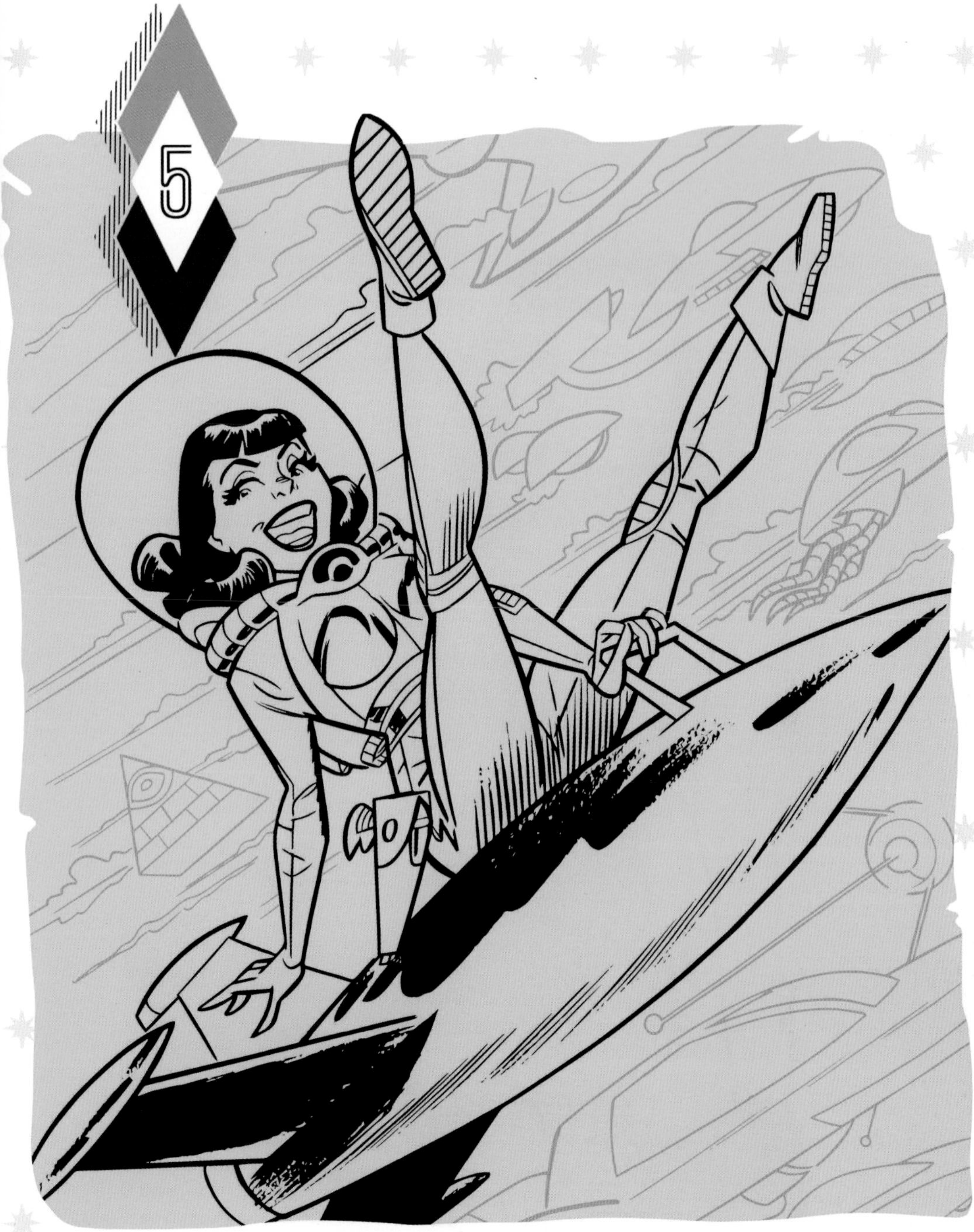
5

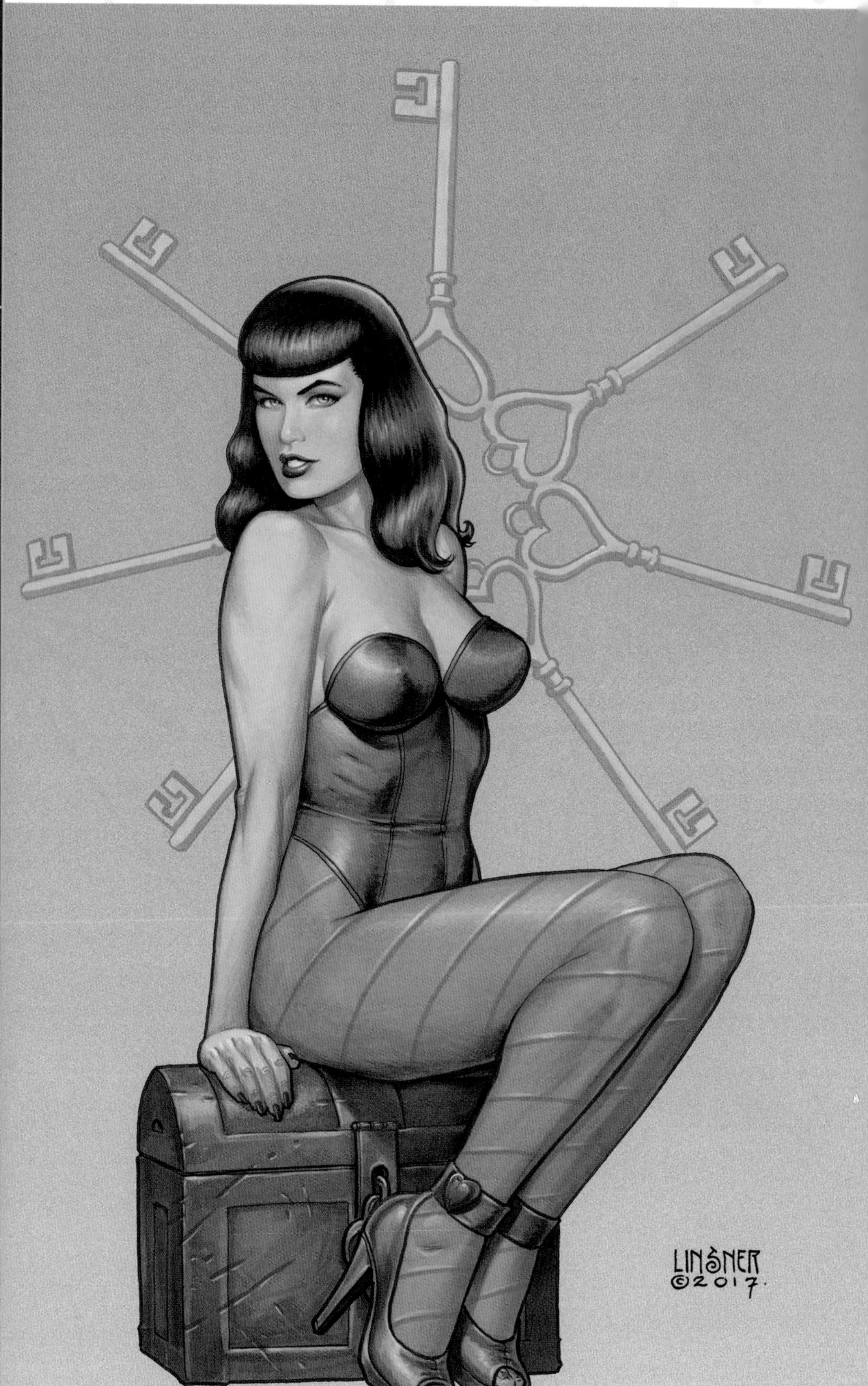
LINSNER
©2017.

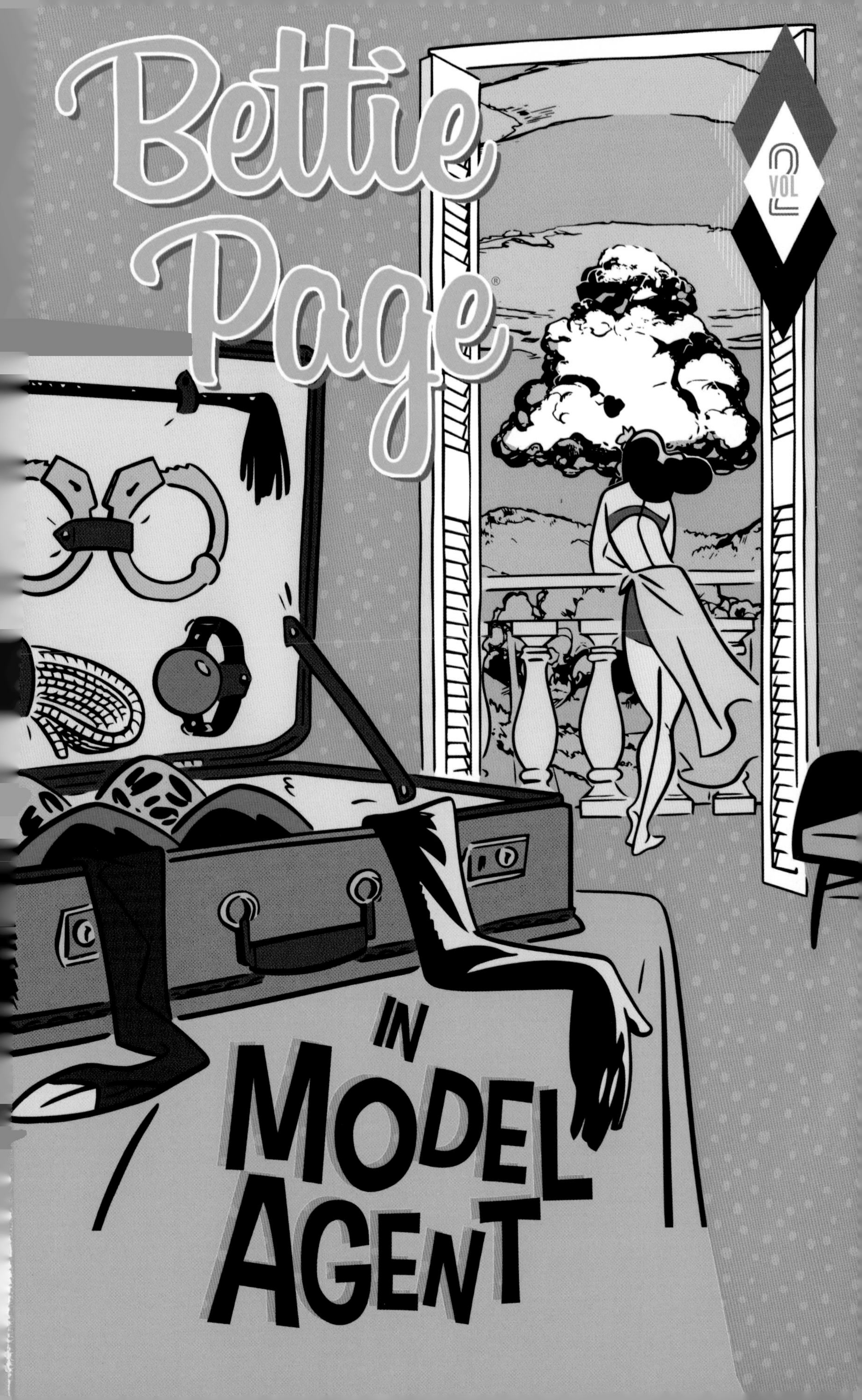
Bettie Page®
VOL 2
IN
MODEL AGENT

ORIGINALLY PUBLISHED IN
BETTIE PAGE #5-8

THE MODEL AGENT

STORY
DAVID AVALLONE

ART
ISSUE 5 BANE WADE
ISSUE 6-8 ESAU FIGUEROA & MATT GAUDIO

LETTERS
TAYLOR ESPOSITO

COLORS
ISSUE 5 MOHAN
ISSUES 6-8 BRITTANY PEZZILLO

EDITORS JOSEPH RYBANDT & ANTHONY MARQUES
COLLECTION DESIGN CATHLEEN HEARD

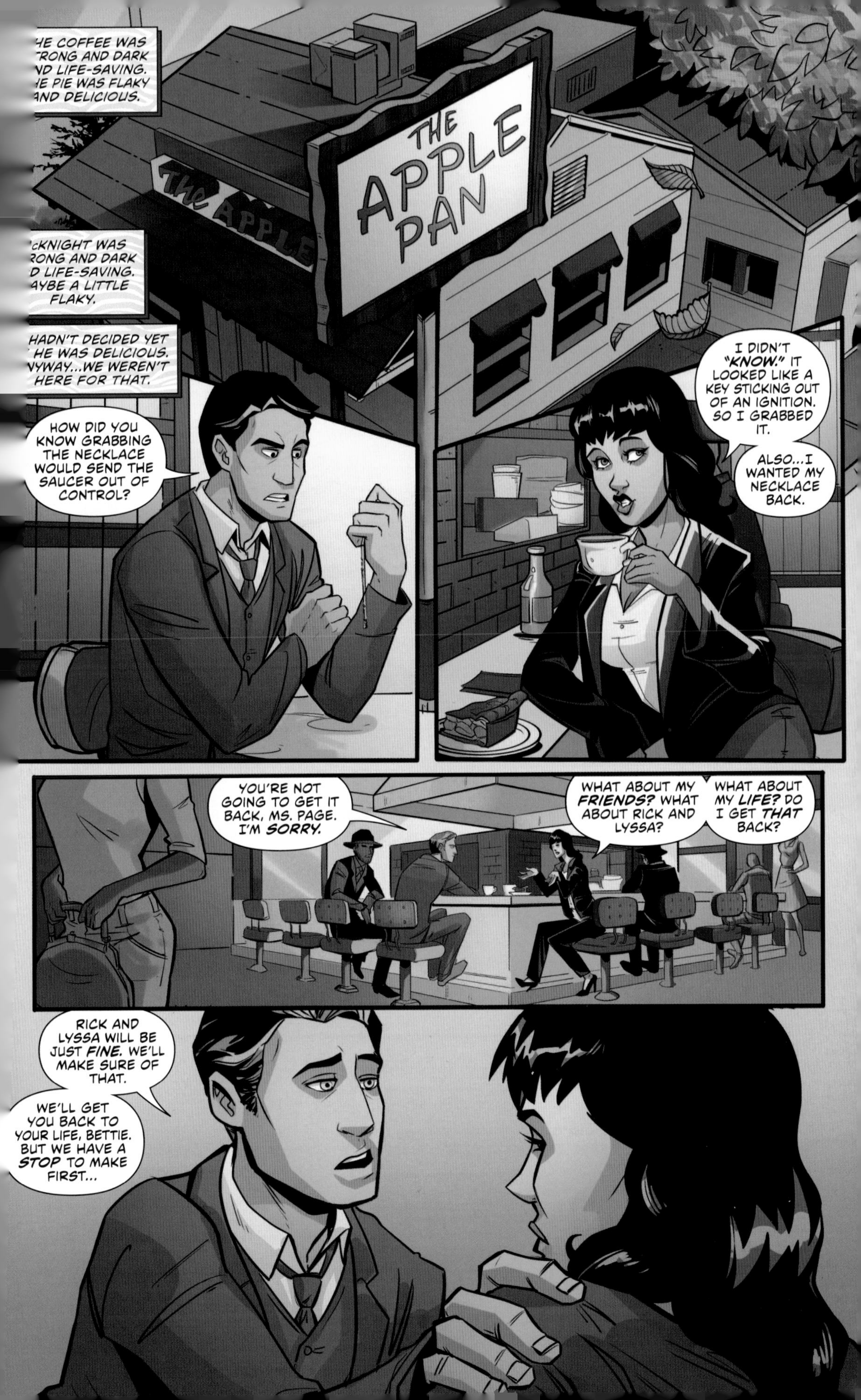
HE COFFEE WAS TRONG AND DARK ND LIFE-SAVING. HE PIE WAS FLAKY AND DELICIOUS.
THE APPLE PAN
THE APPLE
CKNIGHT WAS RONG AND DARK D LIFE-SAVING. AYBE A LITTLE FLAKY.
HADN'T DECIDED YET HE WAS DELICIOUS. NYWAY...WE WEREN'T HERE FOR THAT.
HOW DID YOU KNOW GRABBING THE NECKLACE WOULD SEND THE SAUCER OUT OF CONTROL?
I DIDN'T "KNOW." IT LOOKED LIKE A KEY STICKING OUT OF AN IGNITION. SO I GRABBED IT.
ALSO...I WANTED MY NECKLACE BACK.
YOU'RE NOT GOING TO GET IT BACK, MS. PAGE. I'M SORRY.
WHAT ABOUT MY FRIENDS? WHAT ABOUT RICK AND LYSSA?
WHAT ABOUT MY LIFE? DO I GET THAT BACK?
RICK AND LYSSA WILL BE JUST FINE. WE'LL MAKE SURE OF THAT.
WE'LL GET YOU BACK TO YOUR LIFE, BETTIE. BUT WE HAVE A STOP TO MAKE FIRST...

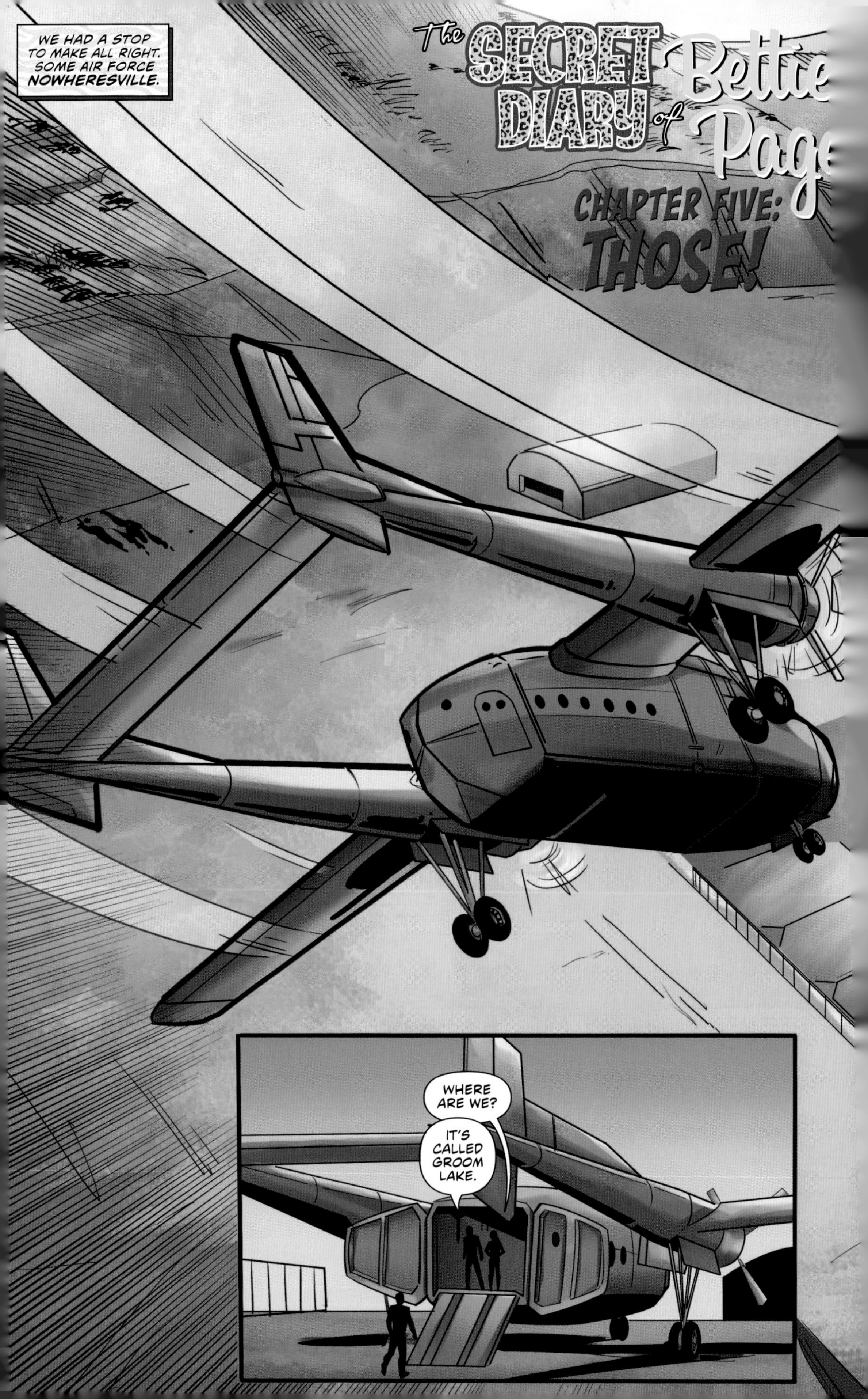
WE HAD A STOP TO MAKE ALL RIGHT. SOME AIR FORCE NOWHERESVILLE.
The SECRET DIARY of Bettie Pag
CHAPTER FIVE: THOSE!
WHERE ARE WE?
IT'S CALLED GROOM LAKE.

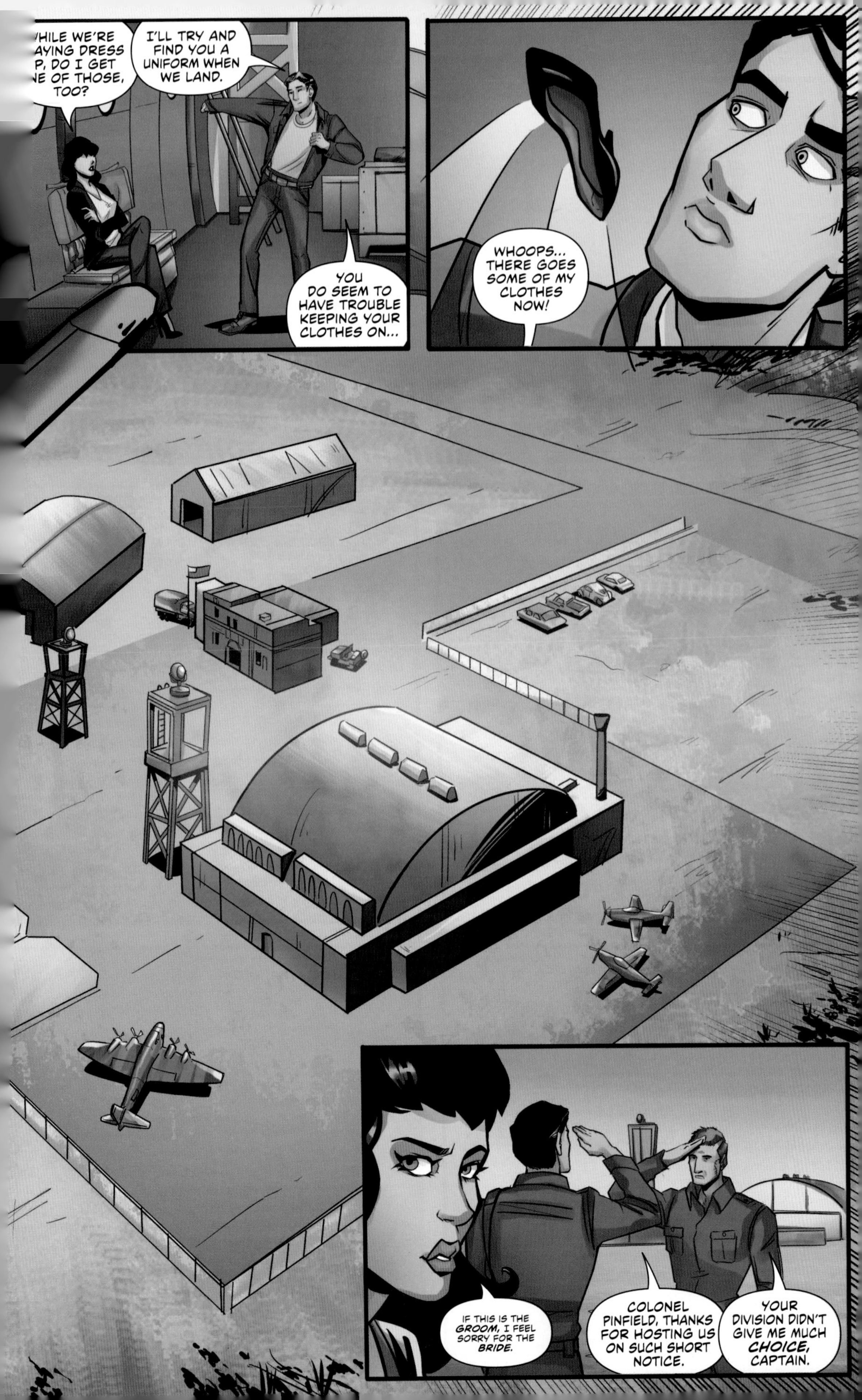
WHILE WE'RE PLAYING DRESS UP, DO I GET ONE OF THOSE, TOO?
I'LL TRY AND FIND YOU A UNIFORM WHEN WE LAND.
YOU DO SEEM TO HAVE TROUBLE KEEPING YOUR CLOTHES ON...
WHOOPS... THERE GOES SOME OF MY CLOTHES NOW!
IF THIS IS THE GROOM, I FEEL SORRY FOR THE BRIDE.
COLONEL PINFIELD, THANKS FOR HOSTING US ON SUCH SHORT NOTICE.
YOUR DIVISION DIDN'T GIVE ME MUCH CHOICE, CAPTAIN.

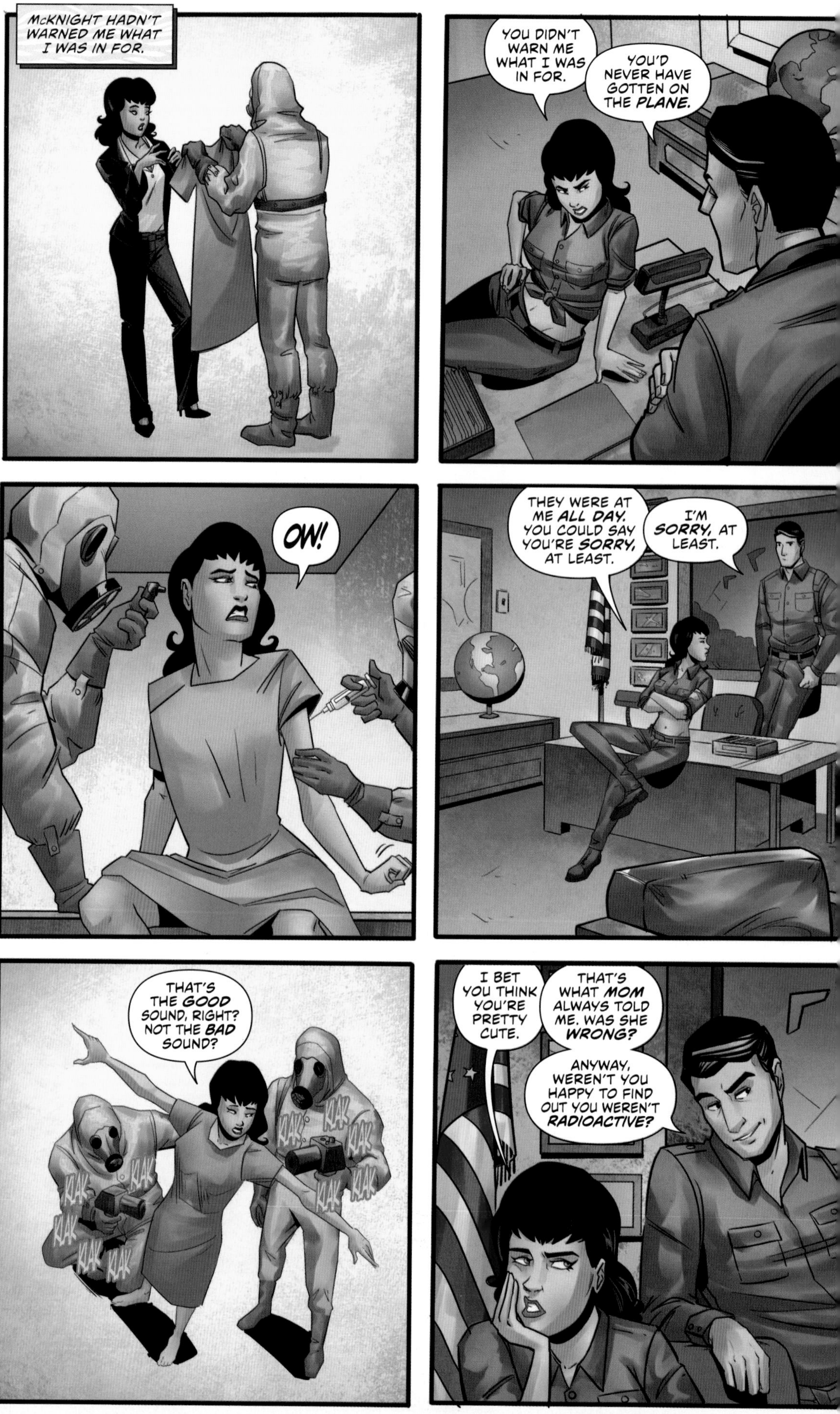
McKNIGHT HADN'T WARNED ME WHAT I WAS IN FOR.
YOU DIDN'T WARN ME WHAT I WAS IN FOR.
YOU'D NEVER HAVE GOTTEN ON THE PLANE.
OW!
THEY WERE AT ME ALL DAY. YOU COULD SAY YOU'RE SORRY, AT LEAST.
I'M SORRY, AT LEAST.
THAT'S THE GOOD SOUND, RIGHT? NOT THE BAD SOUND?
KLAK KLAK KLAK KLAK KLAK KLAK KLAK KLAK KLAK KLAK
I BET YOU THINK YOU'RE PRETTY CUTE.
THAT'S WHAT MOM ALWAYS TOLD ME. WAS SHE WRONG?
ANYWAY, WEREN'T YOU HAPPY TO FIND OUT YOU WEREN'T RADIOACTIVE?

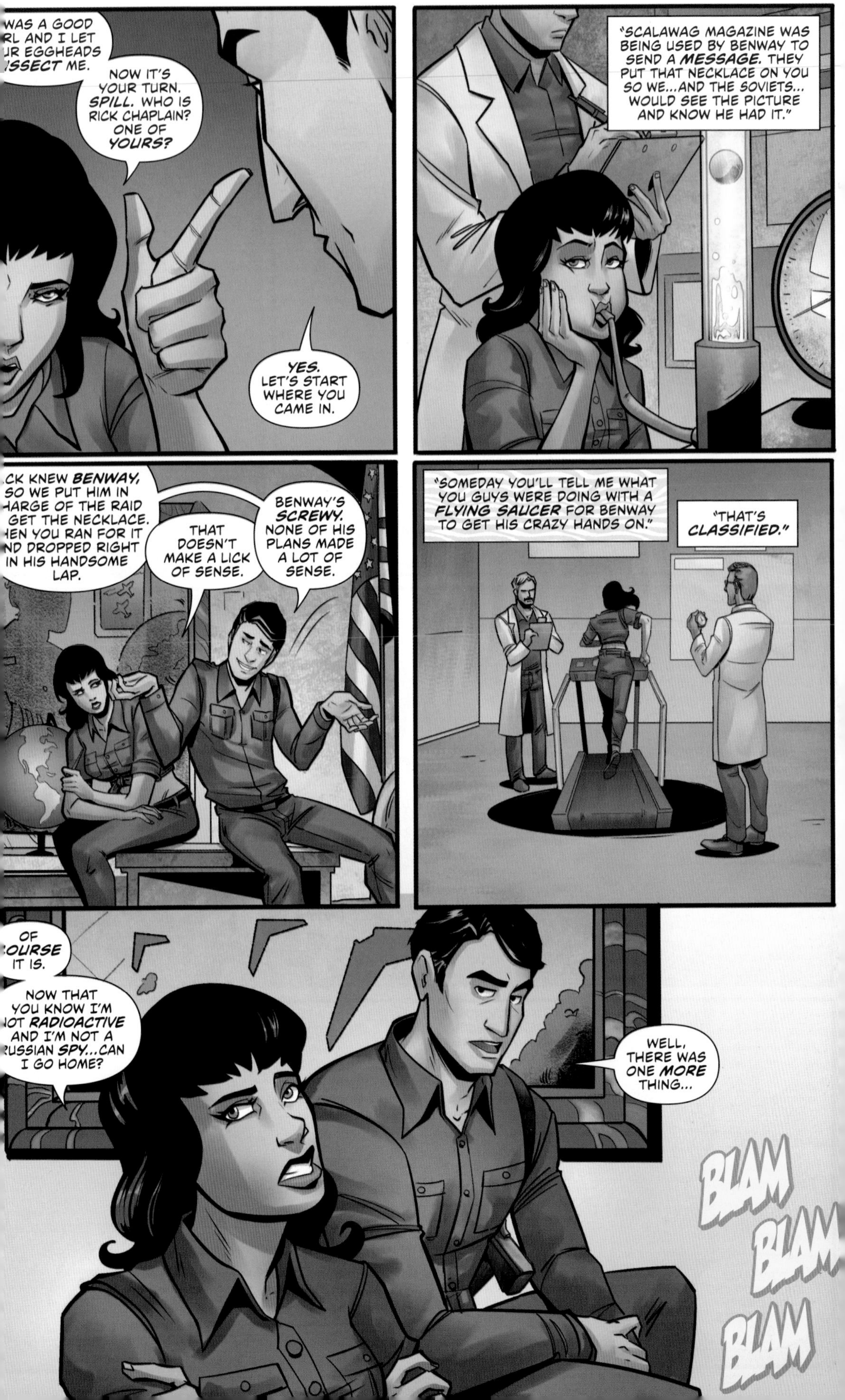

WAS A GOOD
RL AND I LET
UR EGGHEADS
ISSECT ME.
NOW IT'S YOUR TURN. SPILL. WHO IS RICK CHAPLAIN? ONE OF YOURS?
YES. LET'S START WHERE YOU CAME IN.
"SCALAWAG MAGAZINE WAS BEING USED BY BENWAY TO SEND A MESSAGE. THEY PUT THAT NECKLACE ON YOU SO WE...AND THE SOVIETS... WOULD SEE THE PICTURE AND KNOW HE HAD IT."
CK KNEW BENWAY, SO WE PUT HIM IN HARGE OF THE RAID GET THE NECKLACE. HEN YOU RAN FOR IT ND DROPPED RIGHT IN HIS HANDSOME LAP.
THAT DOESN'T MAKE A LICK OF SENSE.
BENWAY'S SCREWY. NONE OF HIS PLANS MADE A LOT OF SENSE.
"SOMEDAY YOU'LL TELL ME WHAT YOU GUYS WERE DOING WITH A FLYING SAUCER FOR BENWAY TO GET HIS CRAZY HANDS ON."
"THAT'S CLASSIFIED."
OF COURSE IT IS.
NOW THAT YOU KNOW I'M OT RADIOACTIVE AND I'M NOT A USSIAN SPY...CAN I GO HOME?
WELL, THERE WAS ONE MORE THING...
BLAM
BLAM
BLAM

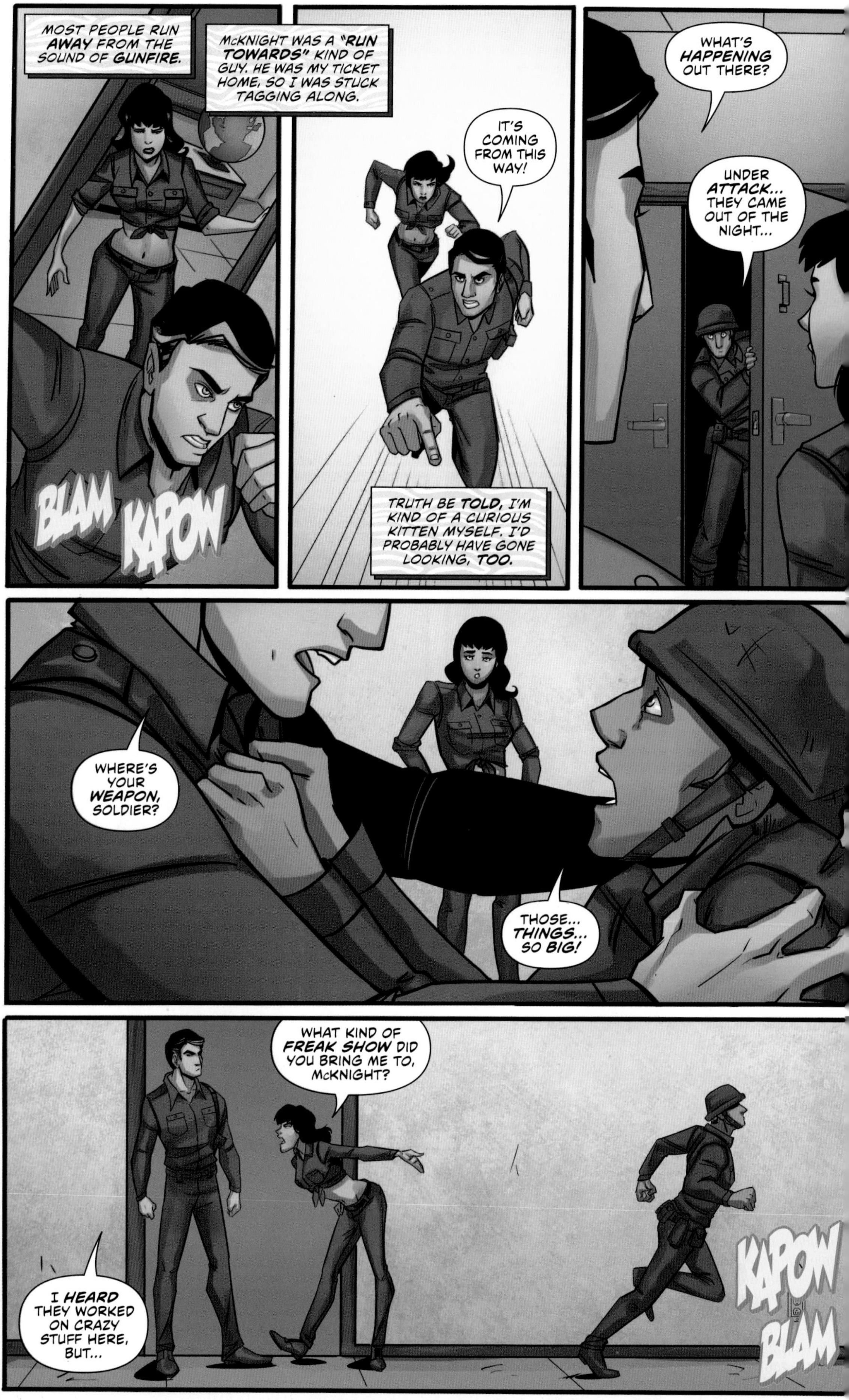
MOST PEOPLE RUN AWAY FROM THE SOUND OF GUNFIRE.
BLAM
KAPOW
McKNIGHT WAS A "RUN TOWARDS" KIND OF GUY. HE WAS MY TICKET HOME, SO I WAS STUCK TAGGING ALONG.
IT'S COMING FROM THIS WAY!
TRUTH BE TOLD, I'M KIND OF A CURIOUS KITTEN MYSELF. I'D PROBABLY HAVE GONE LOOKING, TOO.
WHAT'S HAPPENING OUT THERE?
UNDER ATTACK... THEY CAME OUT OF THE NIGHT...
WHERE'S YOUR WEAPON, SOLDIER?
THOSE... THINGS... SO BIG!
WHAT KIND OF FREAK SHOW DID YOU BRING ME TO, McKNIGHT?
I HEARD THEY WORKED ON CRAZY STUFF HERE, BUT...
KAPOW
BLAM

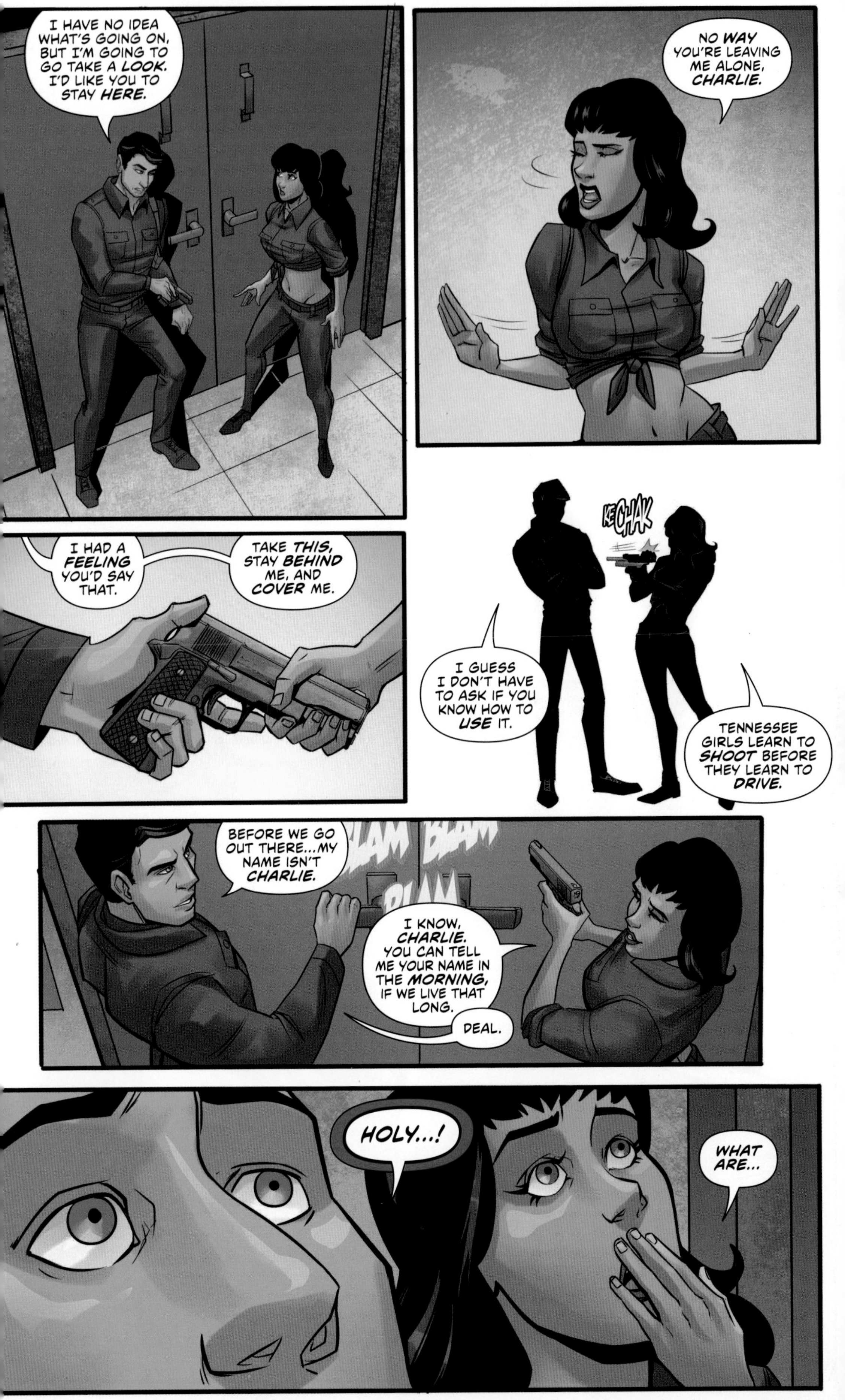

I HAVE NO IDEA WHAT'S GOING ON, BUT I'M GOING TO GO TAKE A *LOOK.* I'D LIKE YOU TO STAY *HERE.*
NO *WAY* YOU'RE LEAVING ME ALONE, *CHARLIE.*
I HAD A *FEELING* YOU'D SAY THAT.
TAKE *THIS,* STAY *BEHIND* ME, AND *COVER* ME.
KE-CHAK
I GUESS I DON'T HAVE TO ASK IF YOU KNOW HOW TO *USE* IT.
TENNESSEE GIRLS LEARN TO *SHOOT* BEFORE THEY LEARN TO *DRIVE.*
BLAM BLAM
BEFORE WE GO OUT THERE...MY NAME ISN'T *CHARLIE.*
I KNOW, *CHARLIE.* YOU CAN TELL ME YOUR NAME IN THE *MORNING,* IF WE LIVE THAT LONG.
DEAL.
HOLY...!
WHAT ARE...

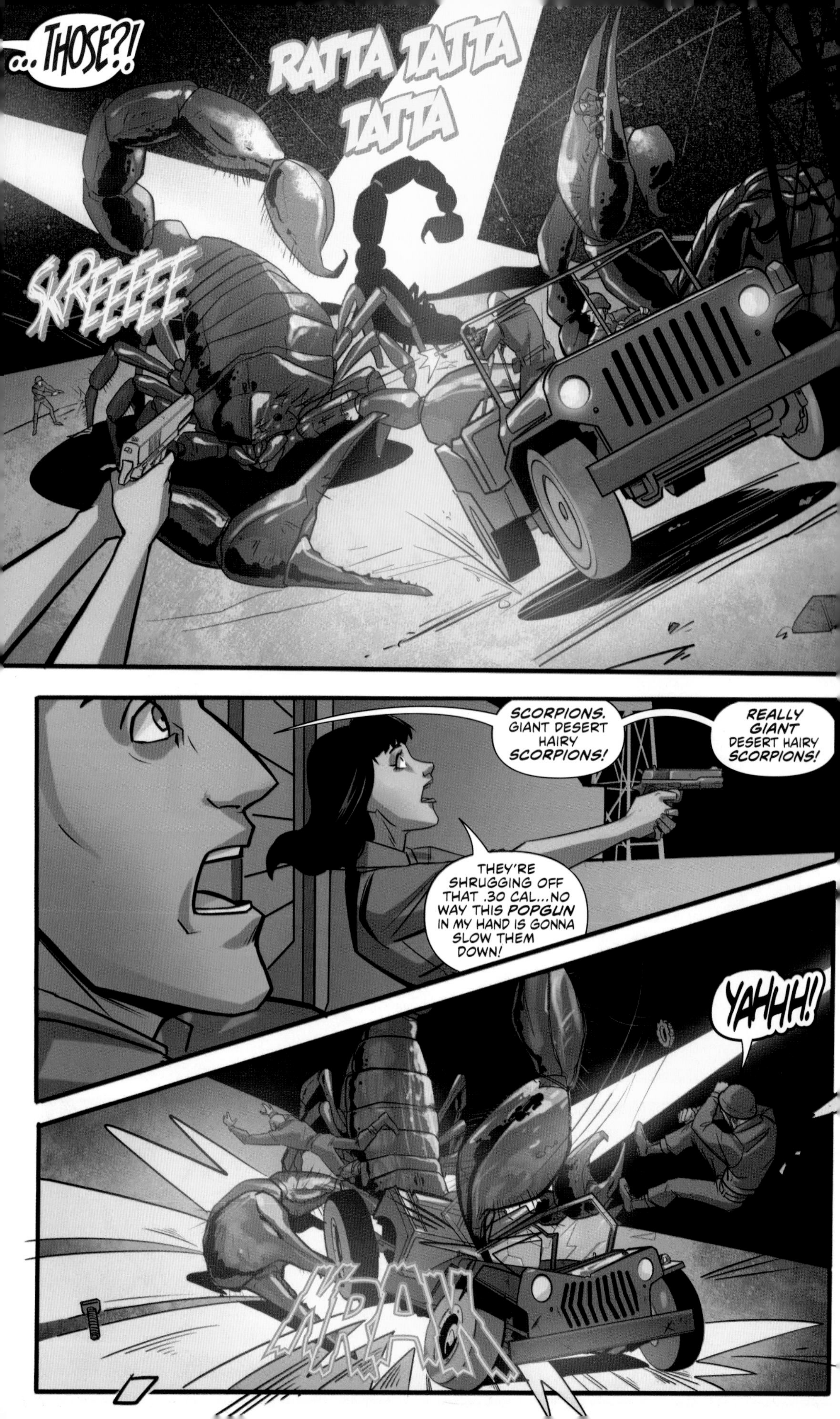
...THOSE?!
RATTA TATTA TATTA
SKREEEEEE
SCORPIONS. GIANT DESERT HAIRY SCORPIONS!
REALLY GIANT DESERT HAIRY SCORPIONS!
THEY'RE SHRUGGING OFF THAT .30 CAL...NO WAY THIS POPGUN IN MY HAND IS GONNA SLOW THEM DOWN!
YAHHH!
KRAK

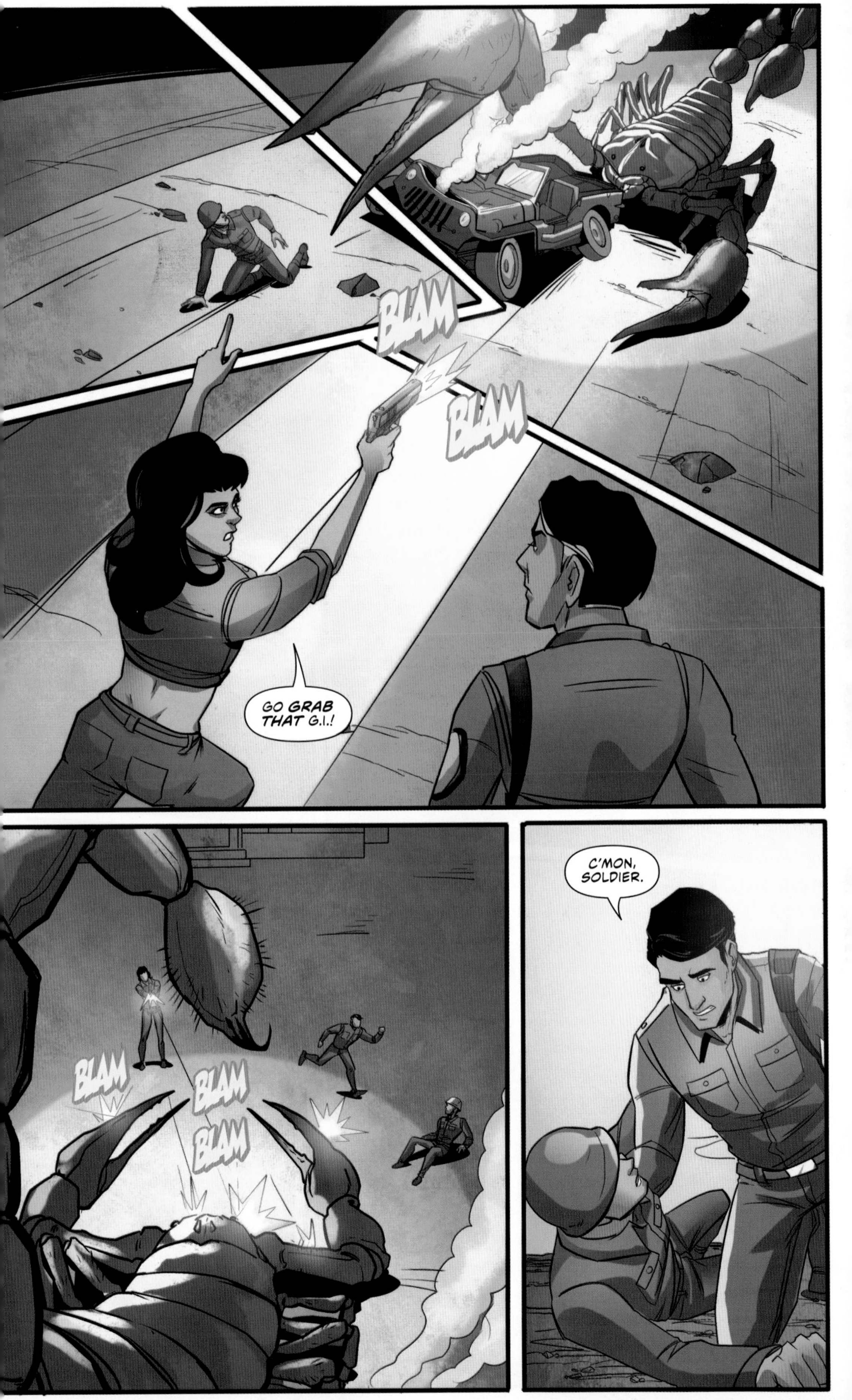
BLAM
BLAM
GO GRAB THAT G.I.!
BLAM
BLAM
BLAM
C'MON, SOLDIER.

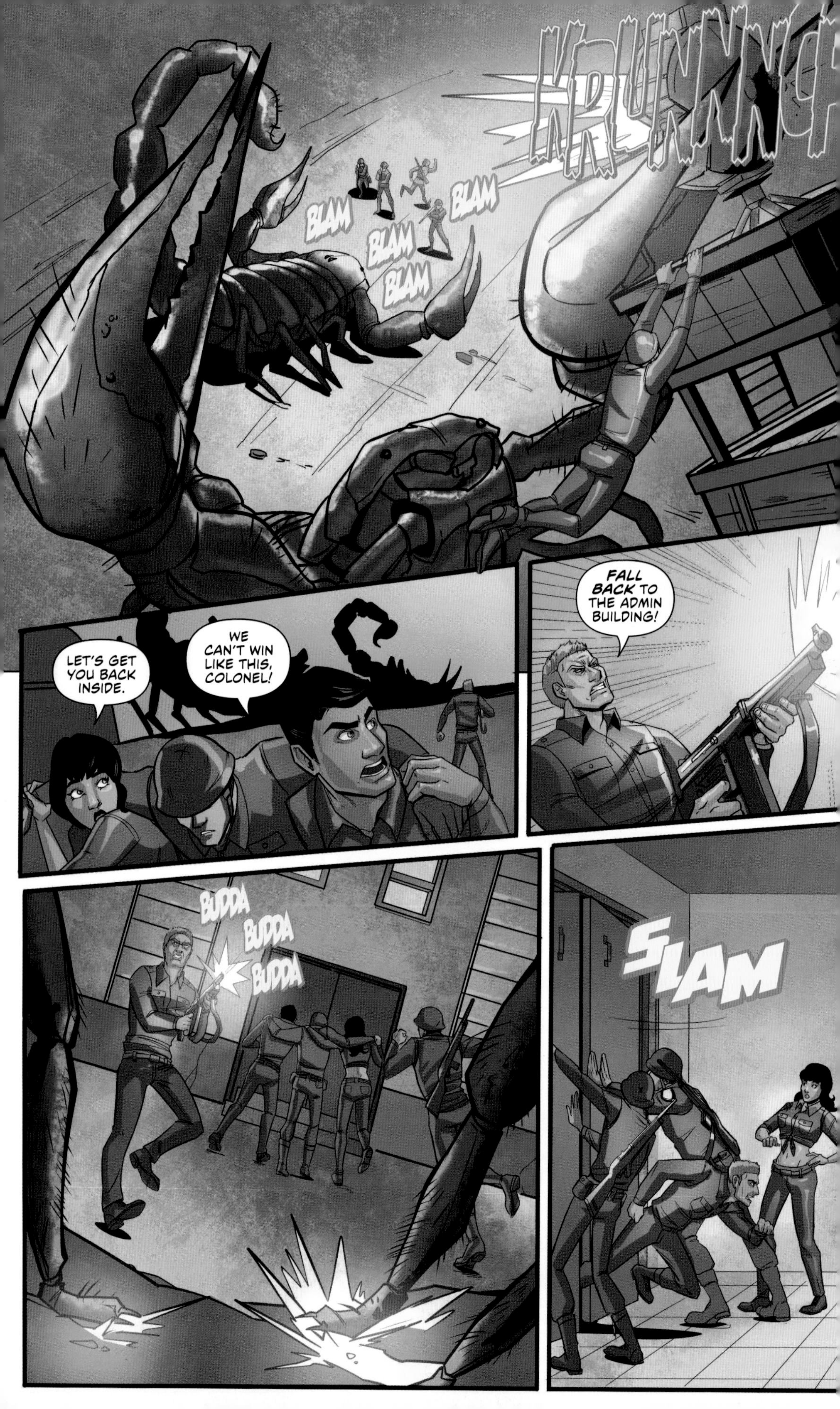
KRUNNNCH
BLAM
BLAM
BLAM
BLAM
LET'S GET YOU BACK INSIDE.
WE CAN'T WIN LIKE THIS, COLONEL!
FALL BACK TO THE ADMIN BUILDING!
BUDDA
BUDDA
BUDDA
SLAM

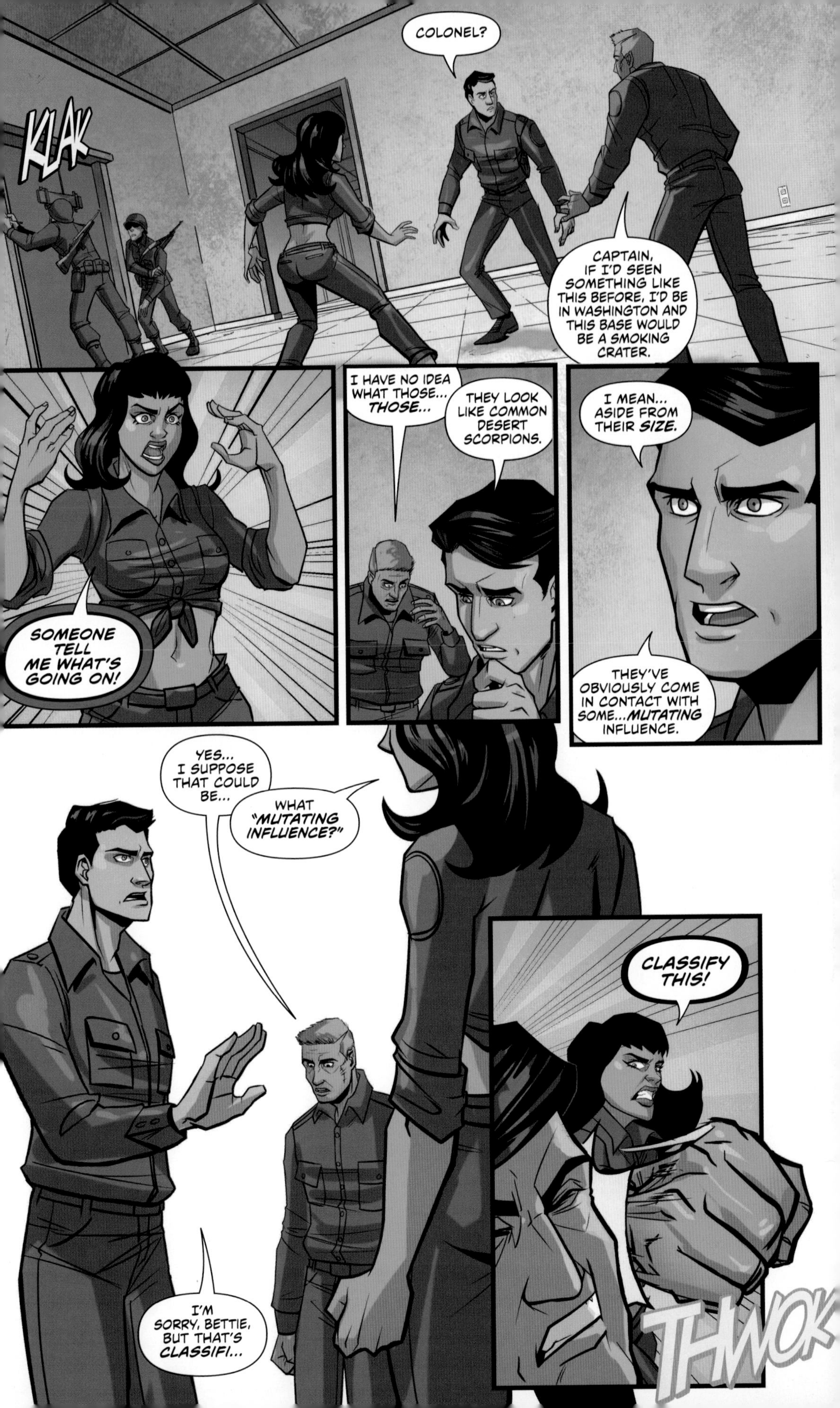
COLONEL?
KLAK
CAPTAIN, IF I'D SEEN SOMETHING LIKE THIS BEFORE, I'D BE IN WASHINGTON AND THIS BASE WOULD BE A SMOKING CRATER.
SOMEONE TELL ME WHAT'S GOING ON!
I HAVE NO IDEA WHAT THOSE... THOSE...
THEY LOOK LIKE COMMON DESERT SCORPIONS.
I MEAN... ASIDE FROM THEIR SIZE.
THEY'VE OBVIOUSLY COME IN CONTACT WITH SOME...MUTATING INFLUENCE.
YES... I SUPPOSE THAT COULD BE...
WHAT "MUTATING INFLUENCE?"
I'M SORRY, BETTIE, BUT THAT'S CLASSIFI...
CLASSIFY THIS!
THWOK

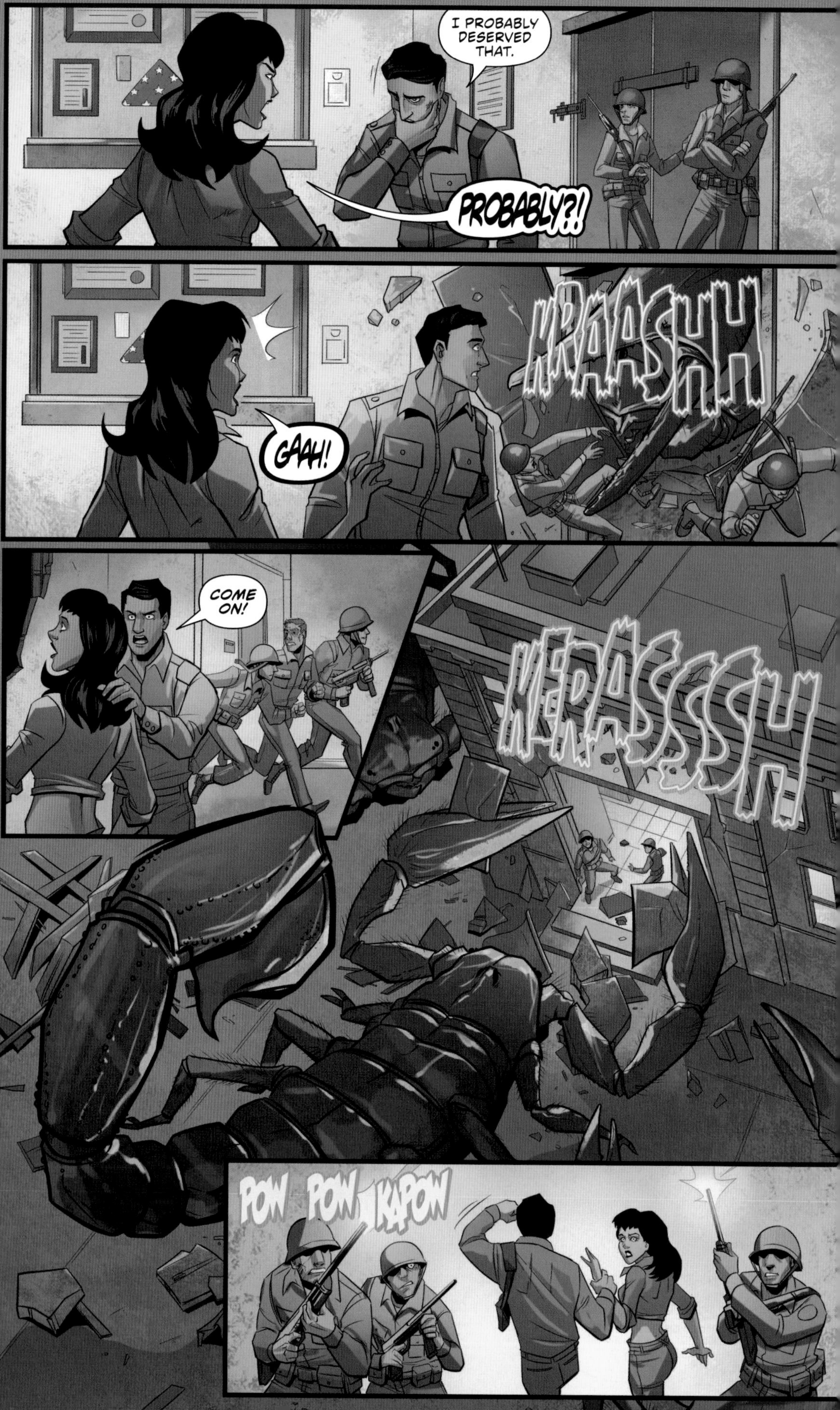
I PROBABLY DESERVED THAT.
PROBABLY?!
GAAH!
KRAASHH
COME ON!
KERASSSSH
POW
POW
KAPOW

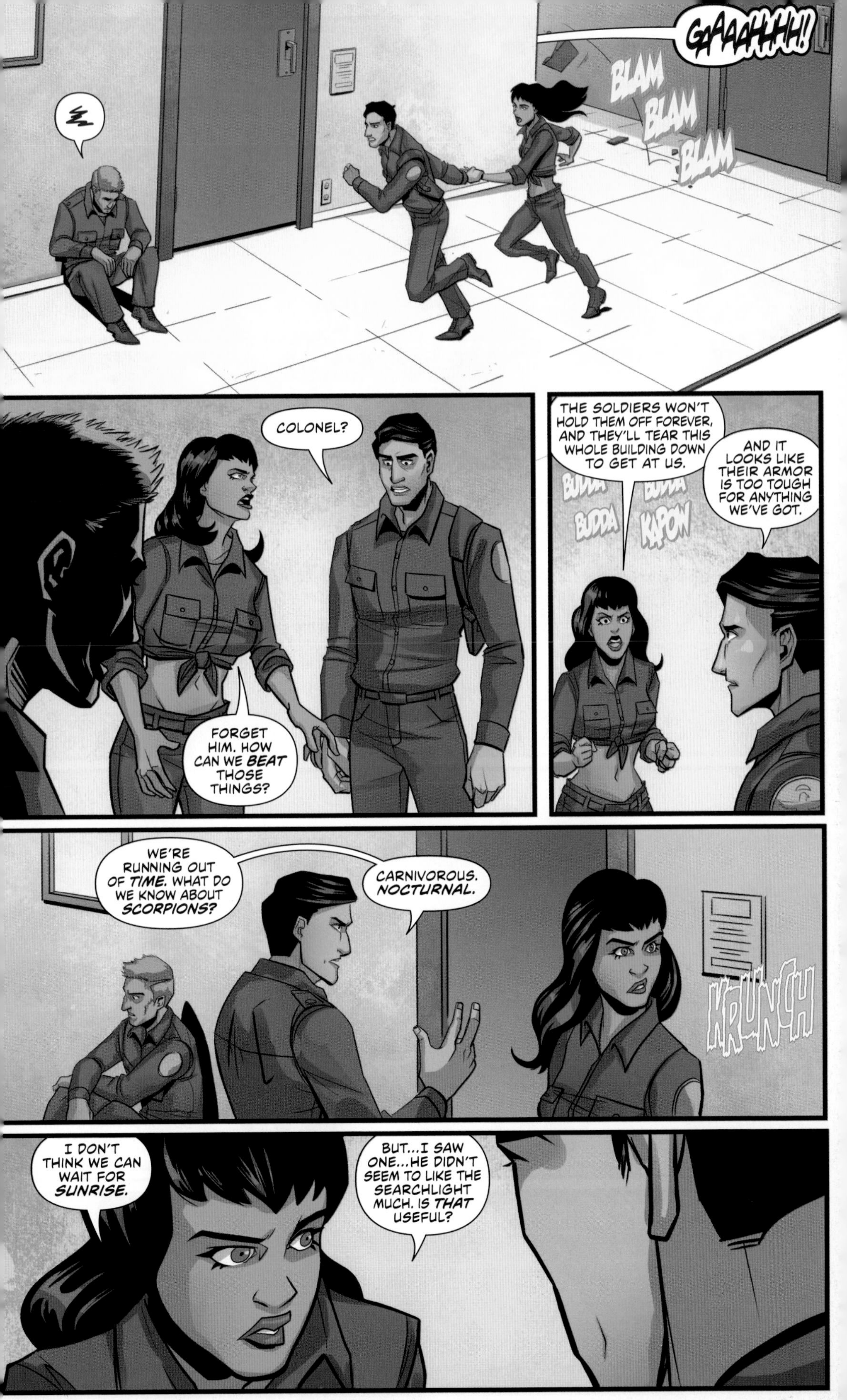
GAAAHHHH!
BLAM
BLAM
BLAM
COLONEL?
FORGET HIM. HOW CAN WE BEAT THOSE THINGS?
THE SOLDIERS WON'T HOLD THEM OFF FOREVER, AND THEY'LL TEAR THIS WHOLE BUILDING DOWN TO GET AT US.
BUDDA BUDDA
BUDDA KAPOW
AND IT LOOKS LIKE THEIR ARMOR IS TOO TOUGH FOR ANYTHING WE'VE GOT.
WE'RE RUNNING OUT OF TIME. WHAT DO WE KNOW ABOUT SCORPIONS?
CARNIVOROUS. NOCTURNAL.
KRUNCH
I DON'T THINK WE CAN WAIT FOR SUNRISE.
BUT...I SAW ONE...HE DIDN'T SEEM TO LIKE THE SEARCHLIGHT MUCH. IS THAT USEFUL?

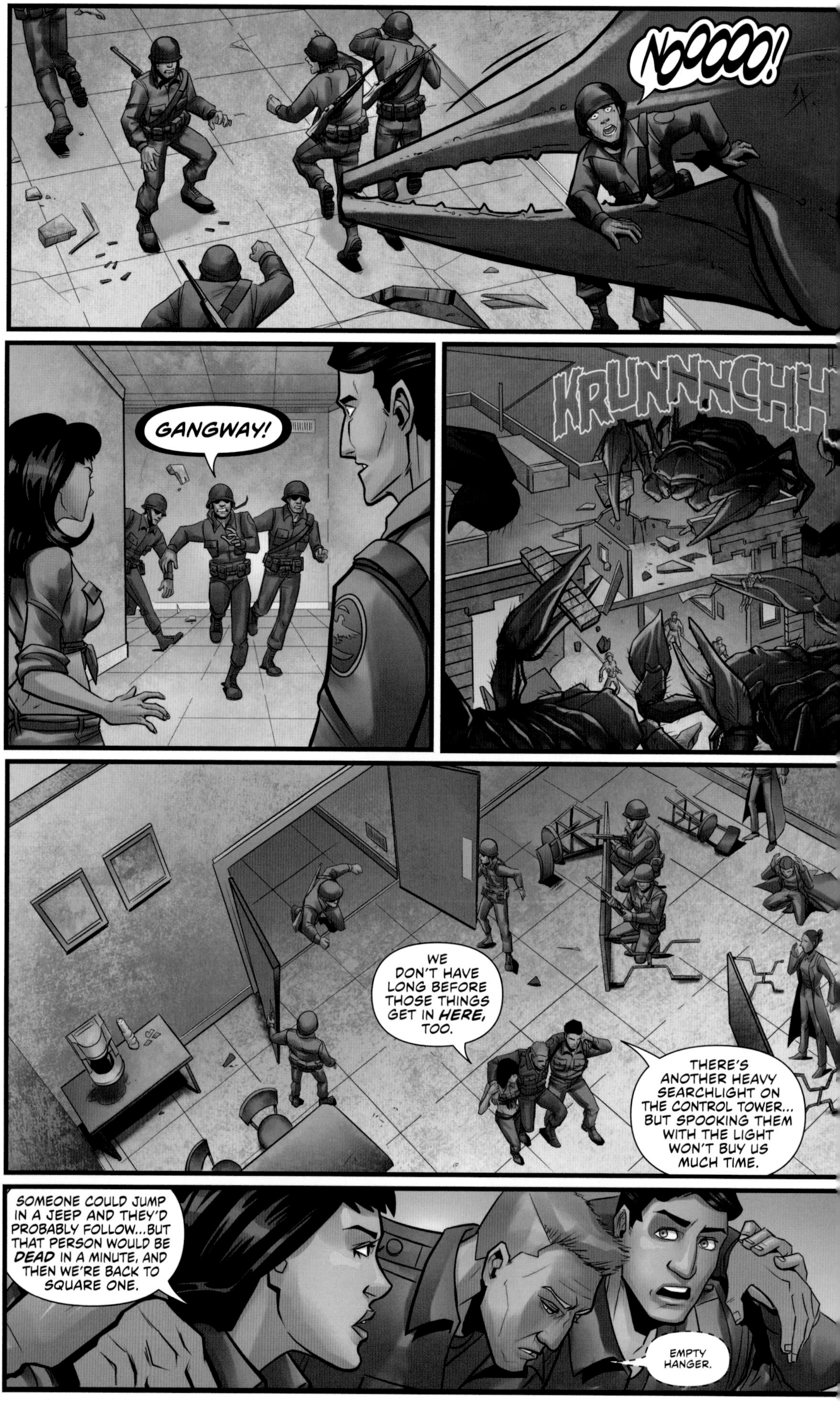
NOOOOO!
GANGWAY!
KRUNNNCHH
WE DON'T HAVE LONG BEFORE THOSE THINGS GET IN *HERE*, TOO.
THERE'S ANOTHER HEAVY SEARCHLIGHT ON THE CONTROL TOWER... BUT SPOOKING THEM WITH THE LIGHT WON'T BUY US MUCH TIME.
SOMEONE COULD JUMP IN A JEEP AND THEY'D PROBABLY FOLLOW...BUT THAT PERSON WOULD BE *DEAD* IN A MINUTE, AND THEN WE'RE BACK TO SQUARE ONE.
EMPTY HANGER.

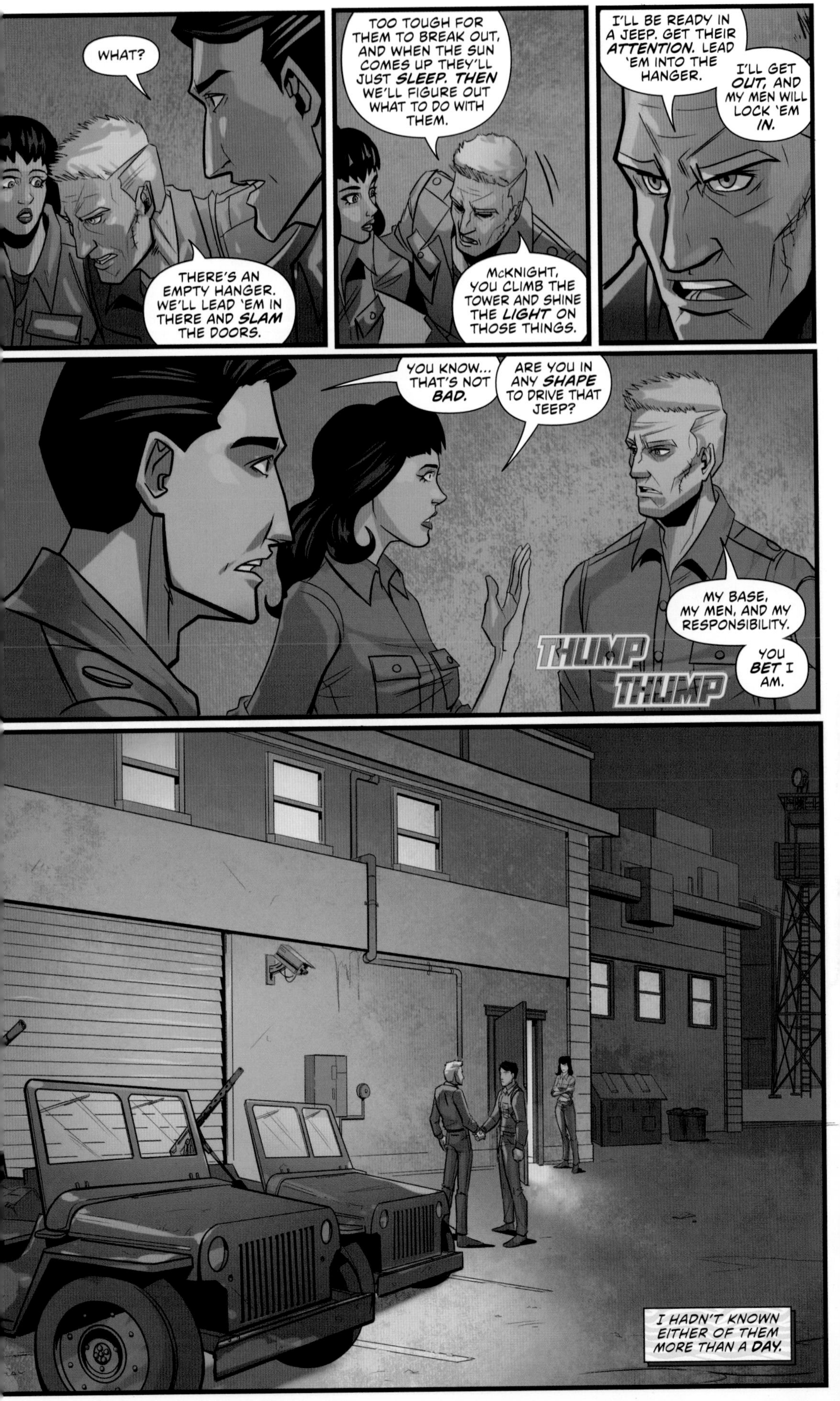
WHAT?
THERE'S AN EMPTY HANGER. WE'LL LEAD 'EM IN THERE AND SLAM THE DOORS.
TOO TOUGH FOR THEM TO BREAK OUT, AND WHEN THE SUN COMES UP THEY'LL JUST SLEEP. THEN WE'LL FIGURE OUT WHAT TO DO WITH THEM.
McKNIGHT, YOU CLIMB THE TOWER AND SHINE THE LIGHT ON THOSE THINGS.
I'LL BE READY IN A JEEP, GET THEIR ATTENTION. LEAD 'EM INTO THE HANGER.
I'LL GET OUT, AND MY MEN WILL LOCK 'EM IN.
YOU KNOW... THAT'S NOT BAD.
ARE YOU IN ANY SHAPE TO DRIVE THAT JEEP?
MY BASE, MY MEN, AND MY RESPONSIBILITY.
THUMP
THUMP
YOU BET I AM.
I HADN'T KNOWN EITHER OF THEM MORE THAN A DAY.

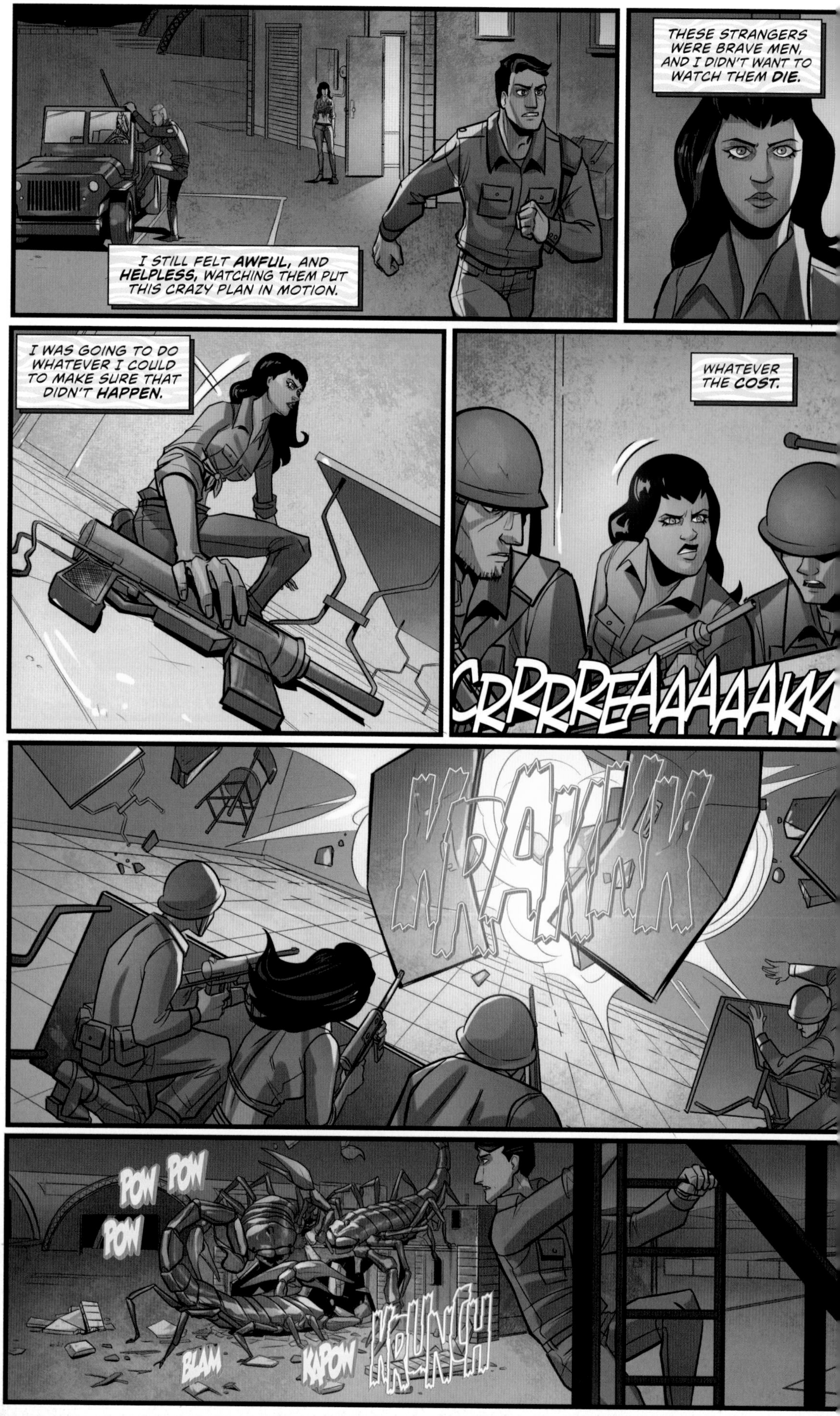
I STILL FELT **AWFUL,** AND **HELPLESS,** WATCHING THEM PUT THIS CRAZY PLAN IN MOTION.
THESE STRANGERS WERE BRAVE MEN, AND I DIDN'T WANT TO WATCH THEM **DIE.**
I WAS GOING TO DO WHATEVER I COULD TO MAKE SURE THAT DIDN'T **HAPPEN.**
WHATEVER THE **COST.**
CRRRREAAAAAKK
POW POW
POW
BLAM
KAPOW
KRUNCH

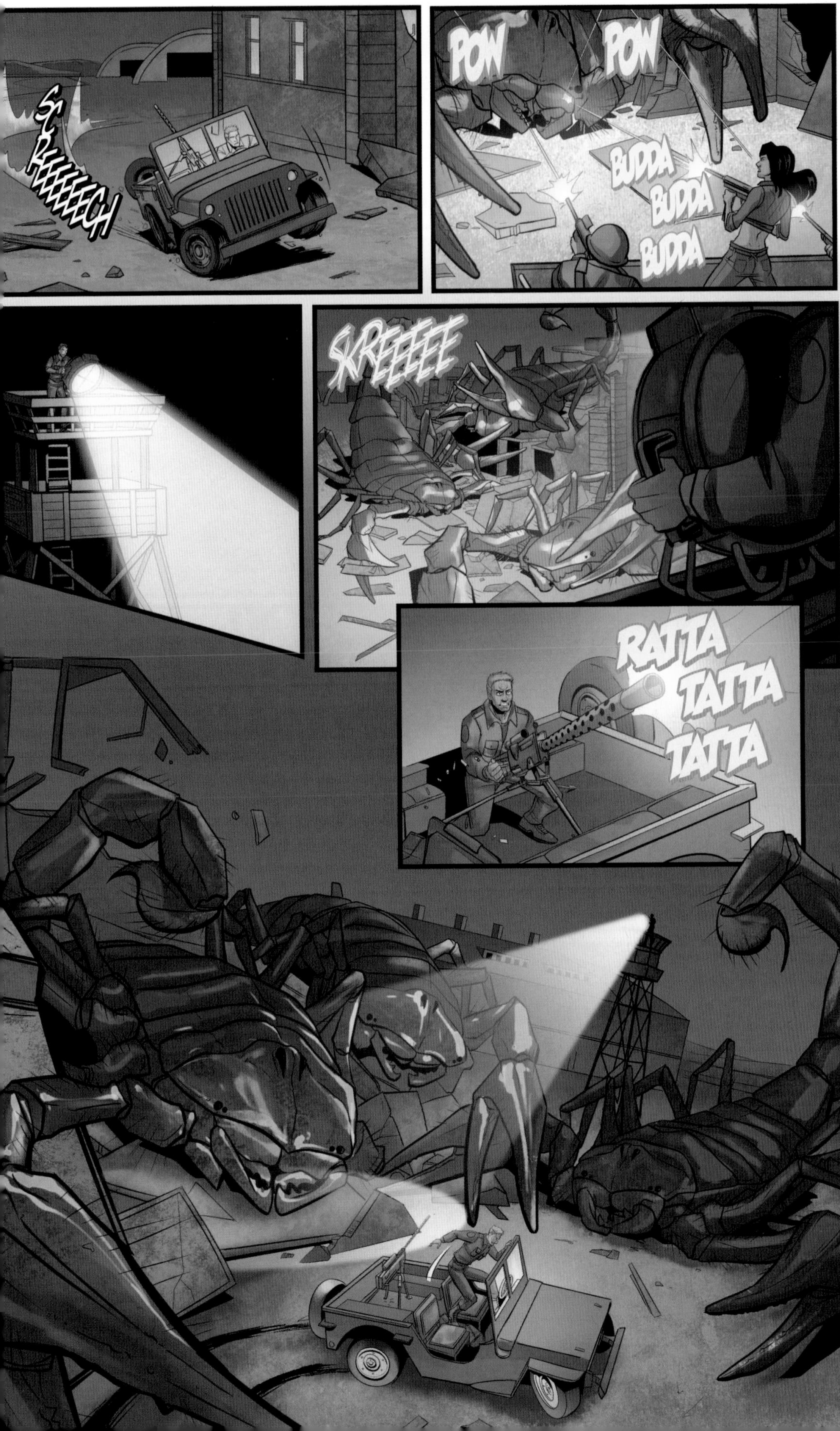
SCREEEEEECH
POW POW
BUDDA BUDDA BUDDA
SKREEEEE
RATTA TATTA TATTA

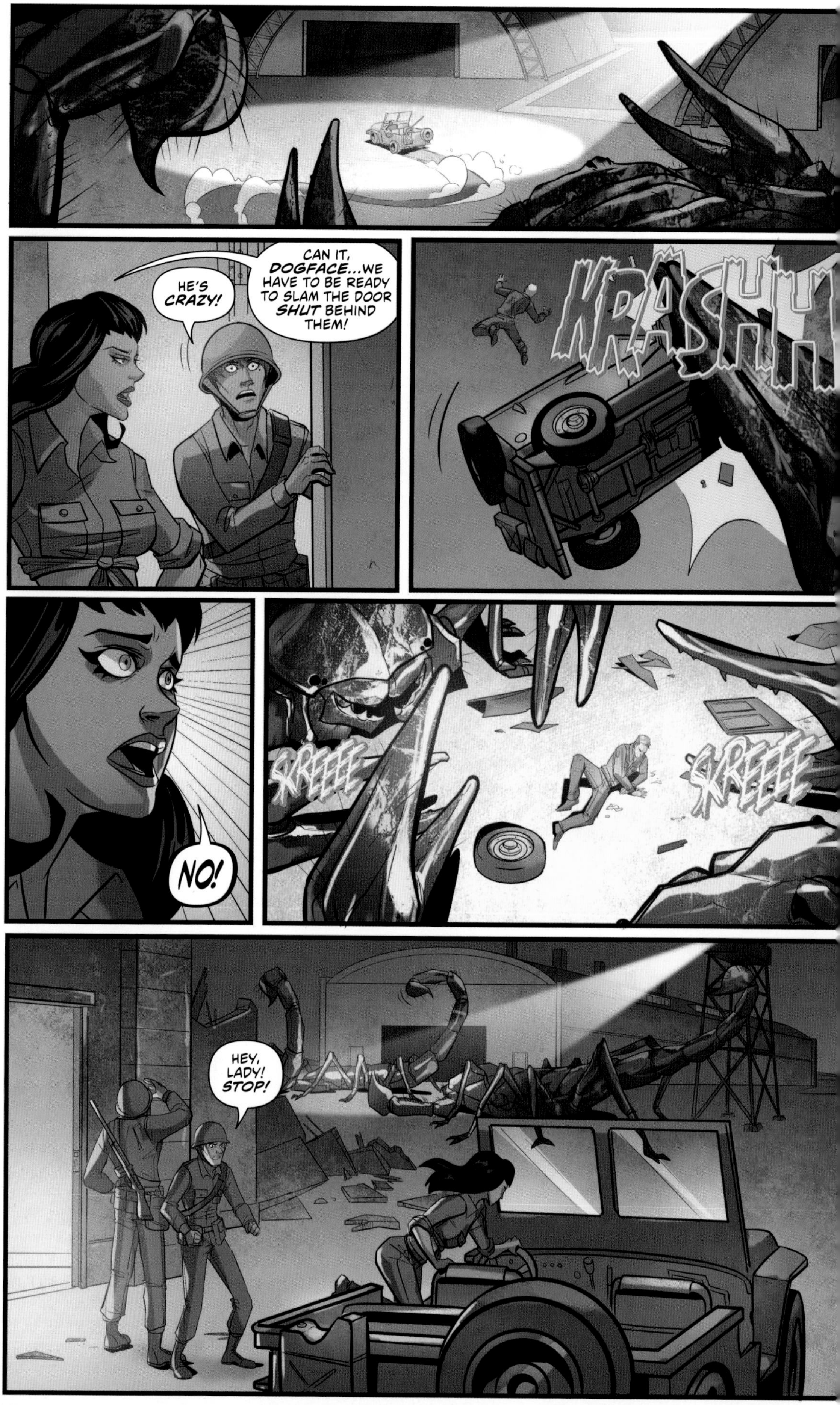

HE'S CRAZY!
CAN IT, DOGFACE...WE HAVE TO BE READY TO SLAM THE DOOR SHUT BEHIND THEM!
KRASHH
NO!
SKREEEE
SKREEEE
HEY, LADY! STOP!

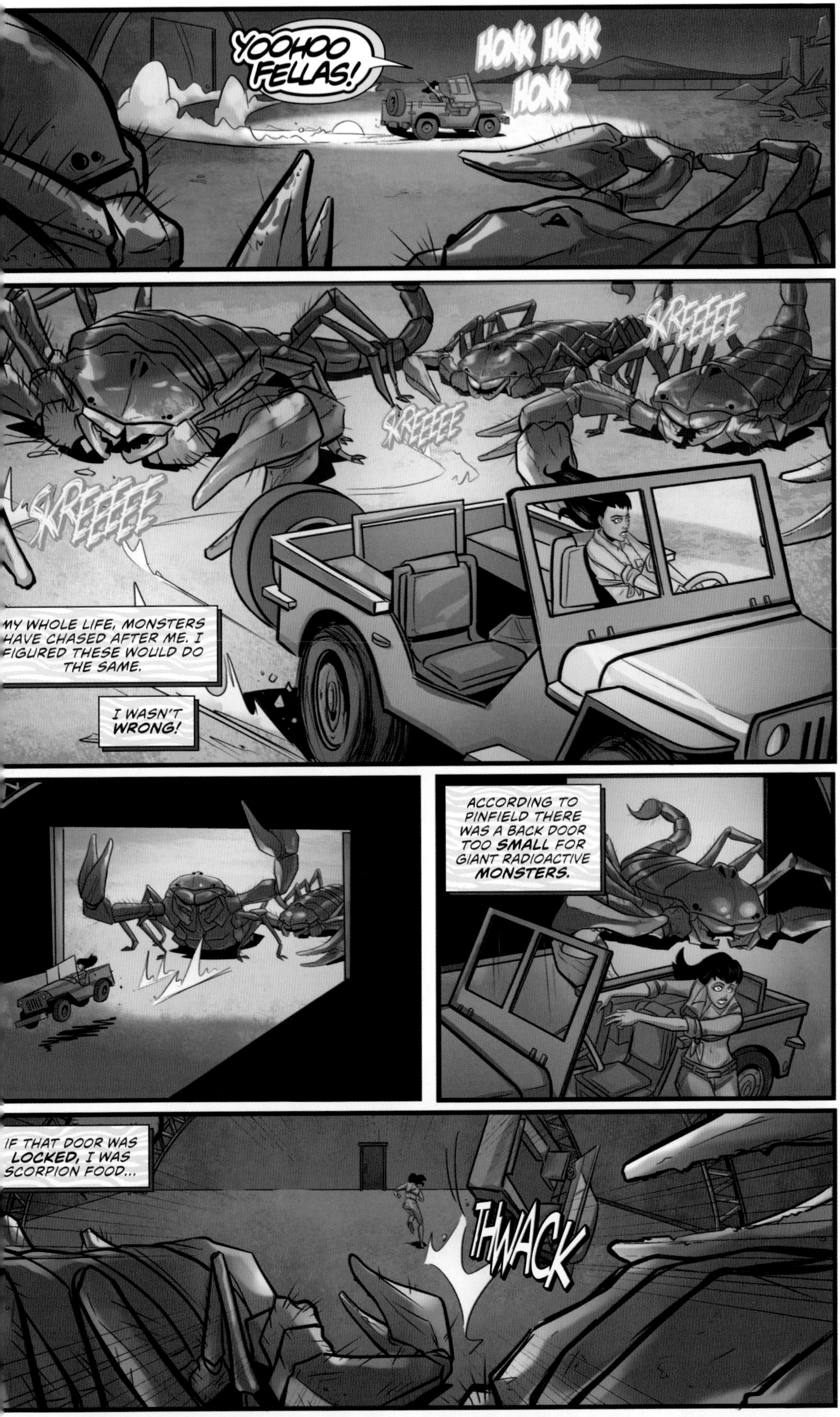
YOOHOO FELLAS!
HONK HONK HONK
SKREEEEE
SKREEEEE
SKREEEEEEEEEE
MY WHOLE LIFE, MONSTERS HAVE CHASED AFTER ME. I FIGURED THESE WOULD DO THE SAME.
I WASN'T **WRONG!**
ACCORDING TO PINFIELD THERE WAS A BACK DOOR TOO **SMALL** FOR GIANT RADIOACTIVE **MONSTERS.**
IF THAT DOOR WAS **LOCKED,** I WAS SCORPION FOOD...
THWACK

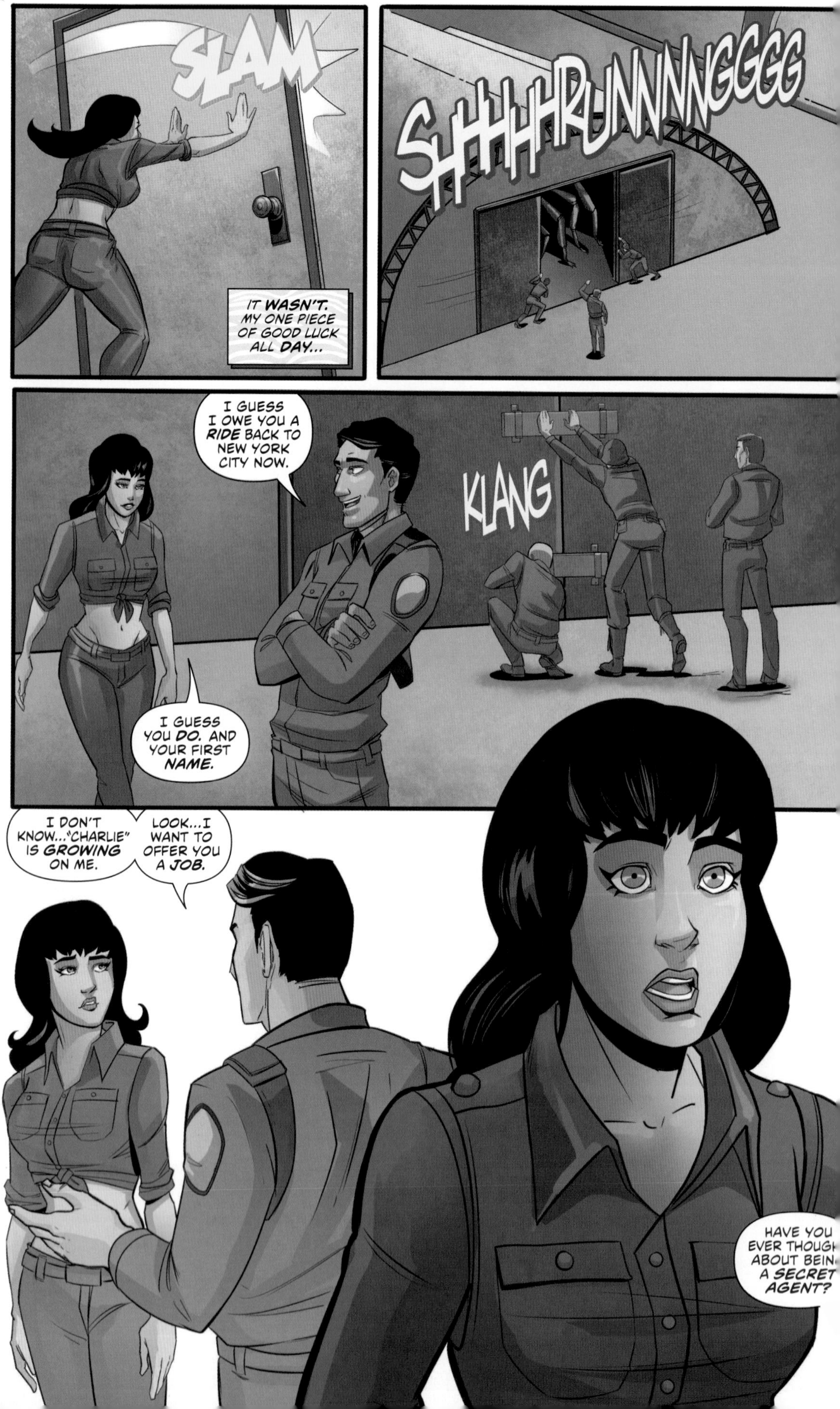
SLAM
IT WASN'T. MY ONE PIECE OF GOOD LUCK ALL DAY...
SHHHHRUNNNNGGGG
I GUESS I OWE YOU A RIDE BACK TO NEW YORK CITY NOW.
KLANG
I GUESS YOU DO. AND YOUR FIRST NAME.
I DON'T KNOW..."CHARLIE" IS GROWING ON ME.
LOOK...I WANT TO OFFER YOU A JOB.
HAVE YOU EVER THOUG ABOUT BEIN A SECRET AGENT?

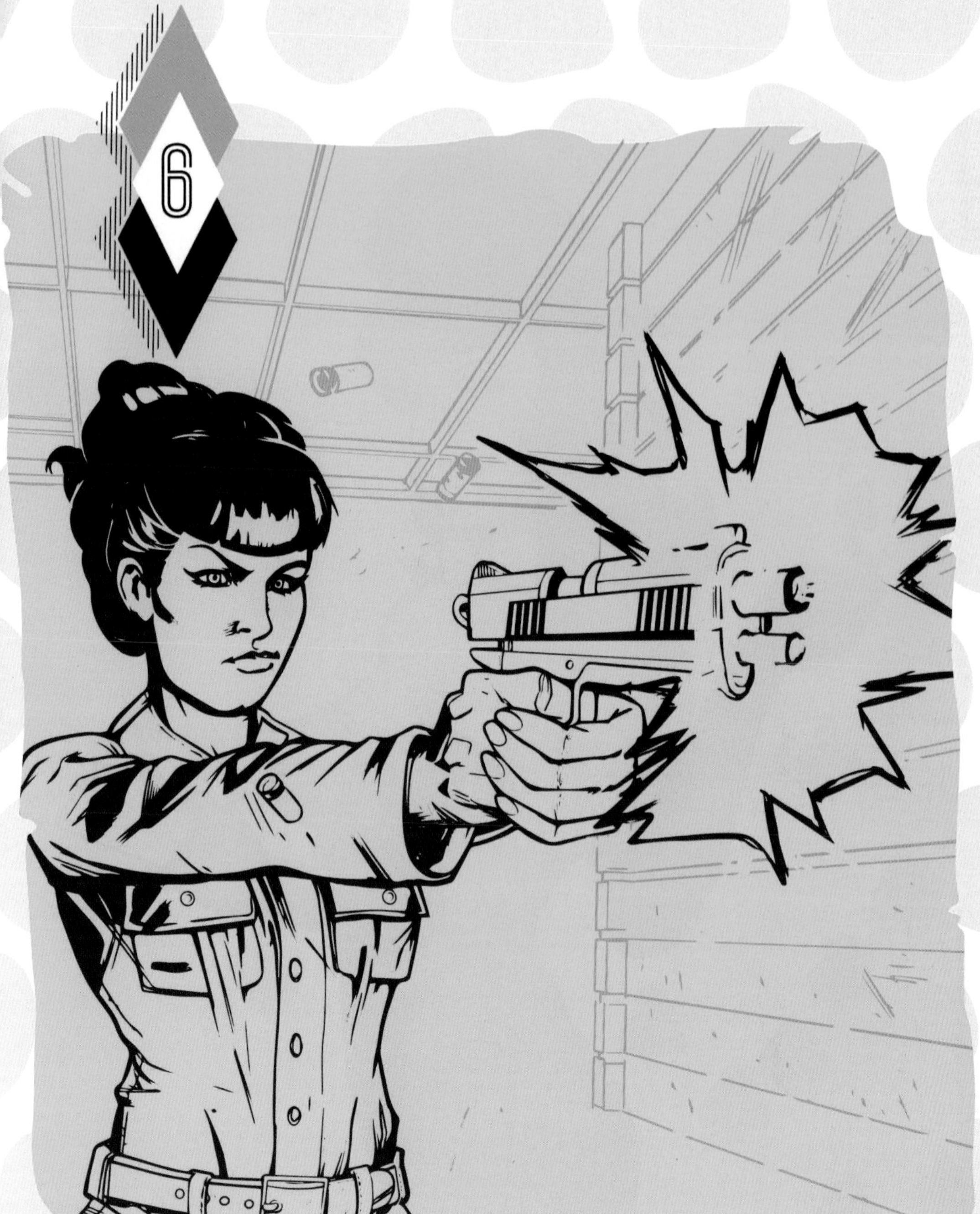
6

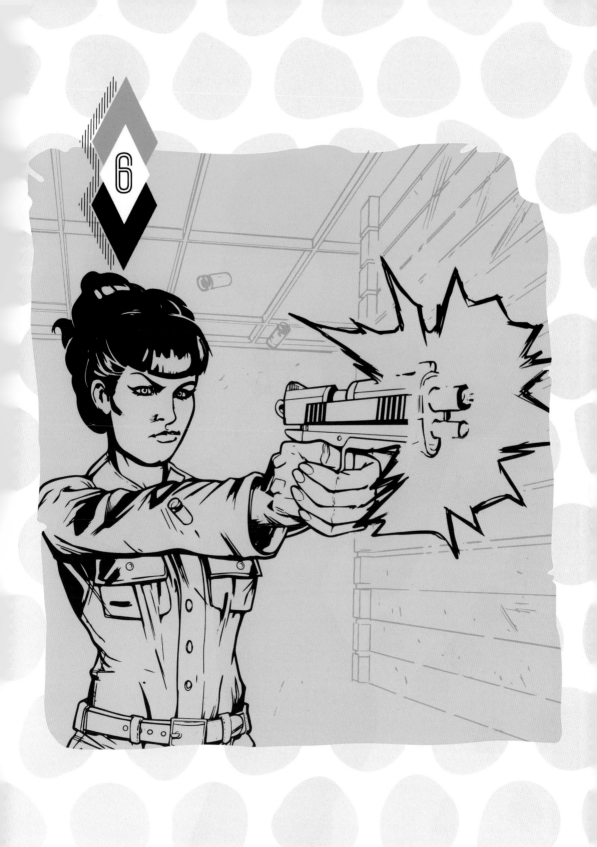

ART: JOSEPH MICHAEL LINSNER

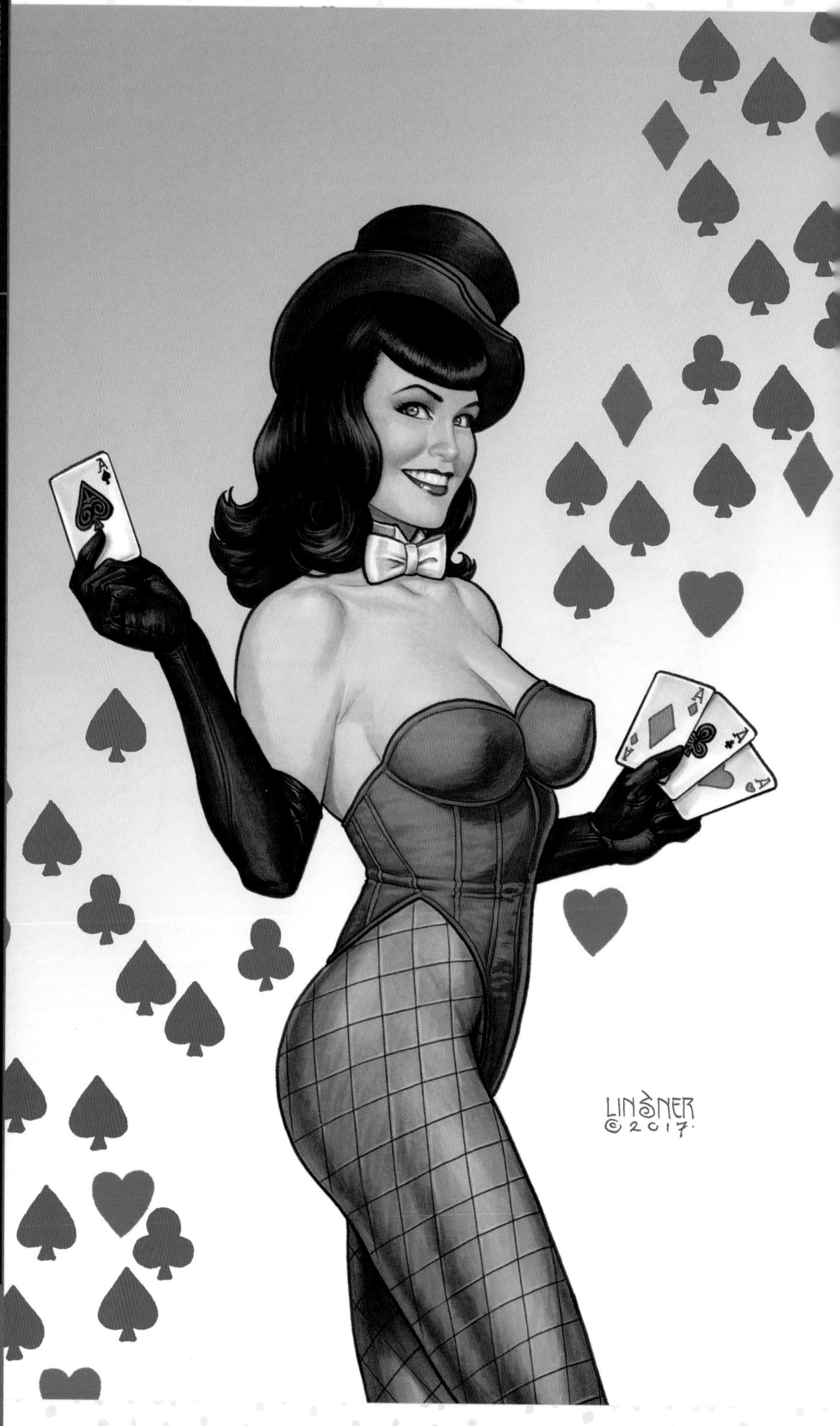
LINSNER
©2017

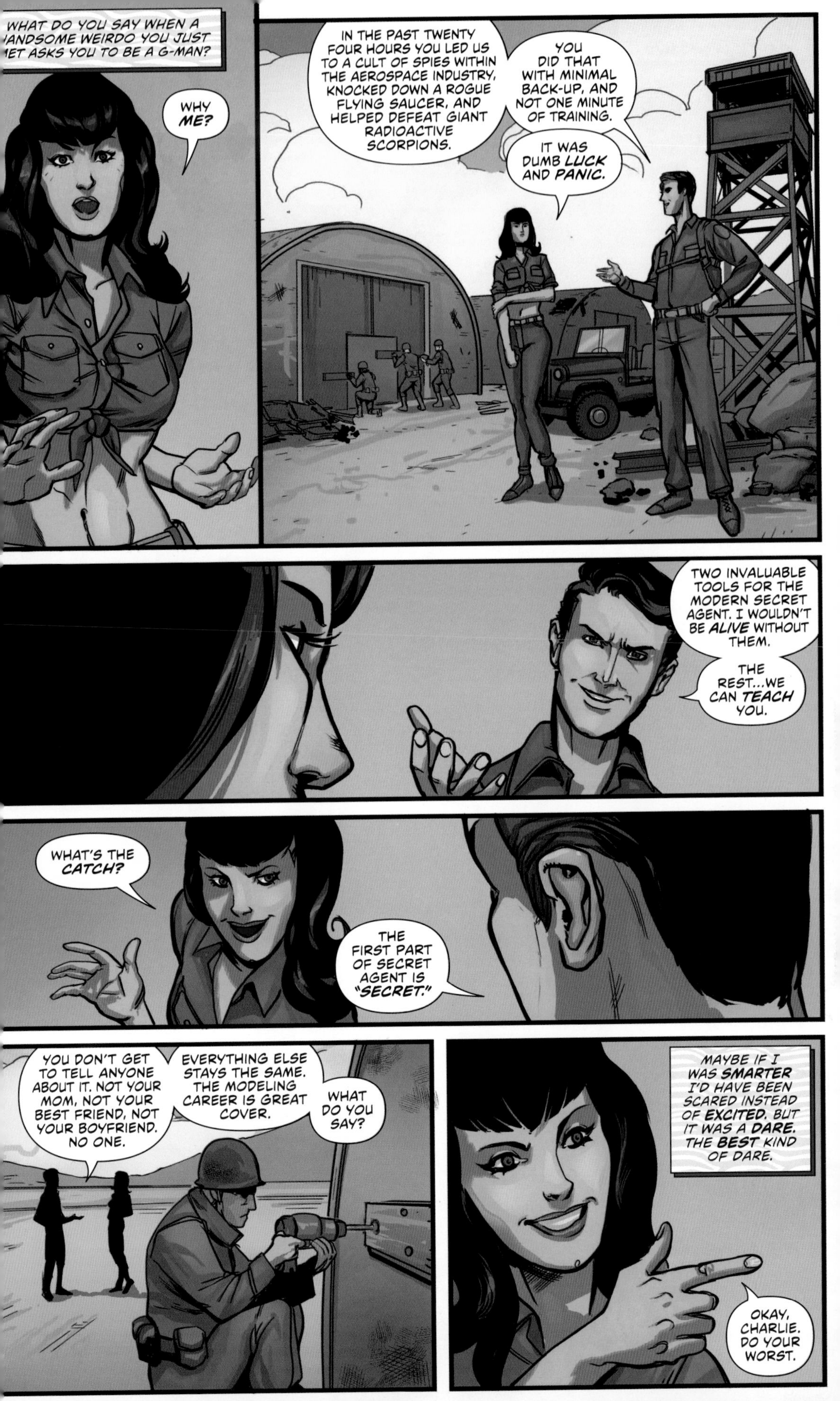
WHAT DO YOU SAY WHEN A HANDSOME WEIRDO YOU JUST MET ASKS YOU TO BE A G-MAN?
WHY ME?
IN THE PAST TWENTY FOUR HOURS YOU LED US TO A CULT OF SPIES WITHIN THE AEROSPACE INDUSTRY, KNOCKED DOWN A ROGUE FLYING SAUCER, AND HELPED DEFEAT GIANT RADIOACTIVE SCORPIONS.
YOU DID THAT WITH MINIMAL BACK-UP, AND NOT ONE MINUTE OF TRAINING.
IT WAS DUMB LUCK AND PANIC.
TWO INVALUABLE TOOLS FOR THE MODERN SECRET AGENT. I WOULDN'T BE ALIVE WITHOUT THEM.
THE REST...WE CAN TEACH YOU.
WHAT'S THE CATCH?
THE FIRST PART OF SECRET AGENT IS "SECRET."
YOU DON'T GET TO TELL ANYONE ABOUT IT. NOT YOUR MOM, NOT YOUR BEST FRIEND, NOT YOUR BOYFRIEND. NO ONE.
EVERYTHING ELSE STAYS THE SAME. THE MODELING CAREER IS GREAT COVER.
WHAT DO YOU SAY?
MAYBE IF I WAS SMARTER I'D HAVE BEEN SCARED INSTEAD OF EXCITED. BUT IT WAS A DARE. THE BEST KIND OF DARE.
OKAY, CHARLIE. DO YOUR WORST.

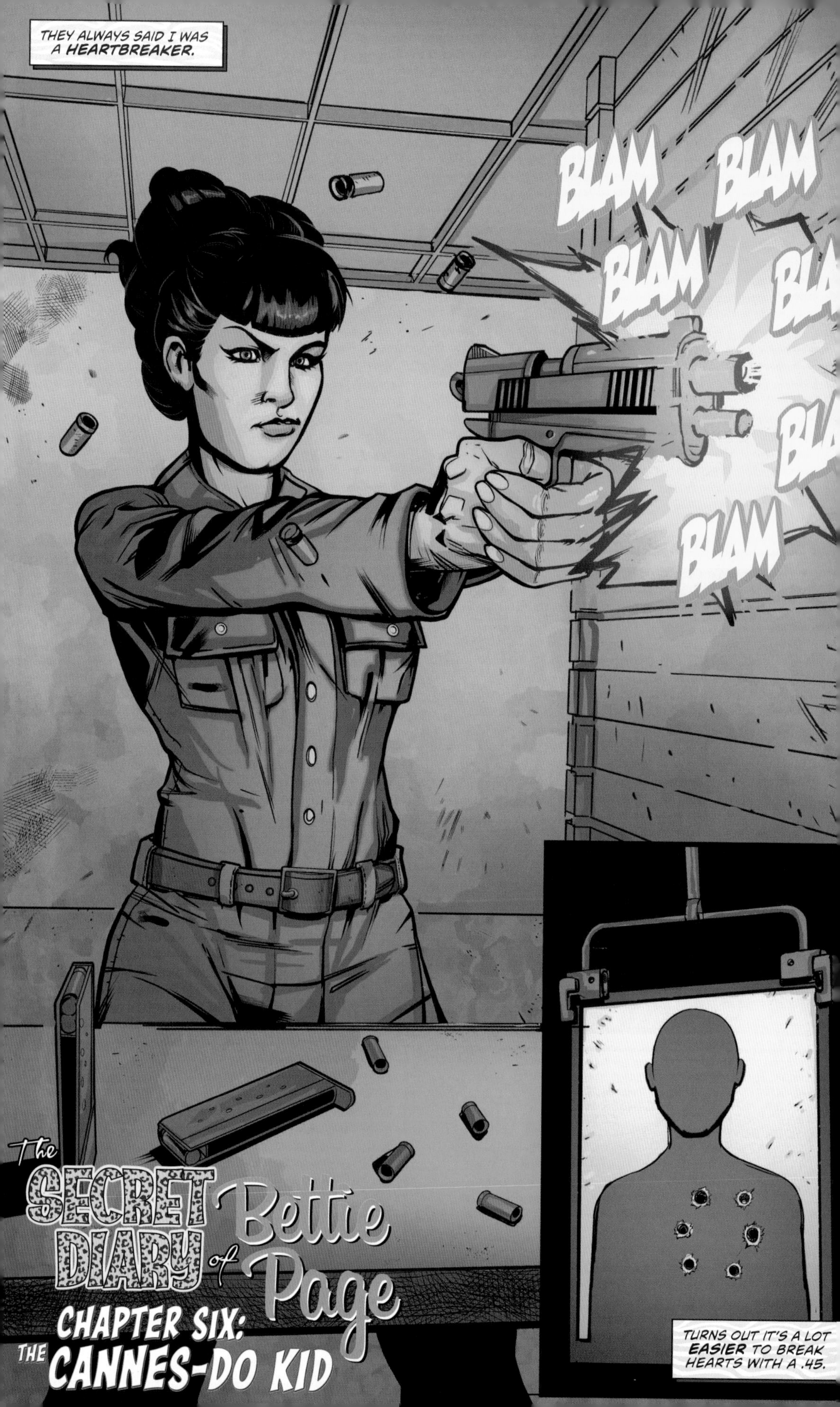
THEY ALWAYS SAID I WAS A HEARTBREAKER.
BLAM BLAM
BLAM
BLAM
BLAM
The SECRET DIARY of Bettie Page
CHAPTER SIX:
THE CANNES-DO KID
TURNS OUT IT'S A LOT EASIER TO BREAK HEARTS WITH A .45.

IT WASN'T ALL FUN AND GAMES.

MY FELLOW TRAINEES WERE MOSTLY BUZZ-CUT *GORILLAS.*

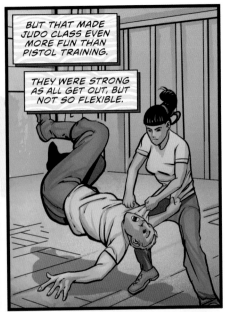

BUT THAT MADE JUDO CLASS EVEN MORE FUN THAN PISTOL TRAINING.

THEY WERE STRONG AS ALL GET OUT, BUT NOT SO FLEXIBLE.

I WANTED TO ASK McKNIGHT IF THEY NEEDED ME TO TEACH THE CADETS A COURSE ON "HOW TO TALK TO A LADY", BUT I HADN'T SEEN HIM SINCE I LANDED HERE.

WHEREVER *"HERE"* WAS.

SO IT WAS HIGH *SCHOOL* ALL OVER AGAIN, BUT LONELIER AND *DEADLIER.*

THEN SUDDENLY... IT WAS OVER.

BUS LEAVES IN TWO HOURS.

BUT... WHAT...?

RETURN HOME AND WAIT FOR INSTRUCTIONS.

IF THEY *NEED* YOU, THEY'LL *CALL* YOU. *DISMISSED.*

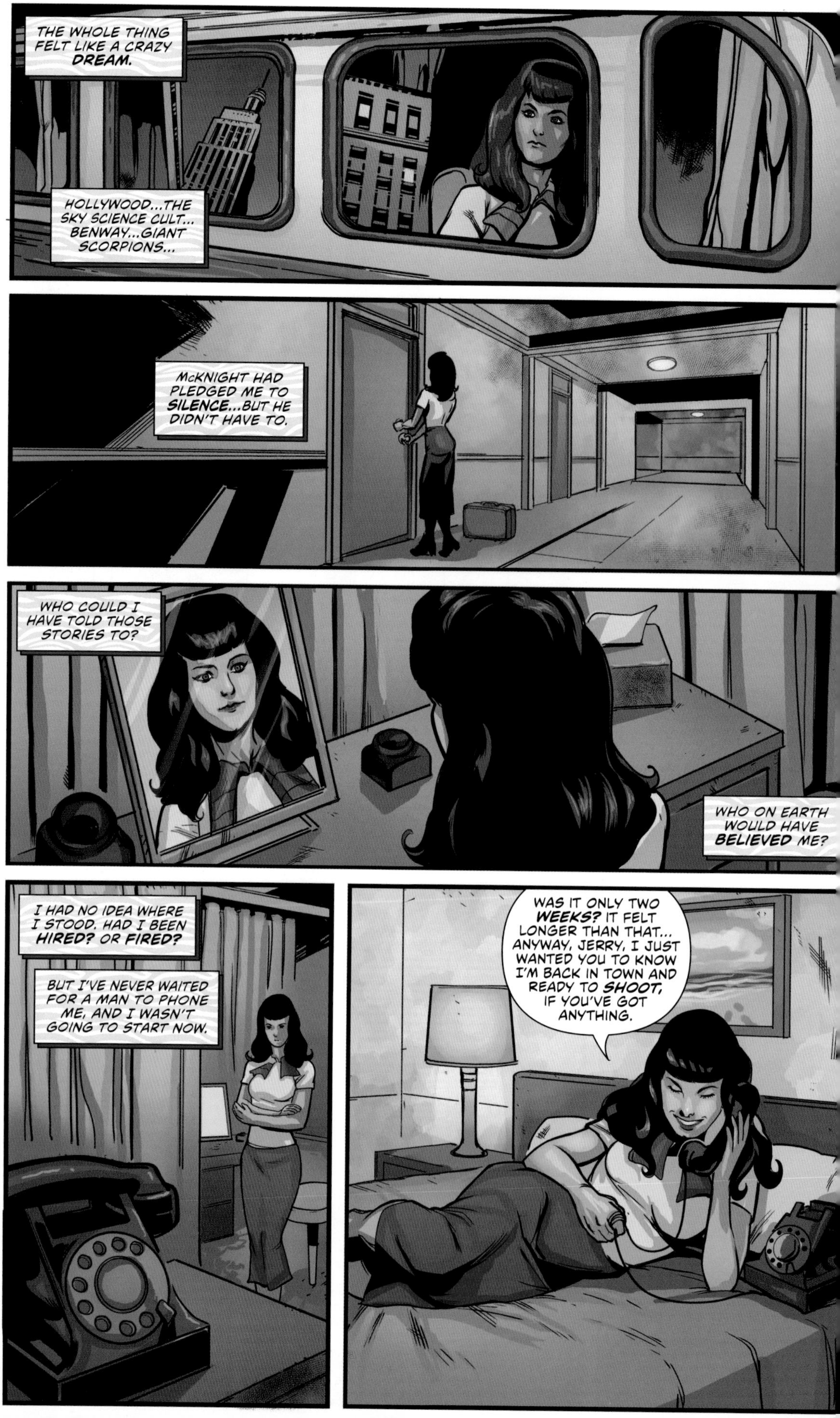
THE WHOLE THING FELT LIKE A CRAZY DREAM.
HOLLYWOOD...THE SKY SCIENCE CULT... BENWAY...GIANT SCORPIONS...
McKNIGHT HAD PLEDGED ME TO SILENCE...BUT HE DIDN'T HAVE TO.
WHO COULD I HAVE TOLD THOSE STORIES TO?
WHO ON EARTH WOULD HAVE BELIEVED ME?
I HAD NO IDEA WHERE I STOOD. HAD I BEEN HIRED? OR FIRED?
BUT I'VE NEVER WAITED FOR A MAN TO PHONE ME, AND I WASN'T GOING TO START NOW.
WAS IT ONLY TWO WEEKS? IT FELT LONGER THAN THAT... ANYWAY, JERRY, I JUST WANTED YOU TO KNOW I'M BACK IN TOWN AND READY TO SHOOT, IF YOU'VE GOT ANYTHING.

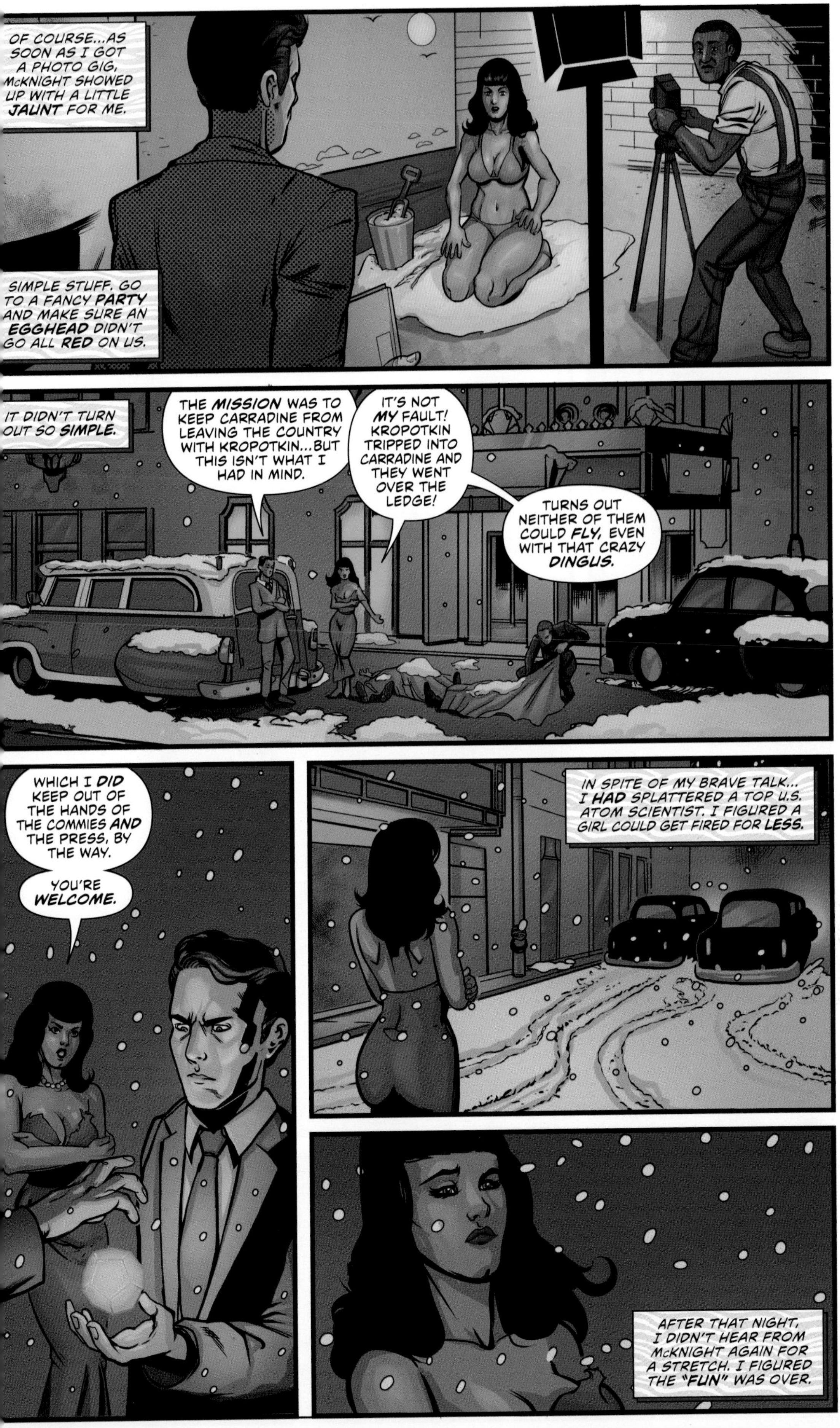
OF COURSE...AS SOON AS I GOT A PHOTO GIG, McKNIGHT SHOWED UP WITH A LITTLE JAUNT FOR ME.
SIMPLE STUFF. GO TO A FANCY PARTY AND MAKE SURE AN EGGHEAD DIDN'T GO ALL RED ON US.
IT DIDN'T TURN OUT SO SIMPLE.
THE MISSION WAS TO KEEP CARRADINE FROM LEAVING THE COUNTRY WITH KROPOTKIN...BUT THIS ISN'T WHAT I HAD IN MIND.
IT'S NOT MY FAULT! KROPOTKIN TRIPPED INTO CARRADINE AND THEY WENT OVER THE LEDGE!
TURNS OUT NEITHER OF THEM COULD FLY, EVEN WITH THAT CRAZY DINGUS.
WHICH I DID KEEP OUT OF THE HANDS OF THE COMMIES AND THE PRESS, BY THE WAY.
YOU'RE WELCOME.
IN SPITE OF MY BRAVE TALK... I HAD SPLATTERED A TOP U.S. ATOM SCIENTIST. I FIGURED A GIRL COULD GET FIRED FOR LESS.
AFTER THAT NIGHT, I DIDN'T HEAR FROM McKNIGHT AGAIN FOR A STRETCH. I FIGURED THE "FUN" WAS OVER.

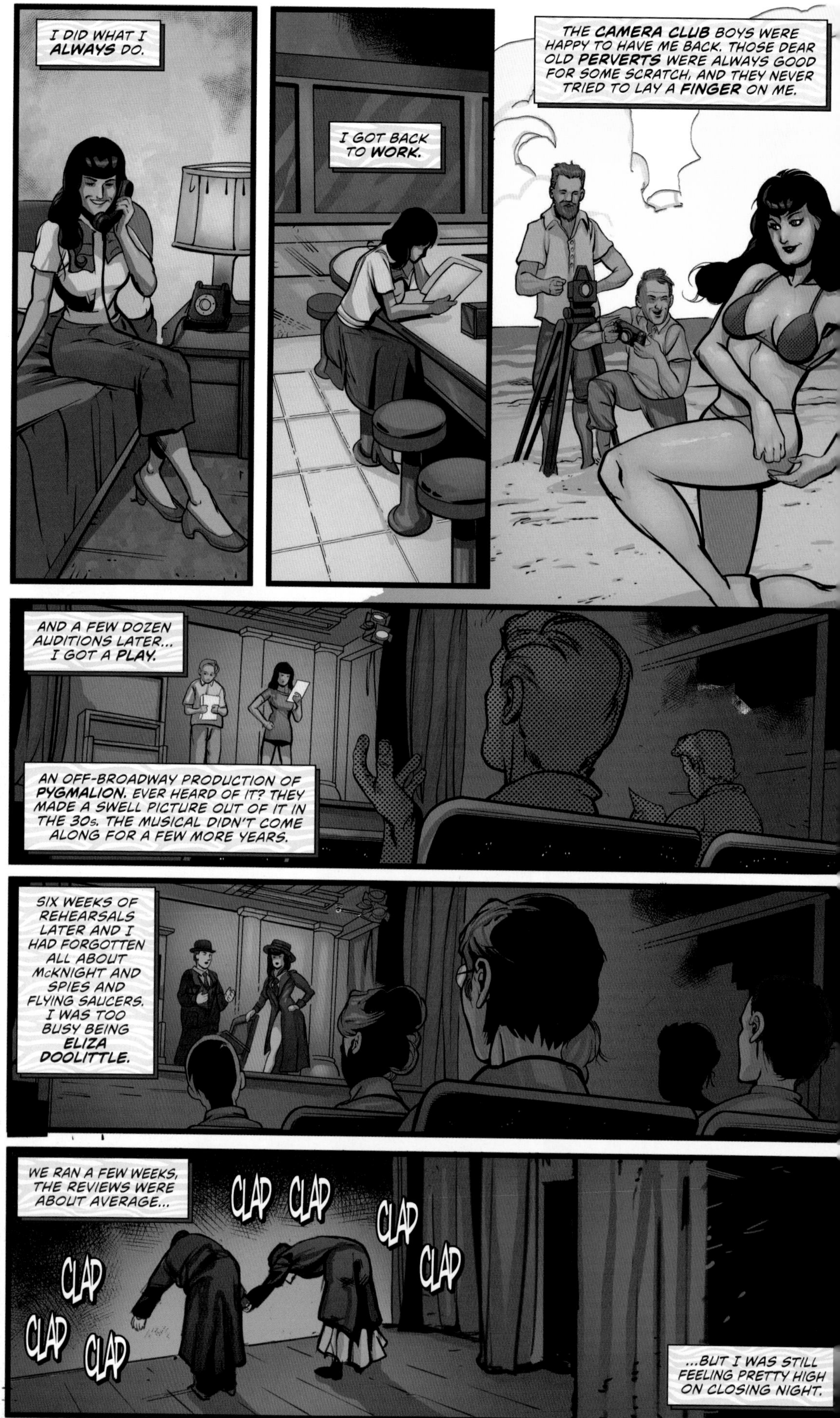
I DID WHAT I ALWAYS DO.
I GOT BACK TO WORK.
THE CAMERA CLUB BOYS WERE HAPPY TO HAVE ME BACK. THOSE DEAR OLD PERVERTS WERE ALWAYS GOOD FOR SOME SCRATCH, AND THEY NEVER TRIED TO LAY A FINGER ON ME.
AND A FEW DOZEN AUDITIONS LATER... I GOT A PLAY.
AN OFF-BROADWAY PRODUCTION OF PYGMALION. EVER HEARD OF IT? THEY MADE A SWELL PICTURE OUT OF IT IN THE 30s. THE MUSICAL DIDN'T COME ALONG FOR A FEW MORE YEARS.
SIX WEEKS OF REHEARSALS LATER AND I HAD FORGOTTEN ALL ABOUT McKNIGHT AND SPIES AND FLYING SAUCERS. I WAS TOO BUSY BEING ELIZA DOOLITTLE.
WE RAN A FEW WEEKS, THE REVIEWS WERE ABOUT AVERAGE...
CLAP CLAP
CLAP
CLAP
CLAP
CLAP
CLAP
...BUT I WAS STILL FEELING PRETTY HIGH ON CLOSING NIGHT.

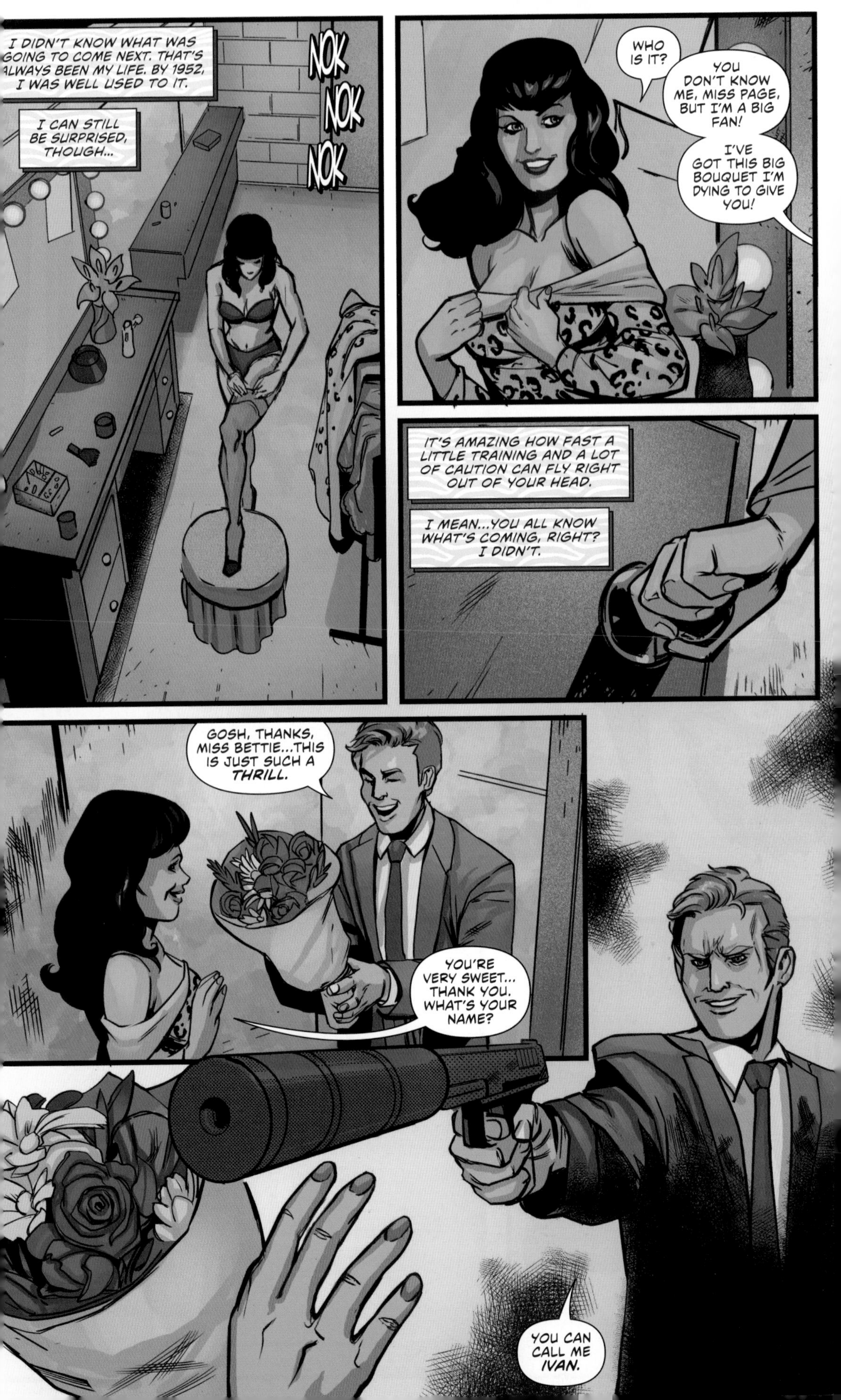

I DIDN'T KNOW WHAT WAS GOING TO COME NEXT. THAT'S ALWAYS BEEN MY LIFE. BY 1952, I WAS WELL USED TO IT.
I CAN STILL BE SURPRISED, THOUGH...
NOK NOK NOK
WHO IS IT?
YOU DON'T KNOW ME, MISS PAGE, BUT I'M A BIG FAN!
I'VE GOT THIS BIG BOUQUET I'M DYING TO GIVE YOU!
IT'S AMAZING HOW FAST A LITTLE TRAINING AND A LOT OF CAUTION CAN FLY RIGHT OUT OF YOUR HEAD.
I MEAN...YOU ALL KNOW WHAT'S COMING, RIGHT? I DIDN'T.
GOSH, THANKS, MISS BETTIE...THIS IS JUST SUCH A THRILL.
YOU'RE VERY SWEET... THANK YOU. WHAT'S YOUR NAME?
YOU CAN CALL ME IVAN.

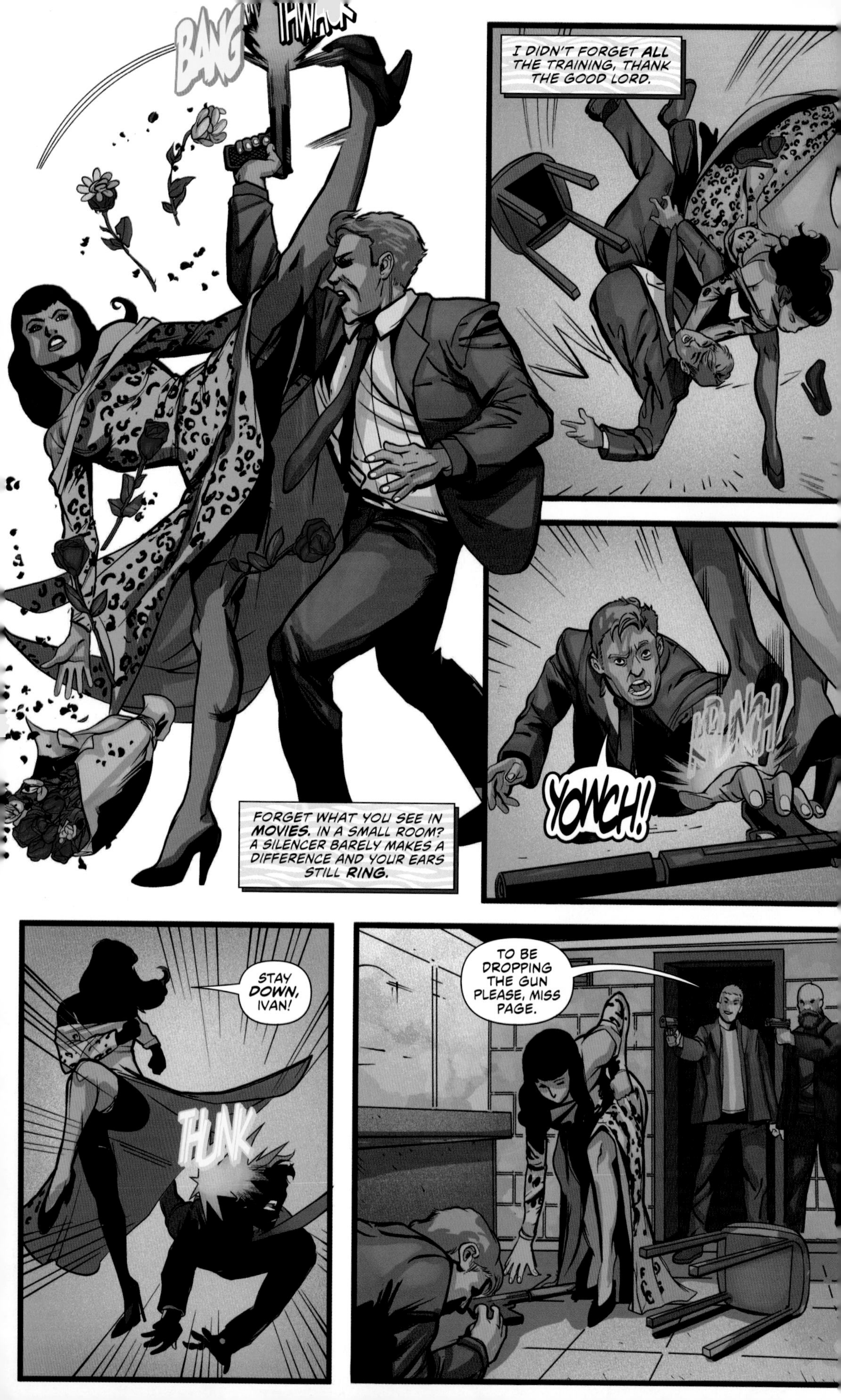
BANG
THWACK
I DIDN'T FORGET ALL THE TRAINING, THANK THE GOOD LORD.
FORGET WHAT YOU SEE IN MOVIES. IN A SMALL ROOM? A SILENCER BARELY MAKES A DIFFERENCE AND YOUR EARS STILL RING.
KRUNCH
YOWCH!
STAY DOWN, IVAN!
THUNK
TO BE DROPPING THE GUN PLEASE, MISS PAGE.

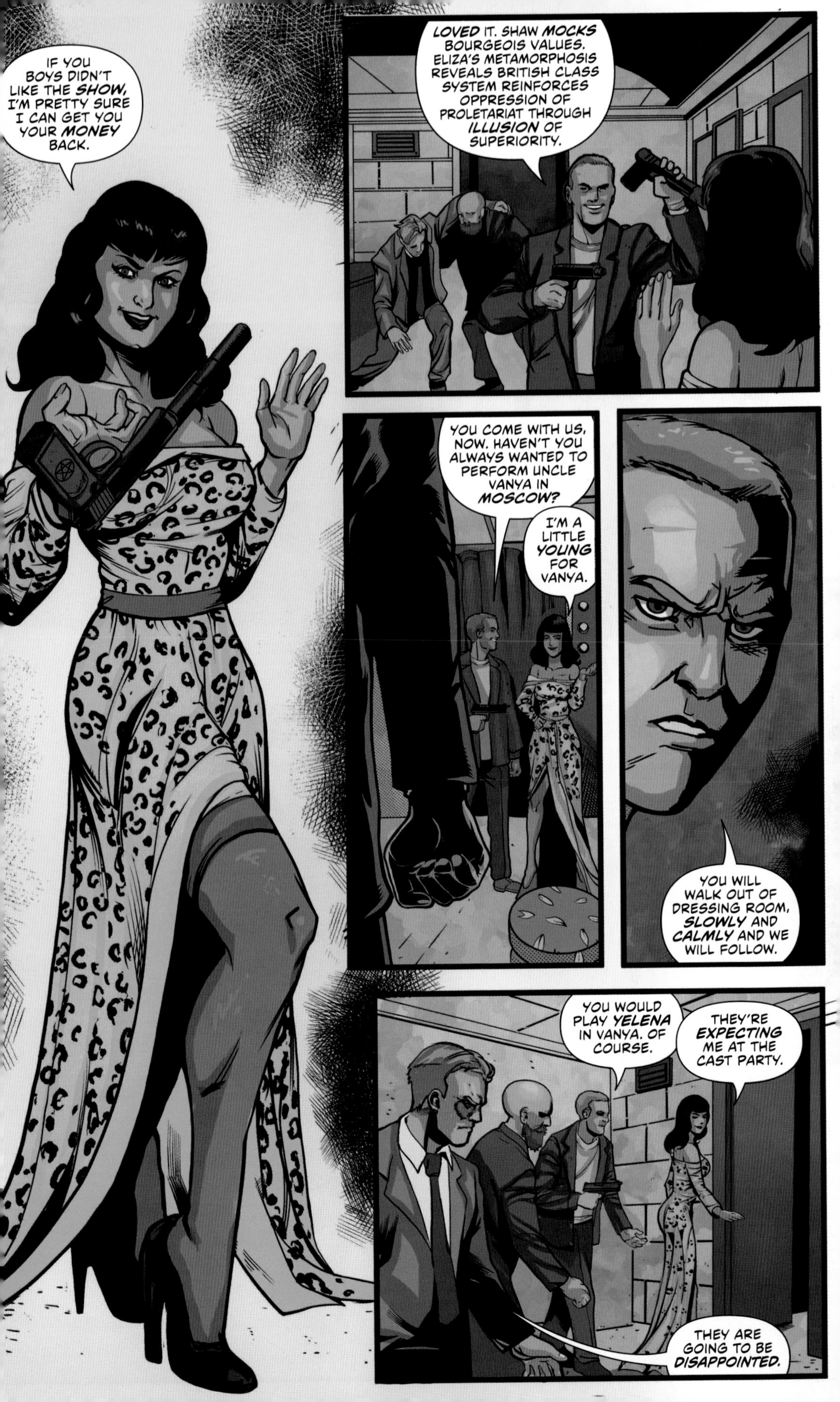

IF YOU BOYS DIDN'T LIKE THE SHOW, I'M PRETTY SURE I CAN GET YOU YOUR MONEY BACK.
LOVED IT. SHAW MOCKS BOURGEOIS VALUES. ELIZA'S METAMORPHOSIS REVEALS BRITISH CLASS SYSTEM REINFORCES OPPRESSION OF PROLETARIAT THROUGH ILLUSION OF SUPERIORITY.
YOU COME WITH US, NOW. HAVEN'T YOU ALWAYS WANTED TO PERFORM UNCLE VANYA IN MOSCOW?
I'M A LITTLE YOUNG FOR VANYA.
YOU WILL WALK OUT OF DRESSING ROOM, SLOWLY AND CALMLY AND WE WILL FOLLOW.
YOU WOULD PLAY YELENA IN VANYA. OF COURSE.
THEY'RE EXPECTING ME AT THE CAST PARTY.
THEY ARE GOING TO BE DISAPPOINTED.

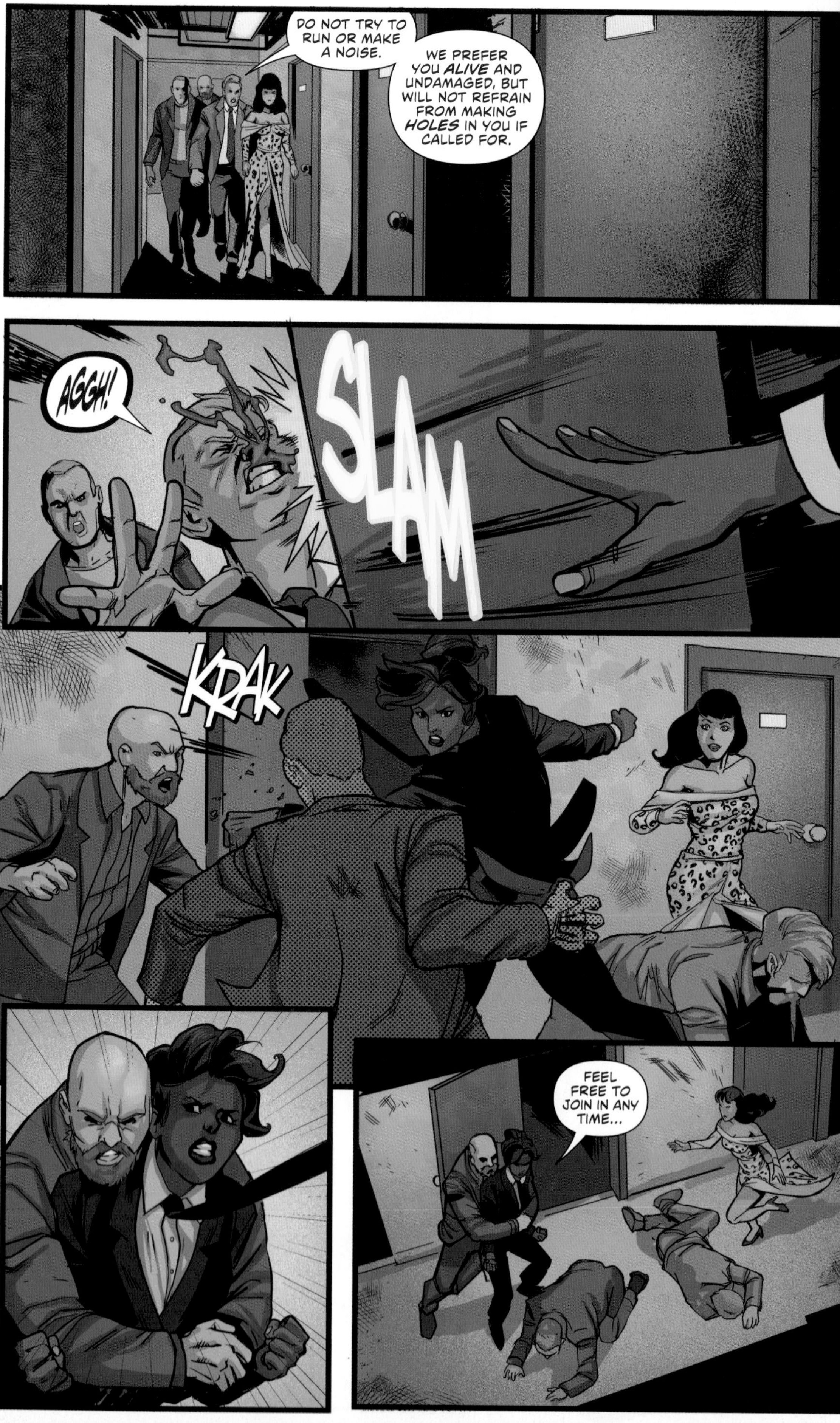
DO NOT TRY TO RUN OR MAKE A NOISE.
WE PREFER YOU ALIVE AND UNDAMAGED, BUT WILL NOT REFRAIN FROM MAKING HOLES IN YOU IF CALLED FOR.
AGGH!
SLAM
KRAK
FEEL FREE TO JOIN IN ANY TIME...

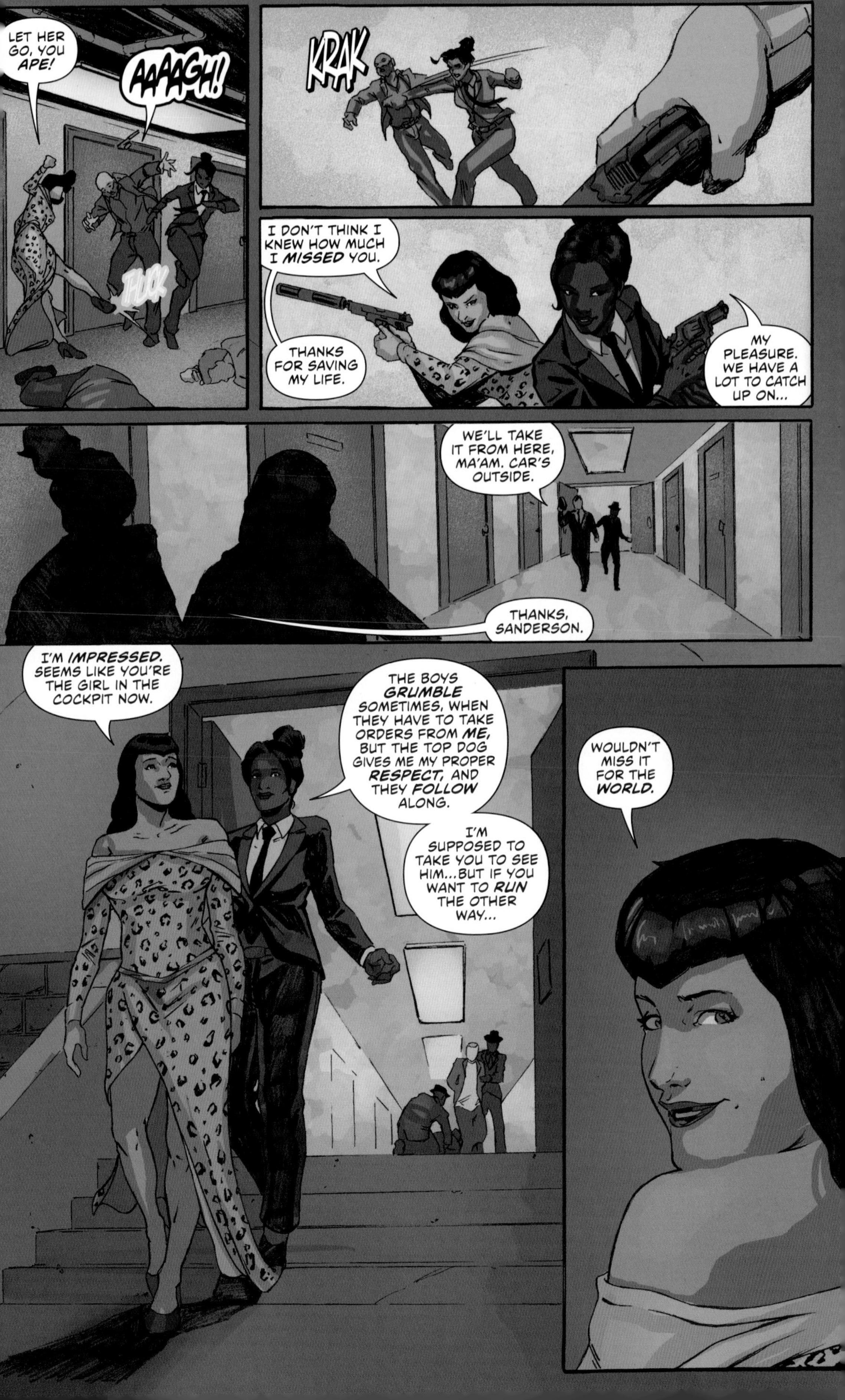

LET HER GO, YOU APE!
AAAAGH!
THUCK
KRAK
I DON'T THINK I KNEW HOW MUCH I MISSED YOU.
THANKS FOR SAVING MY LIFE.
MY PLEASURE. WE HAVE A LOT TO CATCH UP ON...
WE'LL TAKE IT FROM HERE, MA'AM. CAR'S OUTSIDE.
THANKS, SANDERSON.
I'M IMPRESSED. SEEMS LIKE YOU'RE THE GIRL IN THE COCKPIT NOW.
THE BOYS GRUMBLE SOMETIMES, WHEN THEY HAVE TO TAKE ORDERS FROM ME, BUT THE TOP DOG GIVES ME MY PROPER RESPECT, AND THEY FOLLOW ALONG.
I'M SUPPOSED TO TAKE YOU TO SEE HIM...BUT IF YOU WANT TO RUN THE OTHER WAY...
WOULDN'T MISS IT FOR THE WORLD.

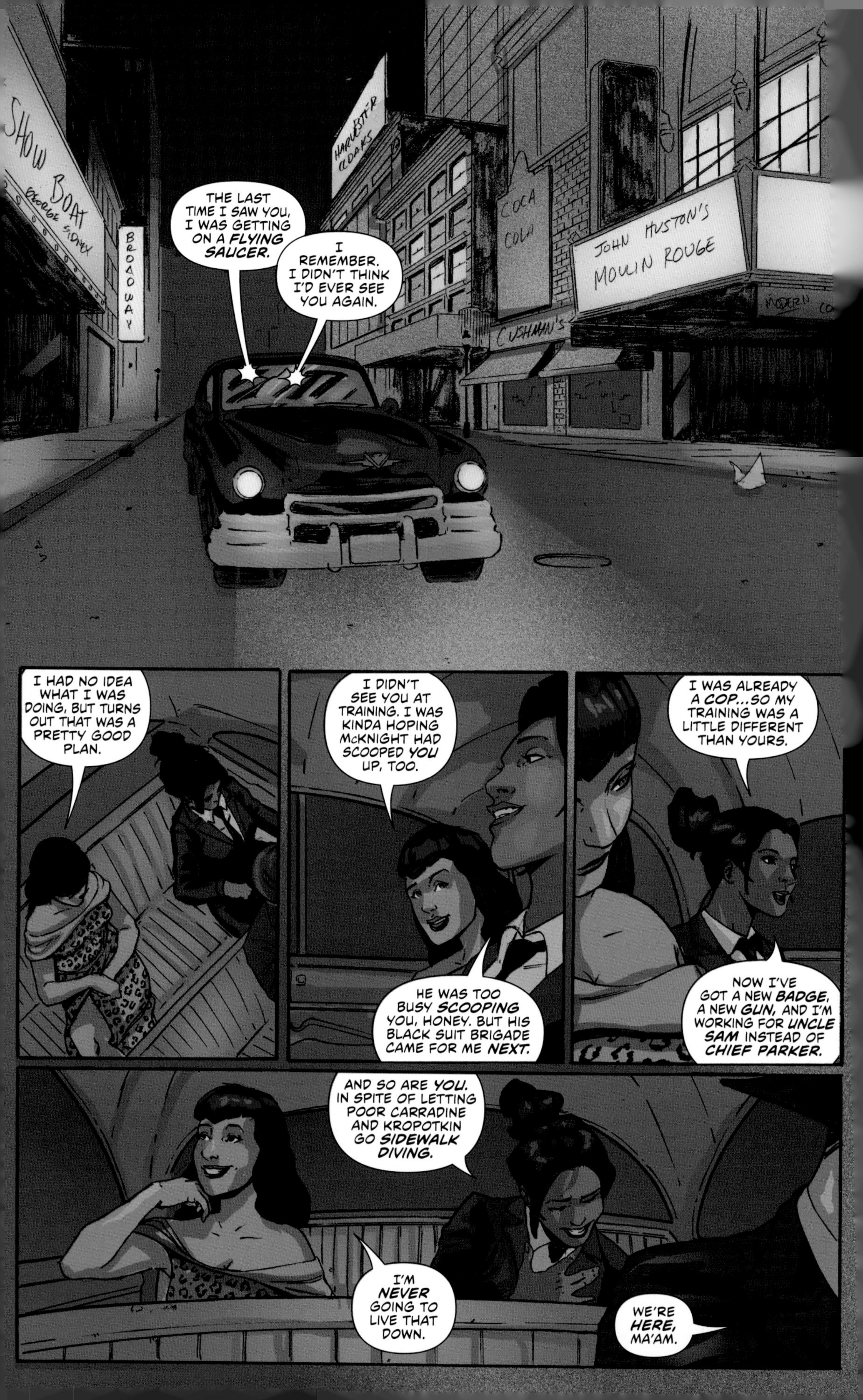
SHOW BOAT
GEORGE SIDNEY
BROADWAY
HARVESTER CLOAKS
COCA COLA
JOHN HUSTON'S
MOULIN ROUGE
CUSHMAN'S
THE LAST TIME I SAW YOU, I WAS GETTING ON A FLYING SAUCER.
I REMEMBER. I DIDN'T THINK I'D EVER SEE YOU AGAIN.
I HAD NO IDEA WHAT I WAS DOING, BUT TURNS OUT THAT WAS A PRETTY GOOD PLAN.
I DIDN'T SEE YOU AT TRAINING. I WAS KINDA HOPING McKNIGHT HAD SCOOPED YOU UP, TOO.
HE WAS TOO BUSY SCOOPING YOU, HONEY. BUT HIS BLACK SUIT BRIGADE CAME FOR ME NEXT.
I WAS ALREADY A COP...SO MY TRAINING WAS A LITTLE DIFFERENT THAN YOURS.
NOW I'VE GOT A NEW BADGE, A NEW GUN, AND I'M WORKING FOR UNCLE SAM INSTEAD OF CHIEF PARKER.
AND SO ARE YOU. IN SPITE OF LETTING POOR CARRADINE AND KROPOTKIN GO SIDEWALK DIVING.
I'M NEVER GOING TO LIVE THAT DOWN.
WE'RE HERE, MA'AM.

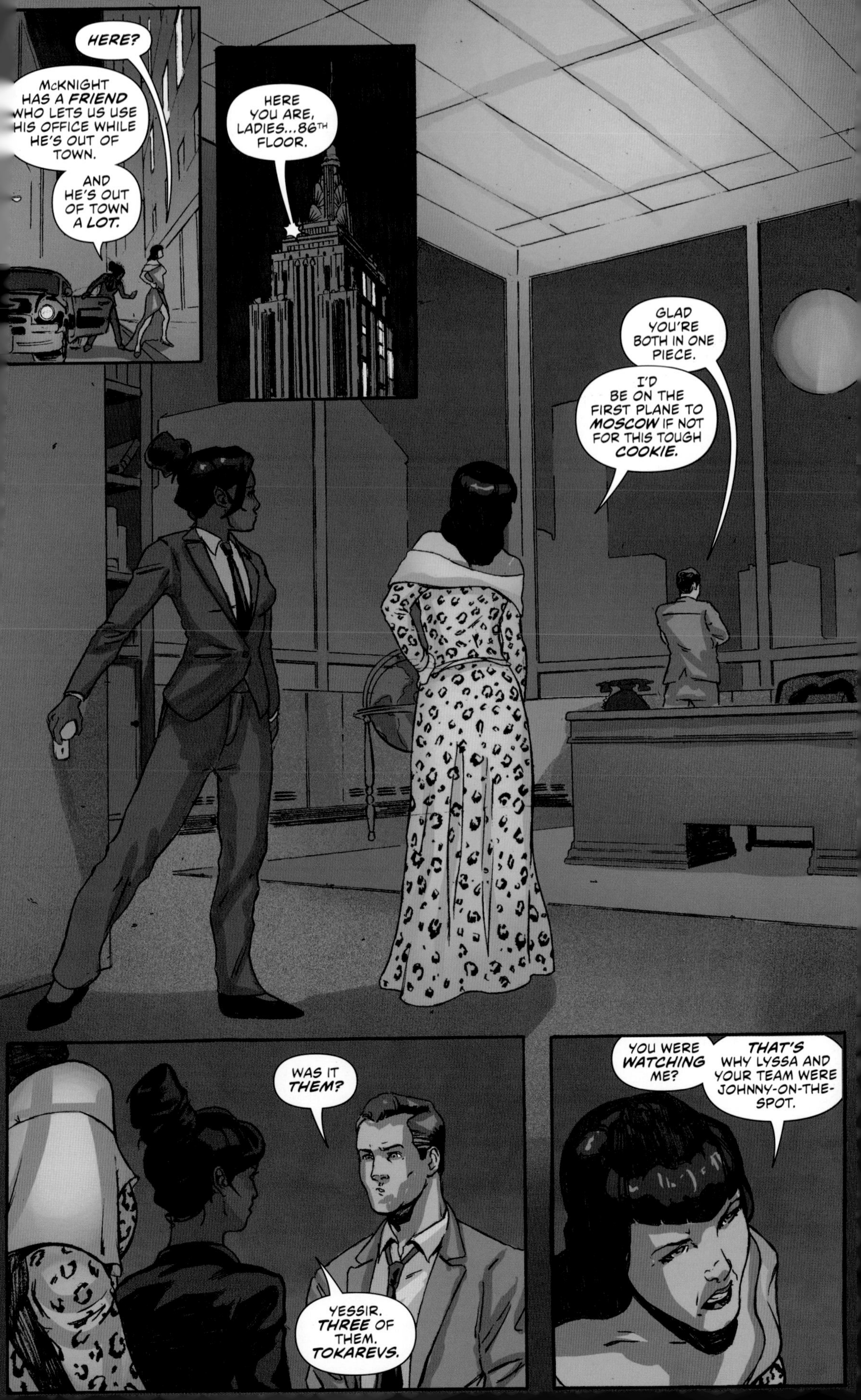
HERE?
McKNIGHT HAS A FRIEND WHO LETS US USE HIS OFFICE WHILE HE'S OUT OF TOWN.
AND HE'S OUT OF TOWN A LOT.
HERE YOU ARE, LADIES...86TH FLOOR.
GLAD YOU'RE BOTH IN ONE PIECE.
I'D BE ON THE FIRST PLANE TO MOSCOW IF NOT FOR THIS TOUGH COOKIE.
WAS IT THEM?
YESSIR. THREE OF THEM. TOKAREVS.
YOU WERE WATCHING ME?
THAT'S WHY LYSSA AND YOUR TEAM WERE JOHNNY-ON-THE-SPOT.

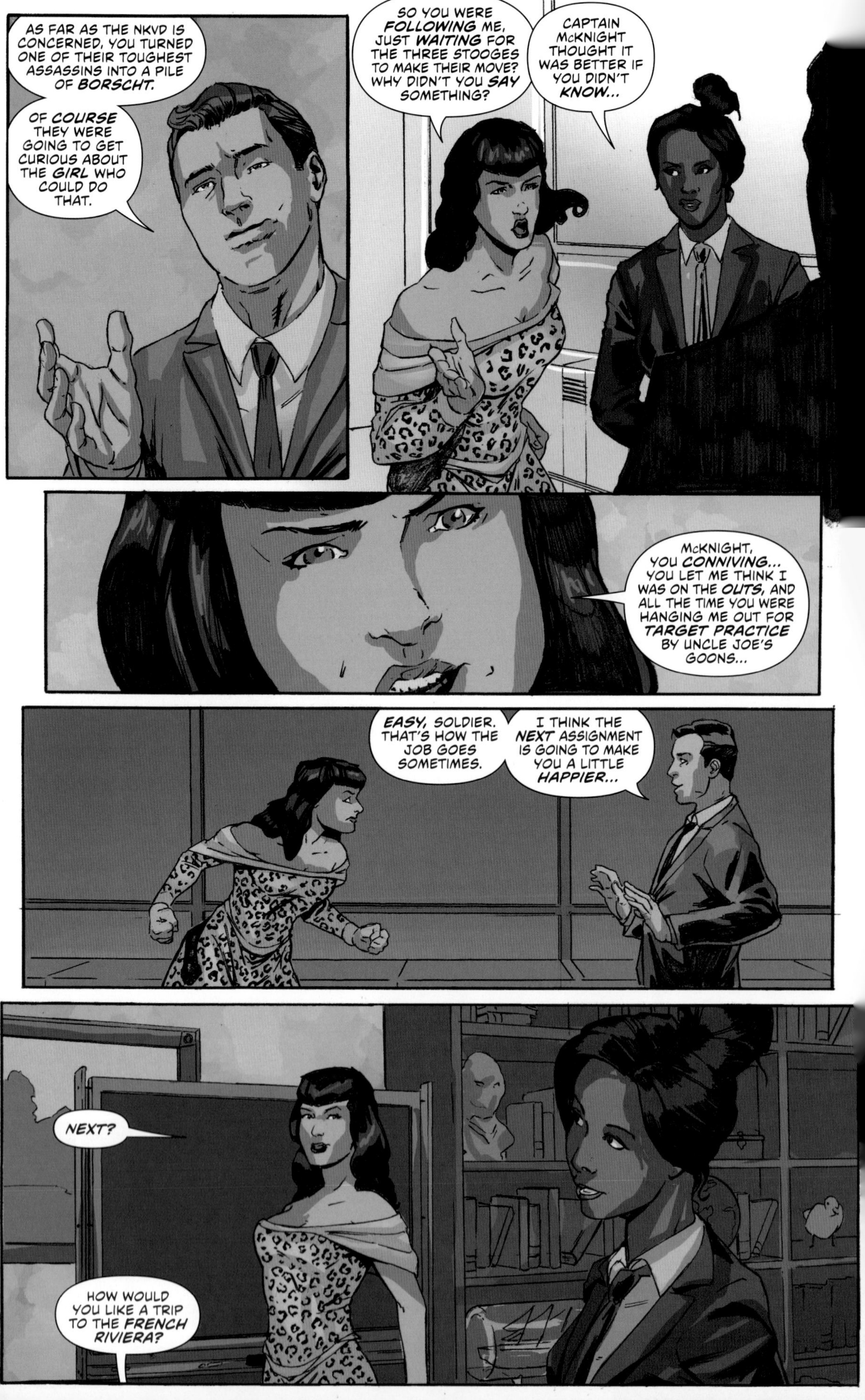
AS FAR AS THE NKVD IS CONCERNED, YOU TURNED ONE OF THEIR TOUGHEST ASSASSINS INTO A PILE OF BORSCHT.
OF COURSE THEY WERE GOING TO GET CURIOUS ABOUT THE GIRL WHO COULD DO THAT.
SO YOU WERE FOLLOWING ME, JUST WAITING FOR THE THREE STOOGES TO MAKE THEIR MOVE? WHY DIDN'T YOU SAY SOMETHING?
CAPTAIN McKNIGHT THOUGHT IT WAS BETTER IF YOU DIDN'T KNOW...
McKNIGHT, YOU CONNIVING... YOU LET ME THINK I WAS ON THE OUTS, AND ALL THE TIME YOU WERE HANGING ME OUT FOR TARGET PRACTICE BY UNCLE JOE'S GOONS...
EASY, SOLDIER. THAT'S HOW THE JOB GOES SOMETIMES.
I THINK THE NEXT ASSIGNMENT IS GOING TO MAKE YOU A LITTLE HAPPIER...
NEXT?
HOW WOULD YOU LIKE A TRIP TO THE FRENCH RIVIERA?

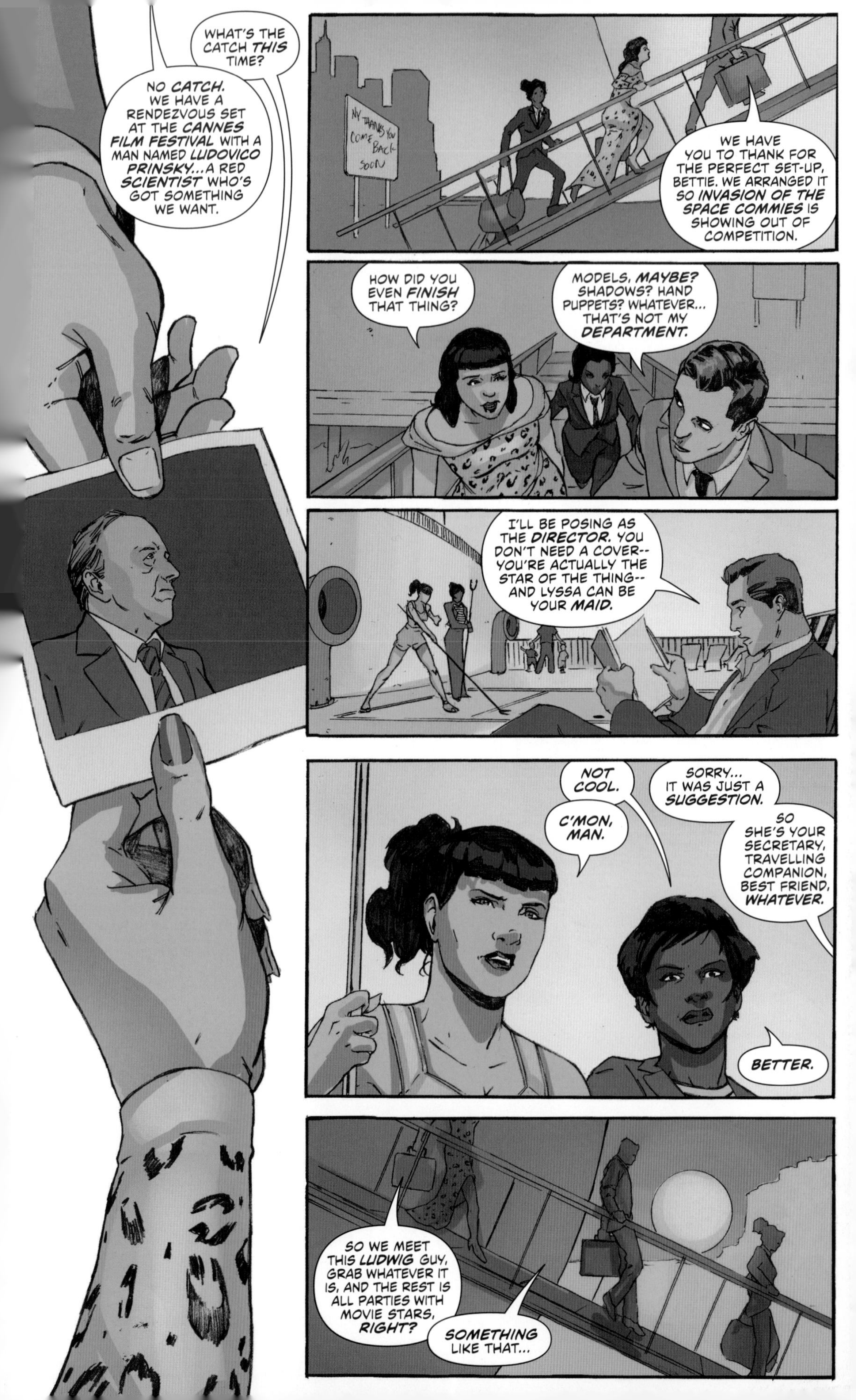
WHAT'S THE CATCH THIS TIME?
NO CATCH. WE HAVE A RENDEZVOUS SET AT THE CANNES FILM FESTIVAL WITH A MAN NAMED LUDOVICO PRINSKY...A RED SCIENTIST WHO'S GOT SOMETHING WE WANT.
NY THANKS YOU COME BACK SOON
WE HAVE YOU TO THANK FOR THE PERFECT SET-UP, BETTIE. WE ARRANGED IT SO INVASION OF THE SPACE COMMIES IS SHOWING OUT OF COMPETITION.
HOW DID YOU EVEN FINISH THAT THING?
MODELS, MAYBE? SHADOWS? HAND PUPPETS? WHATEVER... THAT'S NOT MY DEPARTMENT.
I'LL BE POSING AS THE DIRECTOR. YOU DON'T NEED A COVER-- YOU'RE ACTUALLY THE STAR OF THE THING-- AND LYSSA CAN BE YOUR MAID.
NOT COOL.
C'MON, MAN.
SORRY... IT WAS JUST A SUGGESTION.
SO SHE'S YOUR SECRETARY, TRAVELLING COMPANION, BEST FRIEND, WHATEVER.
BETTER.
SO WE MEET THIS LUDWIG GUY, GRAB WHATEVER IT IS, AND THE REST IS ALL PARTIES WITH MOVIE STARS, RIGHT?
SOMETHING LIKE THAT...

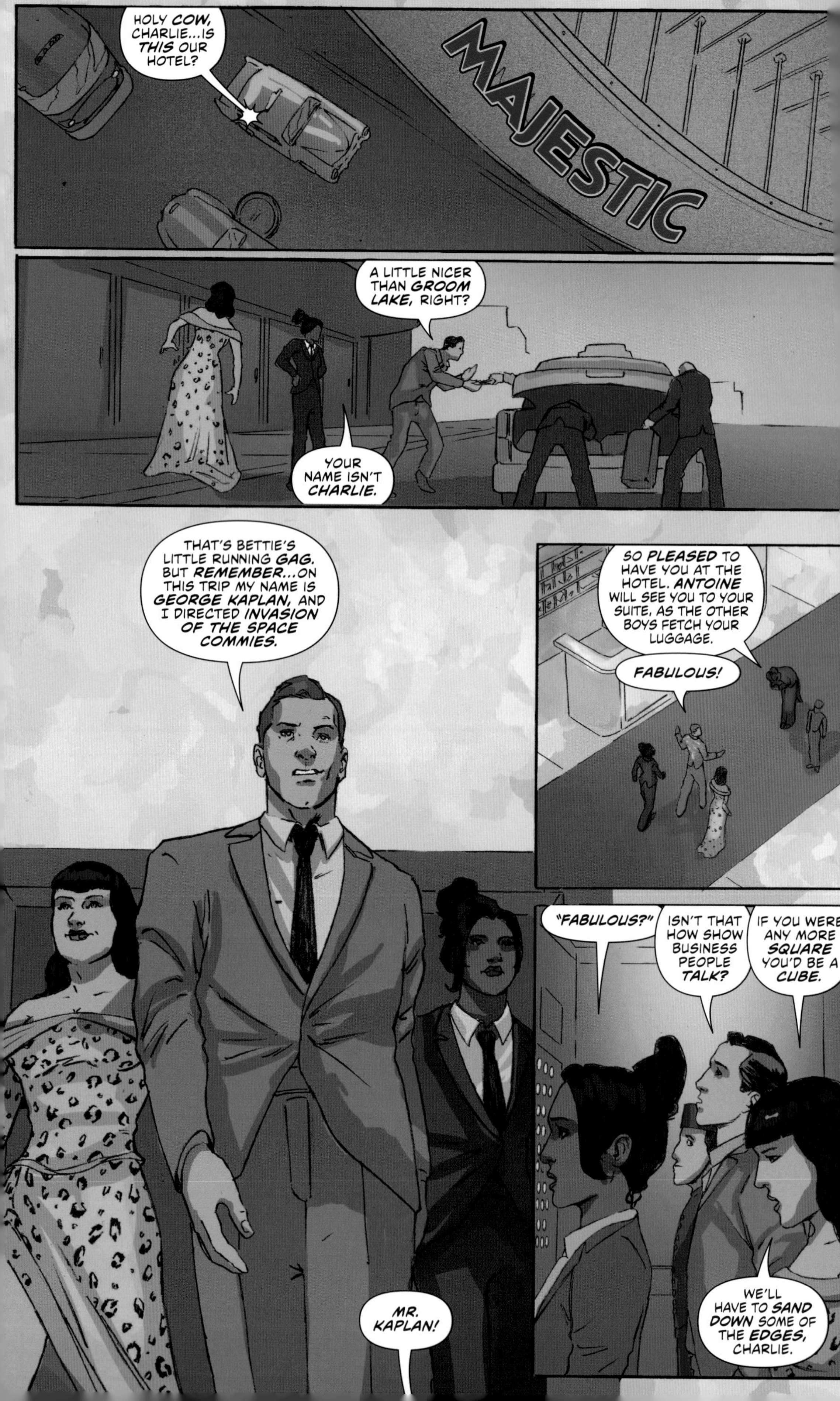
HOLY COW, CHARLIE...IS THIS OUR HOTEL?
MAJESTIC
A LITTLE NICER THAN GROOM LAKE, RIGHT?
YOUR NAME ISN'T CHARLIE.
THAT'S BETTIE'S LITTLE RUNNING GAG. BUT REMEMBER...ON THIS TRIP MY NAME IS GEORGE KAPLAN, AND I DIRECTED INVASION OF THE SPACE COMMIES.
MR. KAPLAN!
SO PLEASED TO HAVE YOU AT THE HOTEL. ANTOINE WILL SEE YOU TO YOUR SUITE, AS THE OTHER BOYS FETCH YOUR LUGGAGE.
FABULOUS!
"FABULOUS?"
ISN'T THAT HOW SHOW BUSINESS PEOPLE TALK?
IF YOU WERE ANY MORE SQUARE YOU'D BE A CUBE.
WE'LL HAVE TO SAND DOWN SOME OF THE EDGES, CHARLIE.

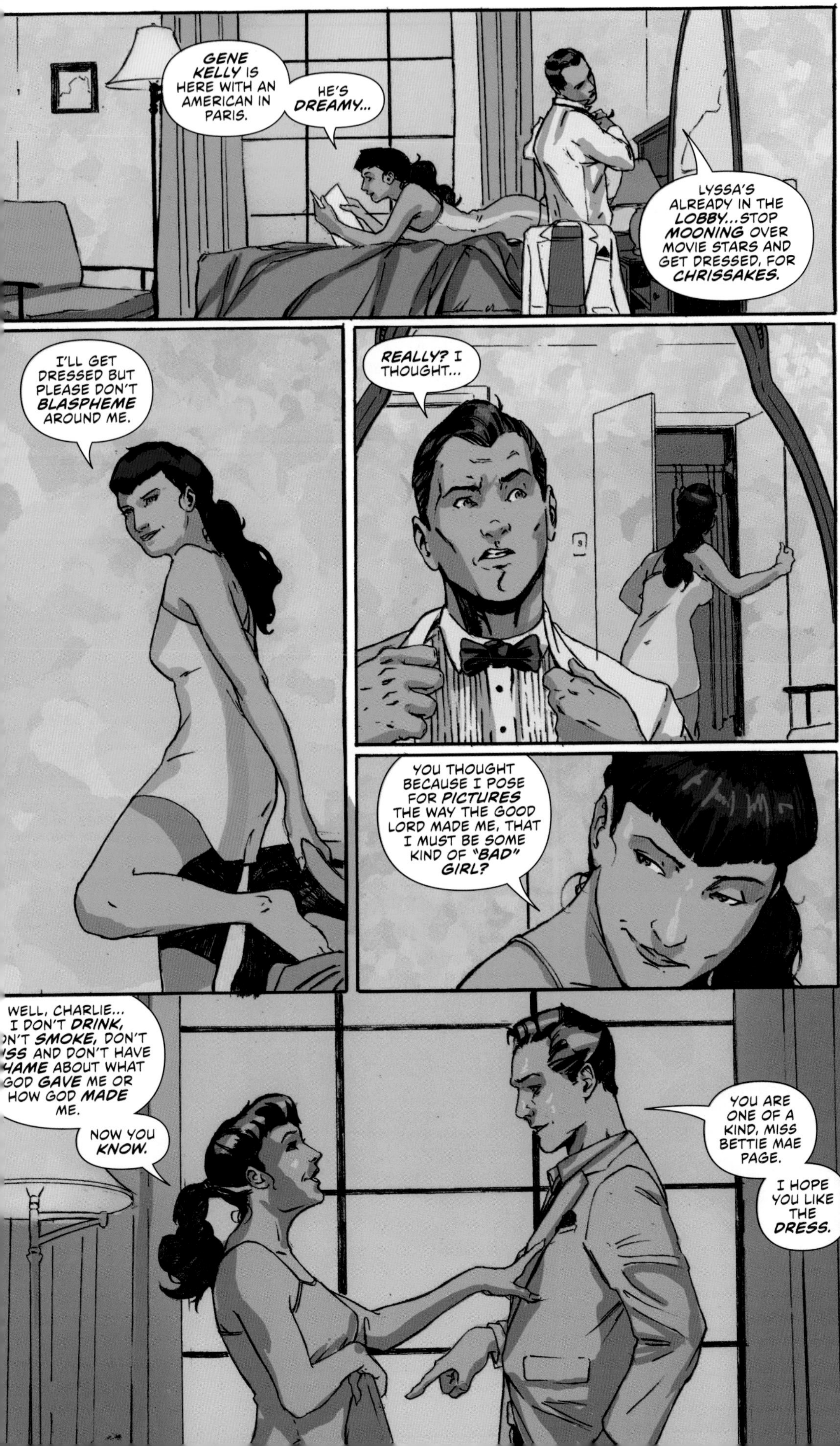
GENE KELLY IS HERE WITH AN AMERICAN IN PARIS.
HE'S DREAMY...
LYSSA'S ALREADY IN THE LOBBY...STOP MOONING OVER MOVIE STARS AND GET DRESSED, FOR CHRISSAKES.
I'LL GET DRESSED BUT PLEASE DON'T BLASPHEME AROUND ME.
REALLY? I THOUGHT...
YOU THOUGHT BECAUSE I POSE FOR PICTURES THE WAY THE GOOD LORD MADE ME, THAT I MUST BE SOME KIND OF "BAD" GIRL?
WELL, CHARLIE... I DON'T DRINK, ON'T SMOKE, DON'T ISS AND DON'T HAVE HAME ABOUT WHAT GOD GAVE ME OR HOW GOD MADE ME.
NOW YOU KNOW.
YOU ARE ONE OF A KIND, MISS BETTIE MAE PAGE.
I HOPE YOU LIKE THE DRESS.

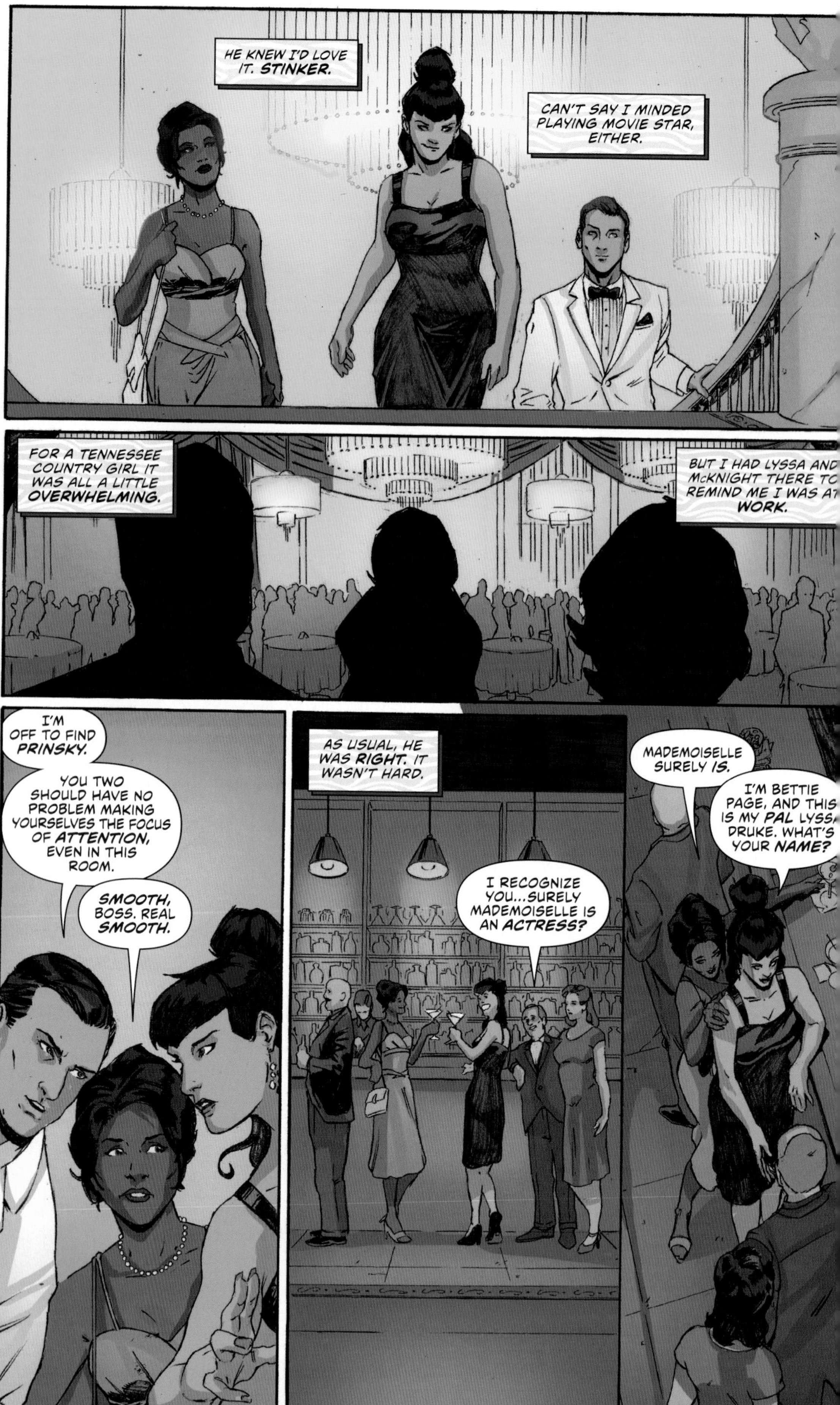

HE KNEW I'D LOVE IT. STINKER.
CAN'T SAY I MINDED PLAYING MOVIE STAR, EITHER.
FOR A TENNESSEE COUNTRY GIRL IT WAS ALL A LITTLE OVERWHELMING.
BUT I HAD LYSSA AND McKNIGHT THERE TO REMIND ME I WAS AT WORK.
I'M OFF TO FIND PRINSKY.
YOU TWO SHOULD HAVE NO PROBLEM MAKING YOURSELVES THE FOCUS OF ATTENTION, EVEN IN THIS ROOM.
SMOOTH, BOSS. REAL SMOOTH.
AS USUAL, HE WAS RIGHT. IT WASN'T HARD.
I RECOGNIZE YOU...SURELY MADEMOISELLE IS AN ACTRESS?
MADEMOISELLE SURELY IS.
I'M BETTIE PAGE, AND THIS IS MY PAL LYSS, DRUKE. WHAT'S YOUR NAME?

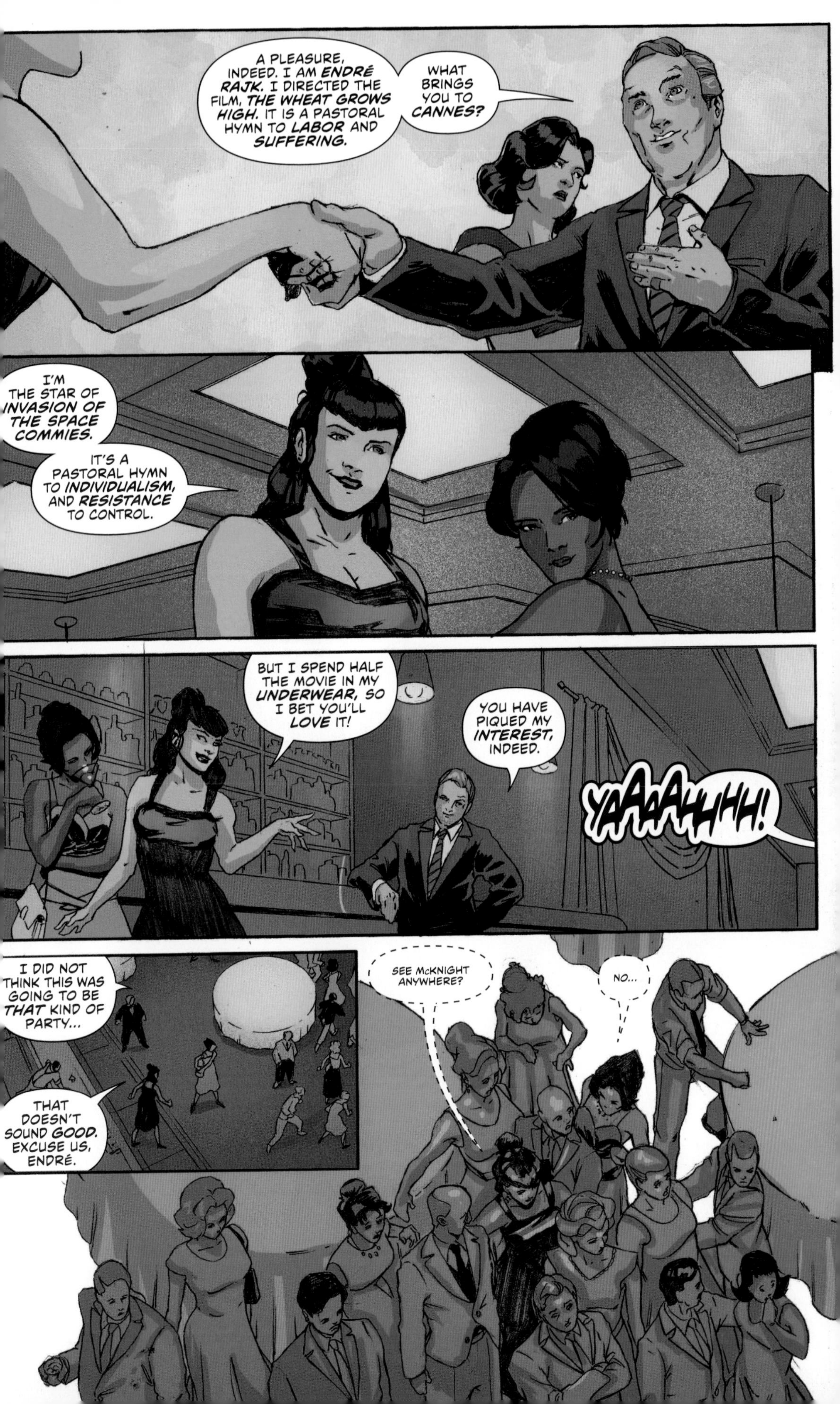

A PLEASURE, INDEED. I AM ENDRÉ RAJK. I DIRECTED THE FILM, THE WHEAT GROWS HIGH. IT IS A PASTORAL HYMN TO LABOR AND SUFFERING.
WHAT BRINGS YOU TO CANNES?
I'M THE STAR OF INVASION OF THE SPACE COMMIES.
IT'S A PASTORAL HYMN TO INDIVIDUALISM, AND RESISTANCE TO CONTROL.
BUT I SPEND HALF THE MOVIE IN MY UNDERWEAR, SO I BET YOU'LL LOVE IT!
YOU HAVE PIQUED MY INTEREST, INDEED.
YAAAAHHHH!
I DID NOT THINK THIS WAS GOING TO BE THAT KIND OF PARTY...
THAT DOESN'T SOUND GOOD. EXCUSE US, ENDRÉ.
SEE McKNIGHT ANYWHERE?
NO...

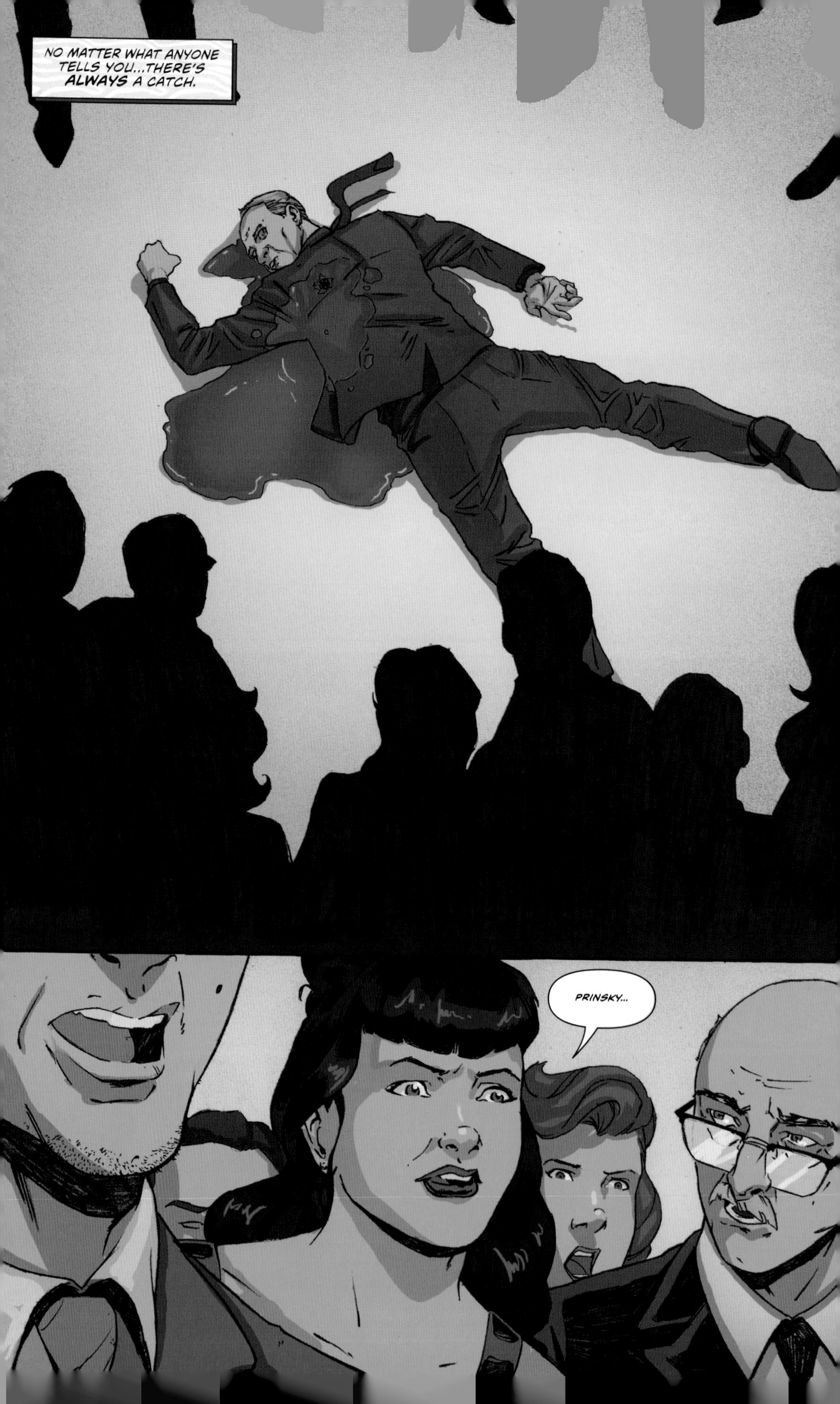
NO MATTER WHAT ANYONE TELLS YOU...THERE'S **ALWAYS** A CATCH.
PRINSKY...

7

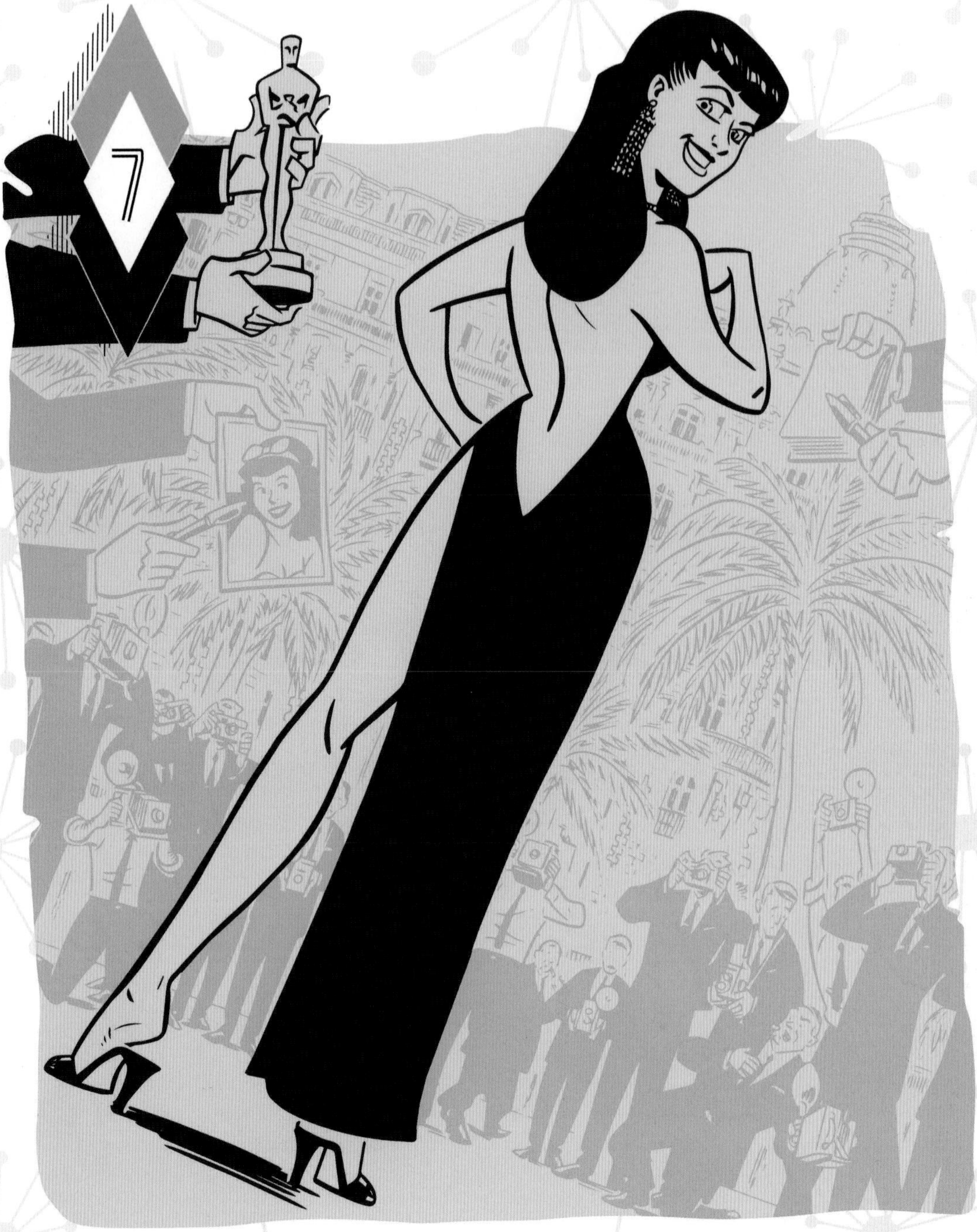

ART: JOSEPH MICHAEL LINSNER

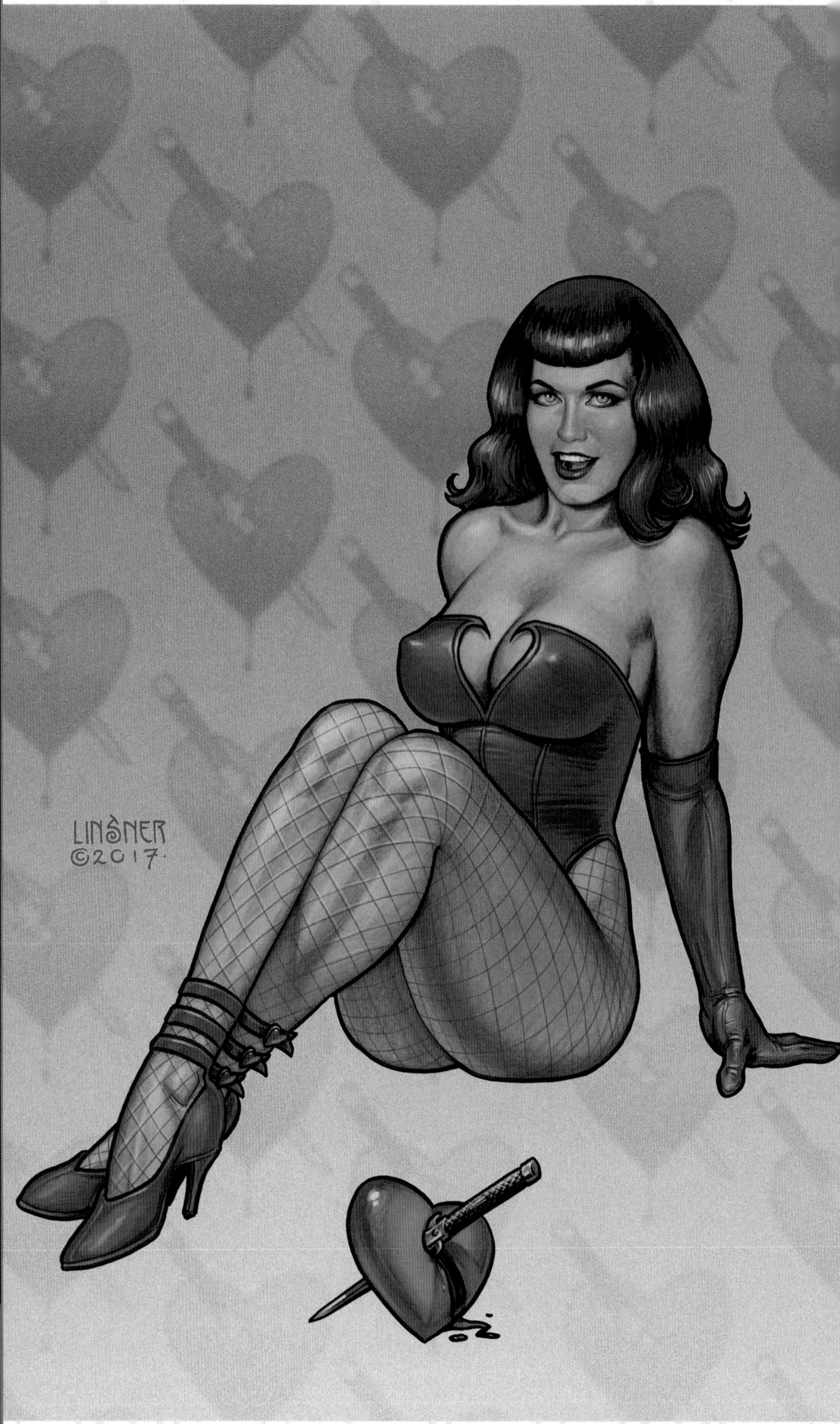
LINSNER
©2017.

7

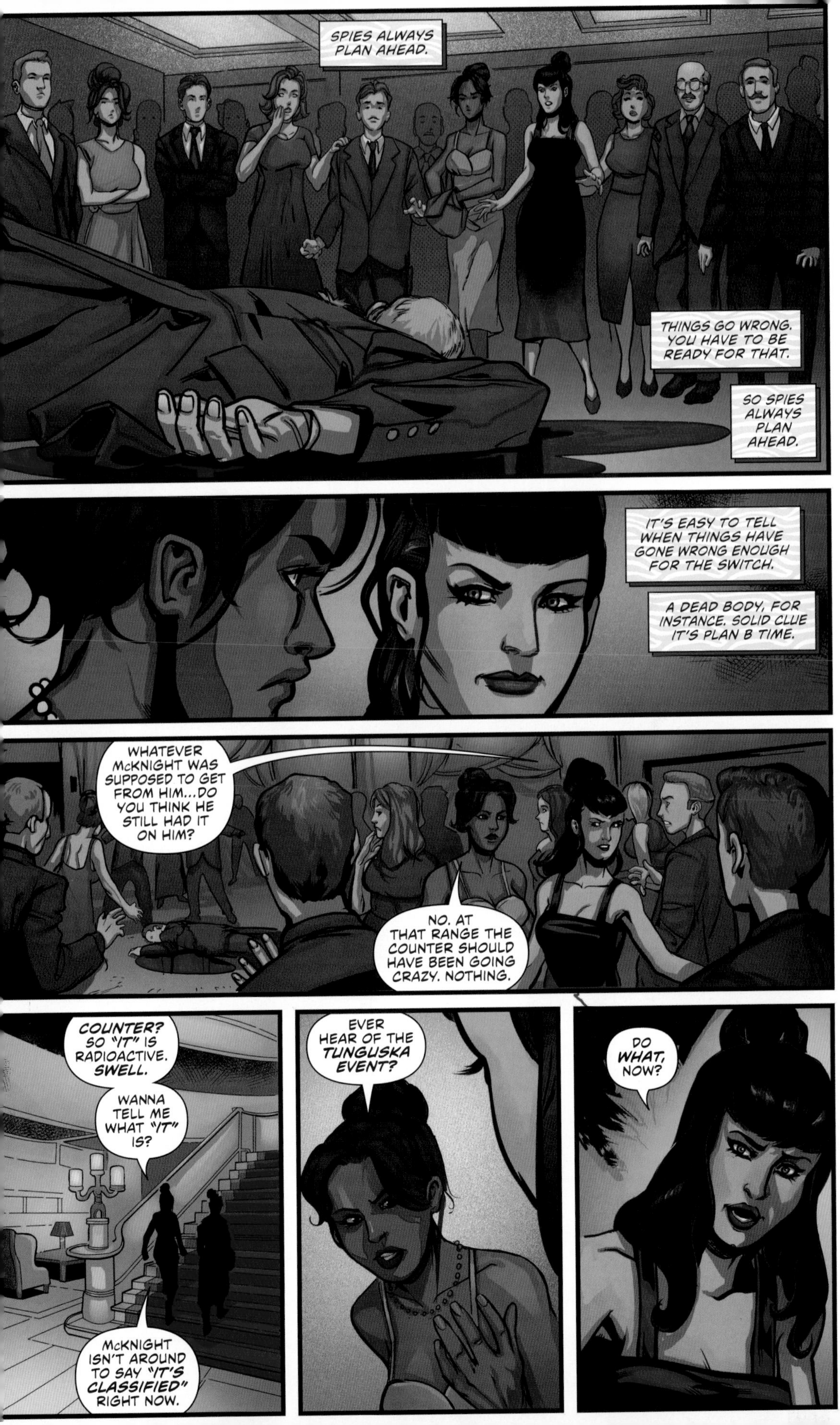
SPIES ALWAYS PLAN AHEAD.
THINGS GO WRONG. YOU HAVE TO BE READY FOR THAT.
SO SPIES ALWAYS PLAN AHEAD.
IT'S EASY TO TELL WHEN THINGS HAVE GONE WRONG ENOUGH FOR THE SWITCH.
A DEAD BODY, FOR INSTANCE. SOLID CLUE IT'S PLAN B TIME.
WHATEVER McKNIGHT WAS SUPPOSED TO GET FROM HIM...DO YOU THINK HE STILL HAD IT ON HIM?
NO. AT THAT RANGE THE COUNTER SHOULD HAVE BEEN GOING CRAZY. NOTHING.
COUNTER? SO "IT" IS RADIOACTIVE. SWELL.
WANNA TELL ME WHAT "IT" IS?
McKNIGHT ISN'T AROUND TO SAY "IT'S CLASSIFIED" RIGHT NOW.
EVER HEAR OF THE TUNGUSKA EVENT?
DO WHAT, NOW?

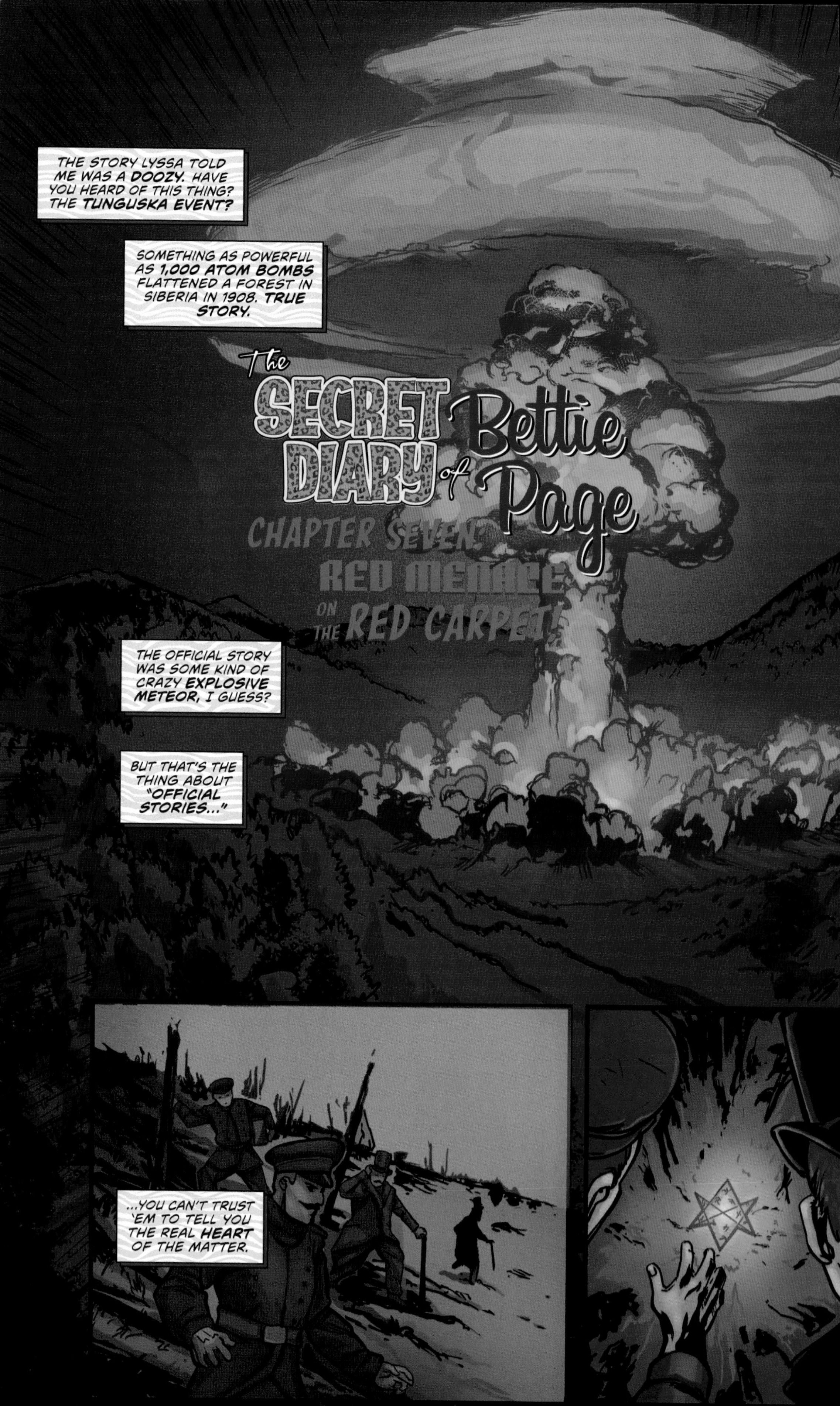
THE STORY LYSSA TOLD ME WAS A DOOZY. HAVE YOU HEARD OF THIS THING? THE TUNGUSKA EVENT?
SOMETHING AS POWERFUL AS 1,000 ATOM BOMBS FLATTENED A FOREST IN SIBERIA IN 1908. TRUE STORY.
The SECRET DIARY of Bettie Page
CHAPTER SEVEN: RED MENACE ON THE RED CARPET!
THE OFFICIAL STORY WAS SOME KIND OF CRAZY EXPLOSIVE METEOR, I GUESS?
BUT THAT'S THE THING ABOUT "OFFICIAL STORIES..."
...YOU CAN'T TRUST 'EM TO TELL YOU THE REAL HEART OF THE MATTER.

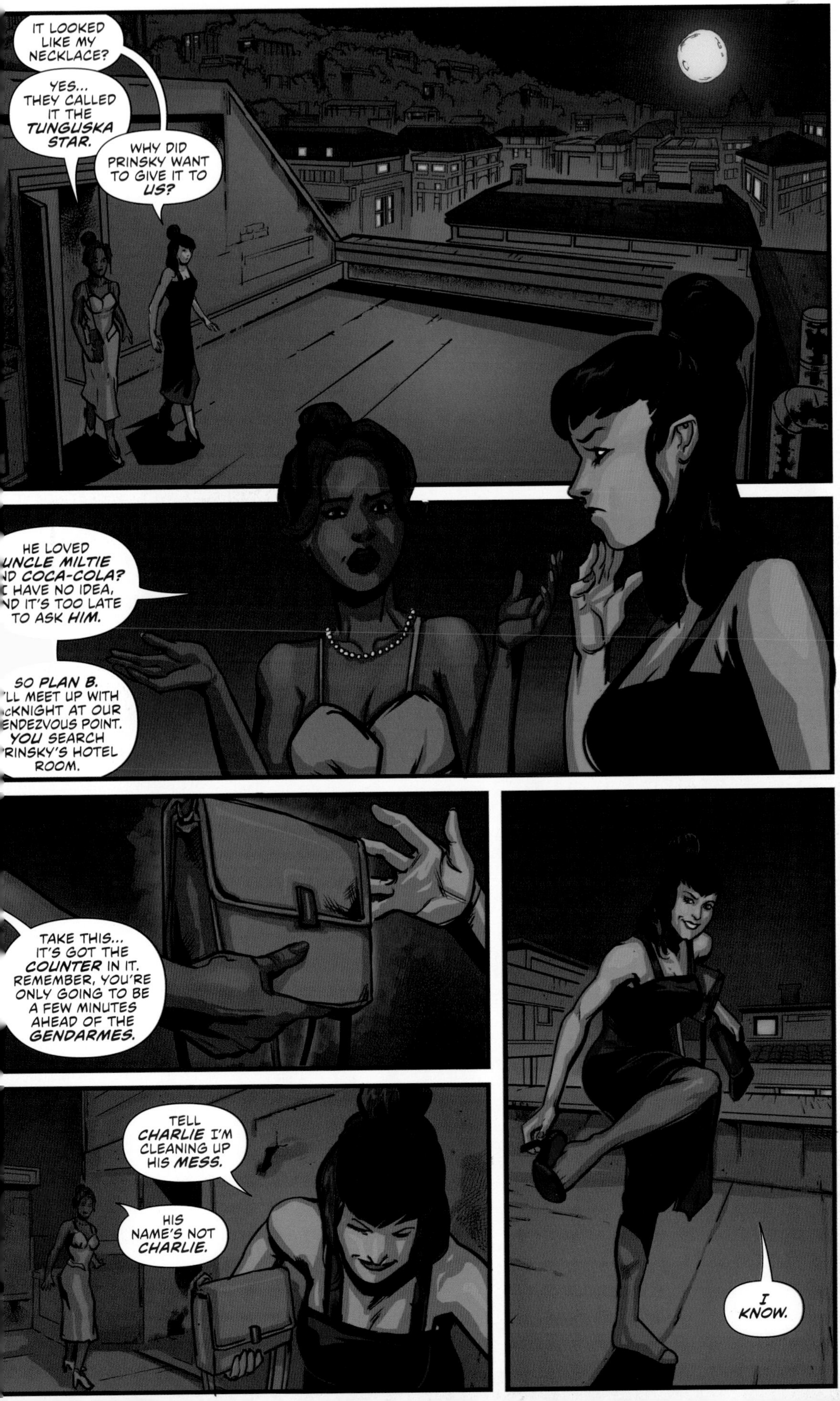
IT LOOKED LIKE MY NECKLACE?
YES... THEY CALLED IT THE TUNGUSKA STAR.
WHY DID PRINSKY WANT TO GIVE IT TO US?
HE LOVED UNCLE MILTIE ND COCA-COLA? I HAVE NO IDEA, ND IT'S TOO LATE TO ASK HIM.
SO PLAN B. 'LL MEET UP WITH CKNIGHT AT OUR ENDEZVOUS POINT. YOU SEARCH RINSKY'S HOTEL ROOM.
TAKE THIS... IT'S GOT THE COUNTER IN IT. REMEMBER, YOU'RE ONLY GOING TO BE A FEW MINUTES AHEAD OF THE GENDARMES.
TELL CHARLIE I'M CLEANING UP HIS MESS.
HIS NAME'S NOT CHARLIE.
I KNOW.

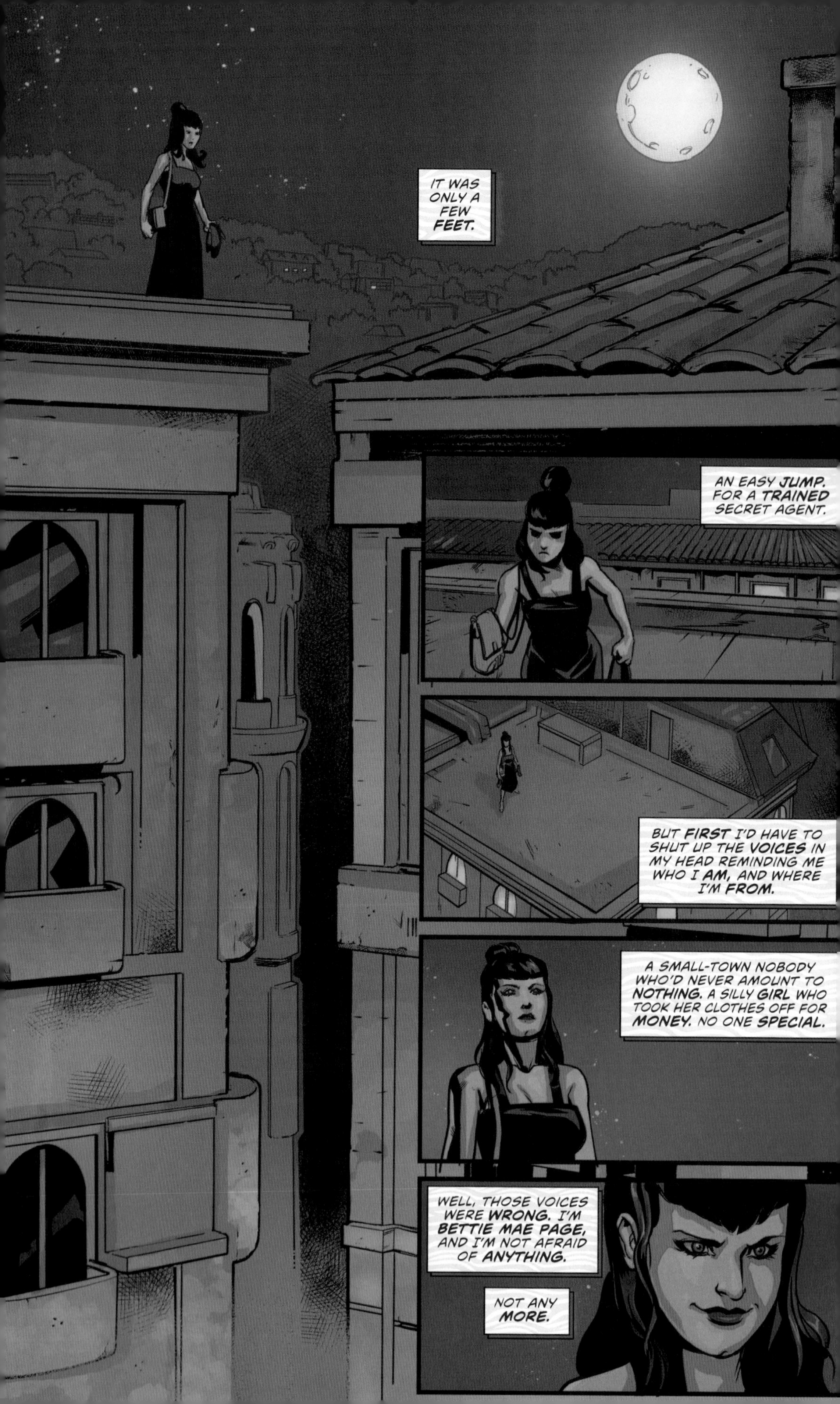
IT WAS ONLY A FEW FEET.
AN EASY JUMP. FOR A TRAINED SECRET AGENT.
BUT FIRST I'D HAVE TO SHUT UP THE VOICES IN MY HEAD REMINDING ME WHO I AM, AND WHERE I'M FROM.
A SMALL-TOWN NOBODY WHO'D NEVER AMOUNT TO NOTHING. A SILLY GIRL WHO TOOK HER CLOTHES OFF FOR MONEY. NO ONE SPECIAL.
WELL, THOSE VOICES WERE WRONG. I'M BETTIE MAE PAGE, AND I'M NOT AFRAID OF ANYTHING.
NOT ANY MORE.

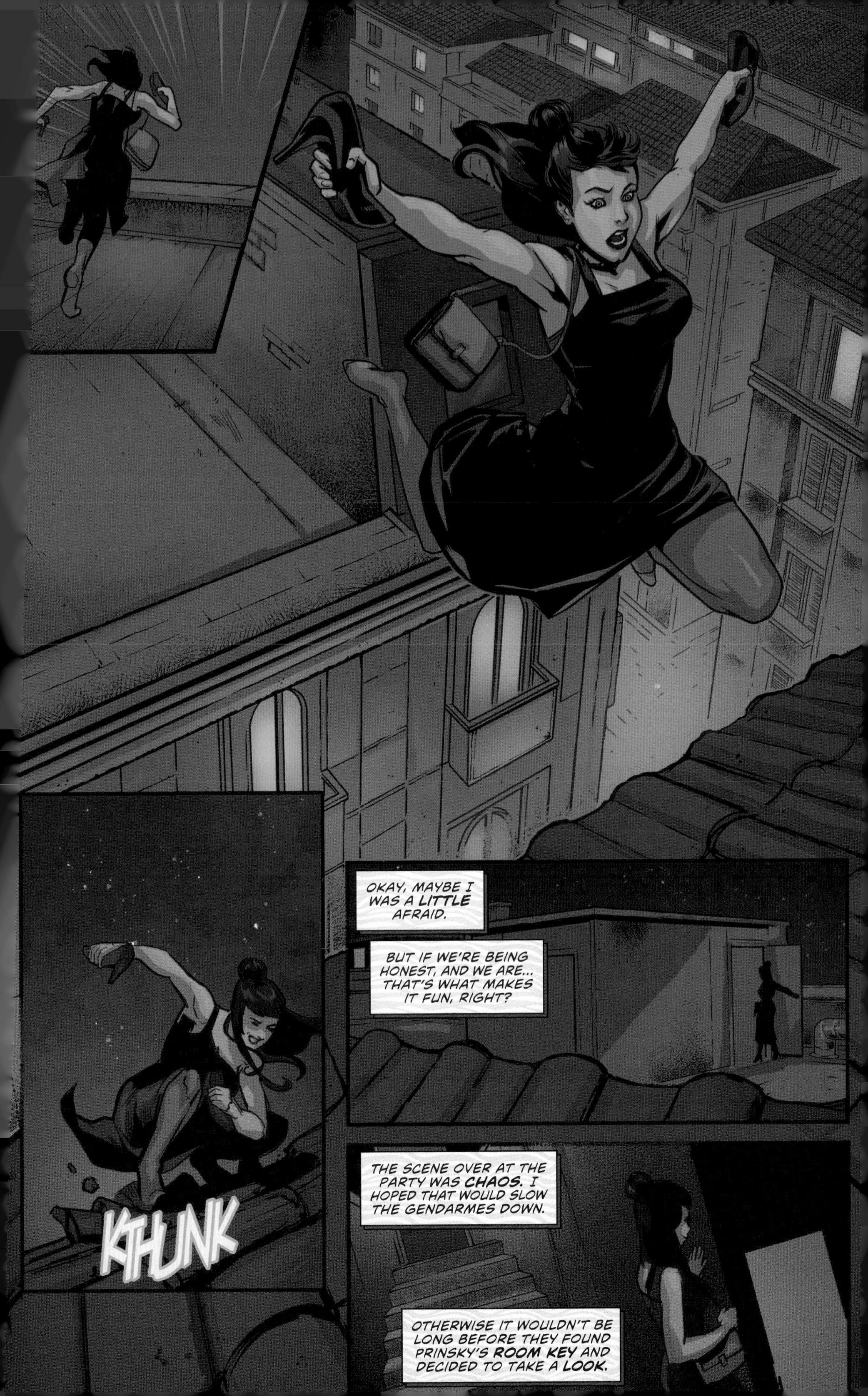
KTHUNK
OKAY, MAYBE I WAS A LITTLE AFRAID.
BUT IF WE'RE BEING HONEST, AND WE ARE... THAT'S WHAT MAKES IT FUN, RIGHT?
THE SCENE OVER AT THE PARTY WAS CHAOS. I HOPED THAT WOULD SLOW THE GENDARMES DOWN.
OTHERWISE IT WOULDN'T BE LONG BEFORE THEY FOUND PRINSKY'S ROOM KEY AND DECIDED TO TAKE A LOOK.

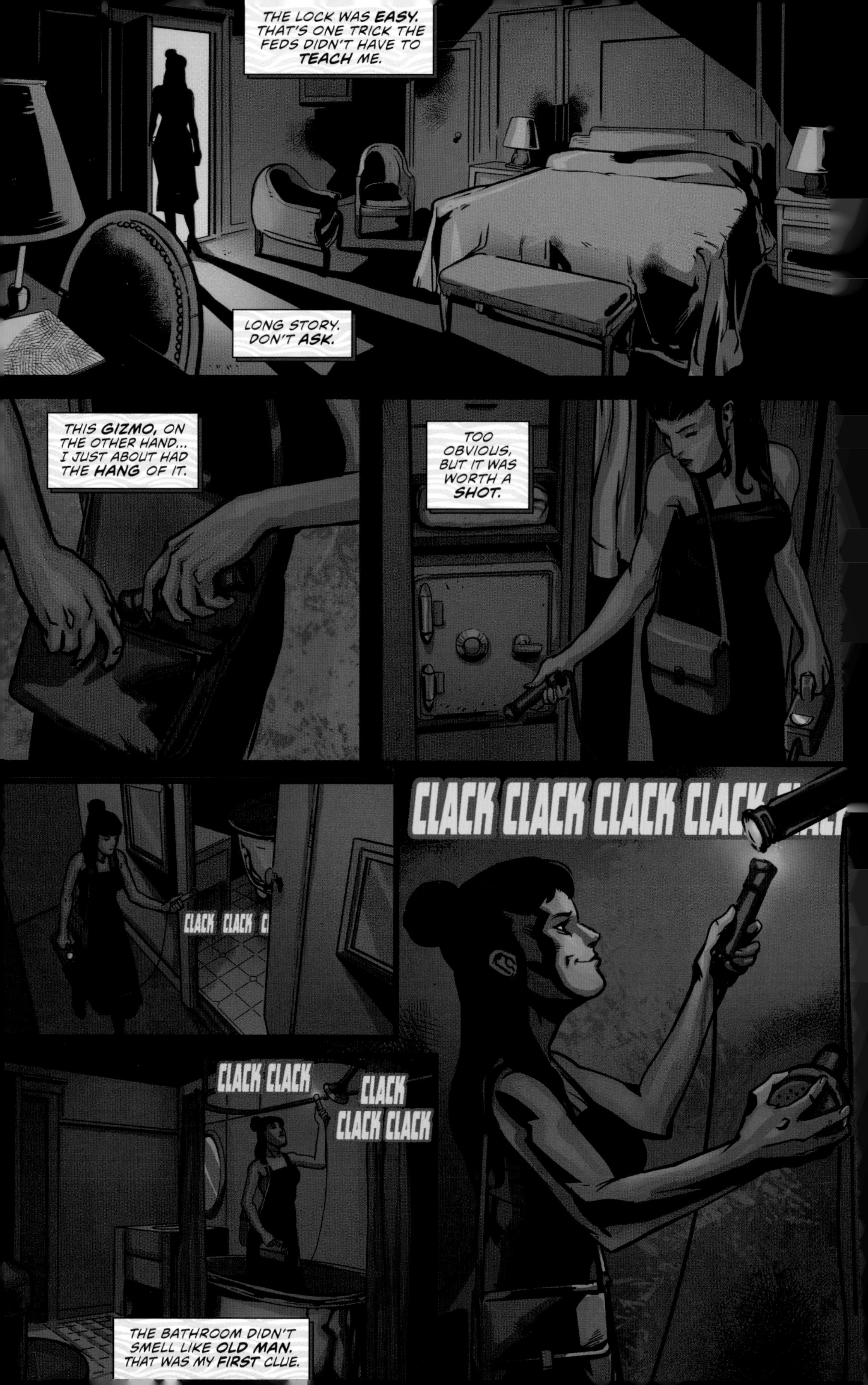
THE LOCK WAS EASY. THAT'S ONE TRICK THE FEDS DIDN'T HAVE TO TEACH ME.
LONG STORY. DON'T ASK.
THIS GIZMO, ON THE OTHER HAND... I JUST ABOUT HAD THE HANG OF IT.
TOO OBVIOUS, BUT IT WAS WORTH A SHOT.
CLACK CLACK
CLACK CLACK CLACK CLACK
CLACK CLACK
CLACK
CLACK CLACK
THE BATHROOM DIDN'T SMELL LIKE OLD MAN. THAT WAS MY FIRST CLUE.

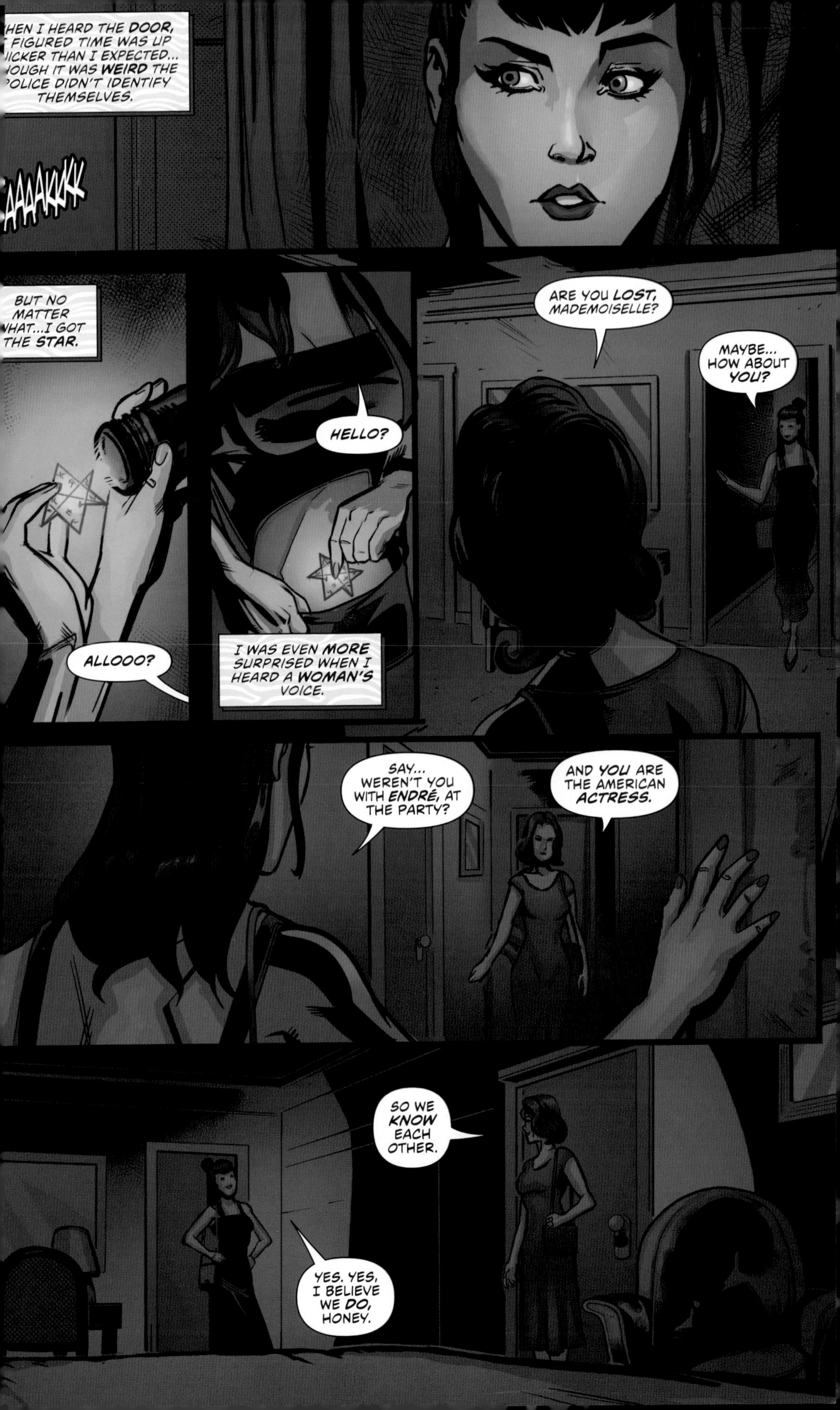
HEN I HEARD THE DOOR, FIGURED TIME WAS UP UICKER THAN I EXPECTED... HOUGH IT WAS WEIRD THE OLICE DIDN'T IDENTIFY THEMSELVES.
AAAAKKK
BUT NO MATTER HAT...I GOT THE STAR.
ALLOOO?
HELLO?
I WAS EVEN MORE SURPRISED WHEN I HEARD A WOMAN'S VOICE.
ARE YOU LOST, MADEMOISELLE?
MAYBE... HOW ABOUT YOU?
SAY... WEREN'T YOU WITH ENDRÉ, AT THE PARTY?
AND YOU ARE THE AMERICAN ACTRESS.
SO WE KNOW EACH OTHER.
YES. YES, I BELIEVE WE DO, HONEY.

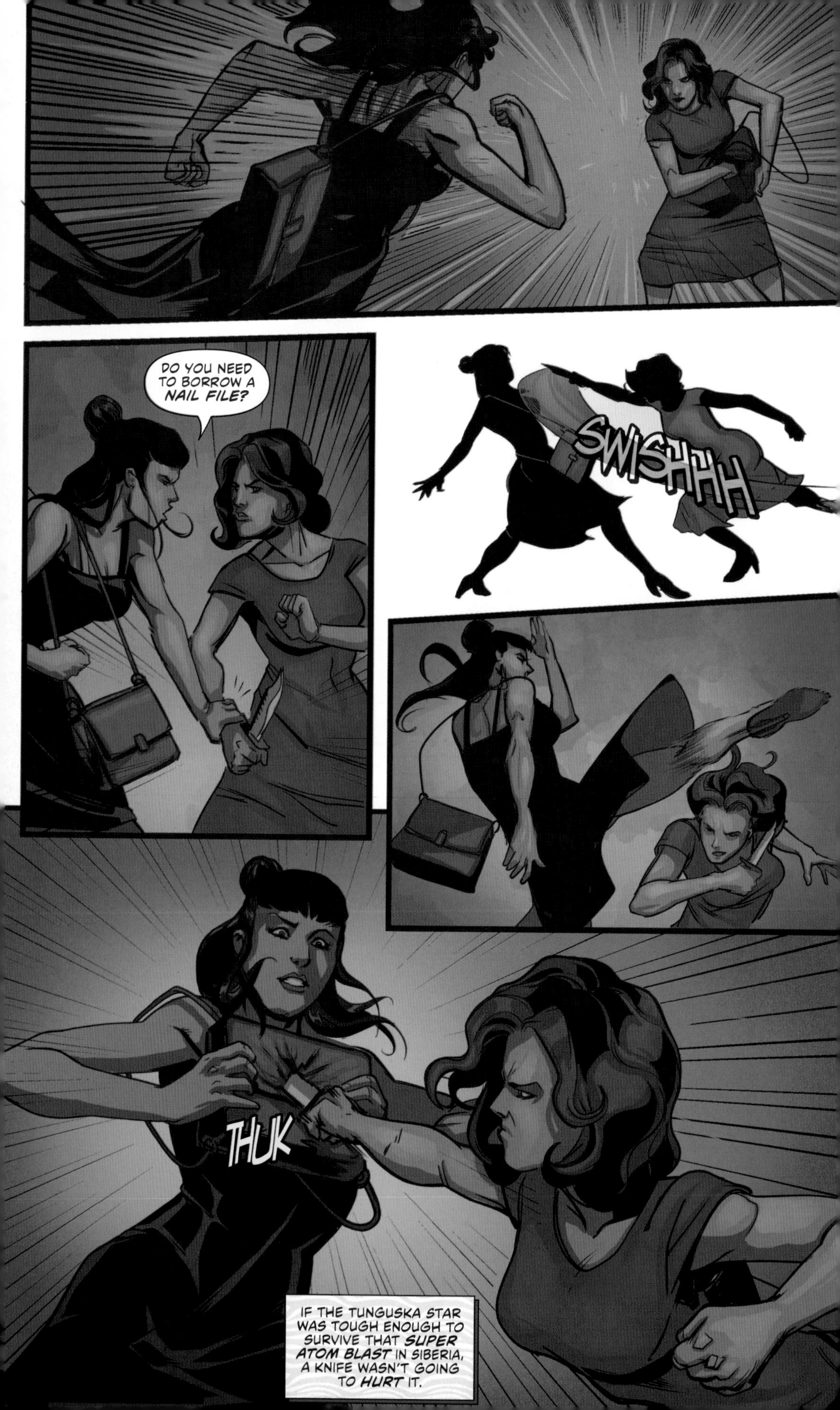
DO YOU NEED TO BORROW A NAIL FILE?
SWISHHH
THUK
IF THE TUNGUSKA STAR WAS TOUGH ENOUGH TO SURVIVE THAT SUPER ATOM BLAST IN SIBERIA, A KNIFE WASN'T GOING TO HURT IT.

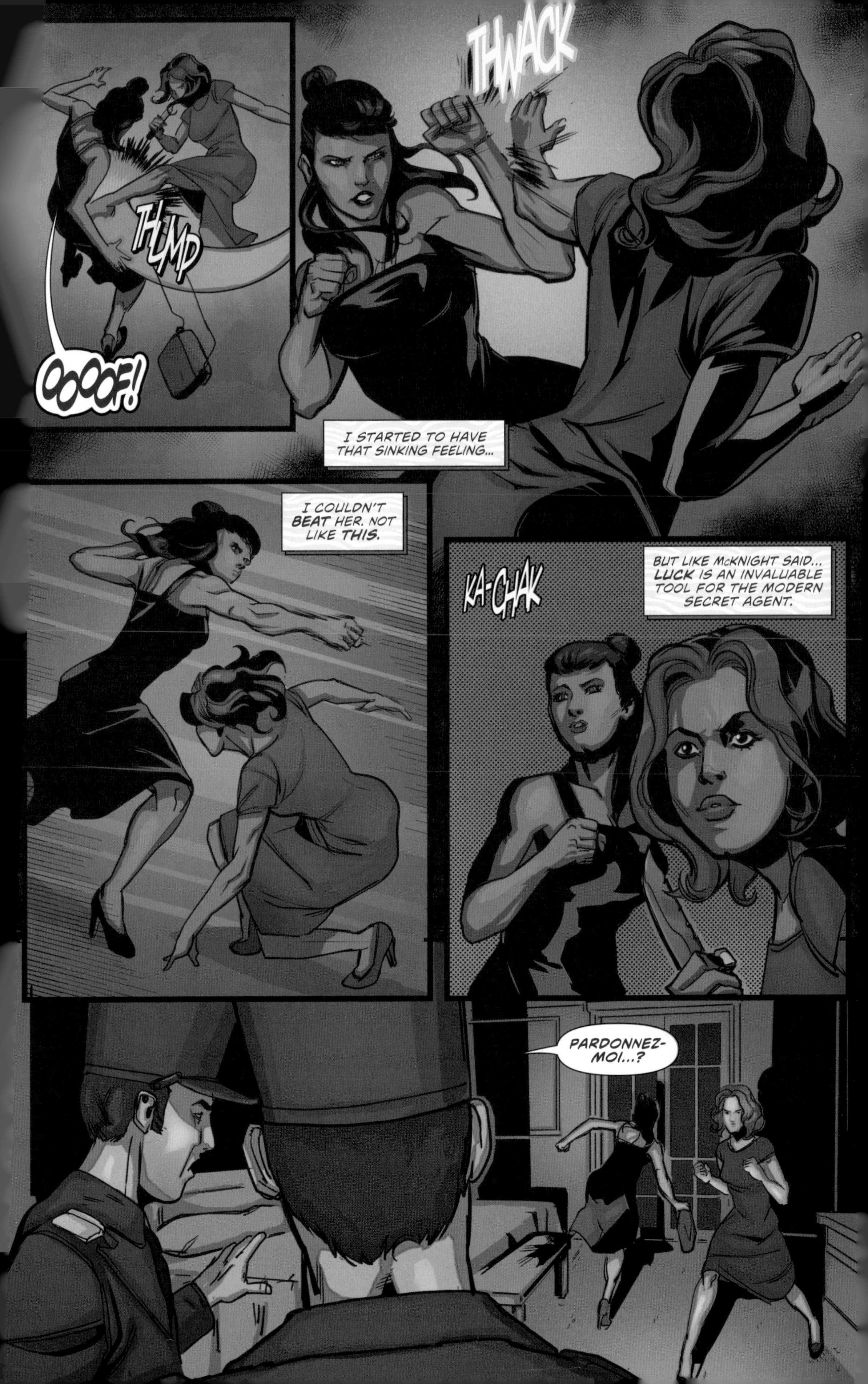

THUMP
OOOOF!
THWACK
I STARTED TO HAVE THAT SINKING FEELING...
I COULDN'T BEAT HER. NOT LIKE THIS.
KA-CHAK
BUT LIKE McKNIGHT SAID... LUCK IS AN INVALUABLE TOOL FOR THE MODERN SECRET AGENT.
PARDONNEZ-MOI...?

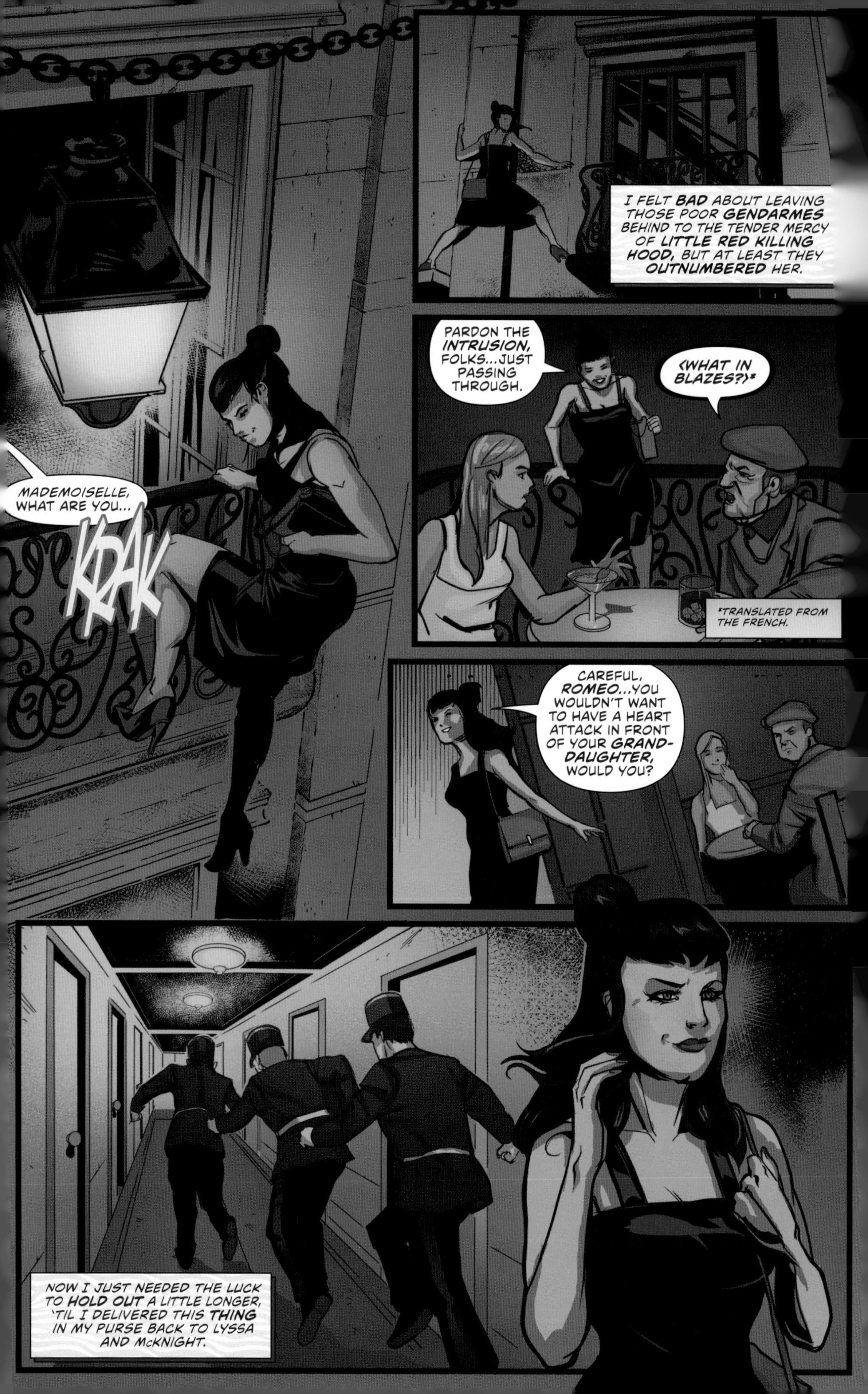
MADEMOISELLE, WHAT ARE YOU...
KRAK
I FELT BAD ABOUT LEAVING THOSE POOR GENDARMES BEHIND TO THE TENDER MERCY OF LITTLE RED KILLING HOOD, BUT AT LEAST THEY OUTNUMBERED HER.
PARDON THE INTRUSION, FOLKS...JUST PASSING THROUGH.
<WHAT IN BLAZES?>*
*TRANSLATED FROM THE FRENCH.
CAREFUL, ROMEO...YOU WOULDN'T WANT TO HAVE A HEART ATTACK IN FRONT OF YOUR GRAND-DAUGHTER, WOULD YOU?
NOW I JUST NEEDED THE LUCK TO HOLD OUT A LITTLE LONGER, 'TIL I DELIVERED THIS THING IN MY PURSE BACK TO LYSSA AND McKNIGHT.

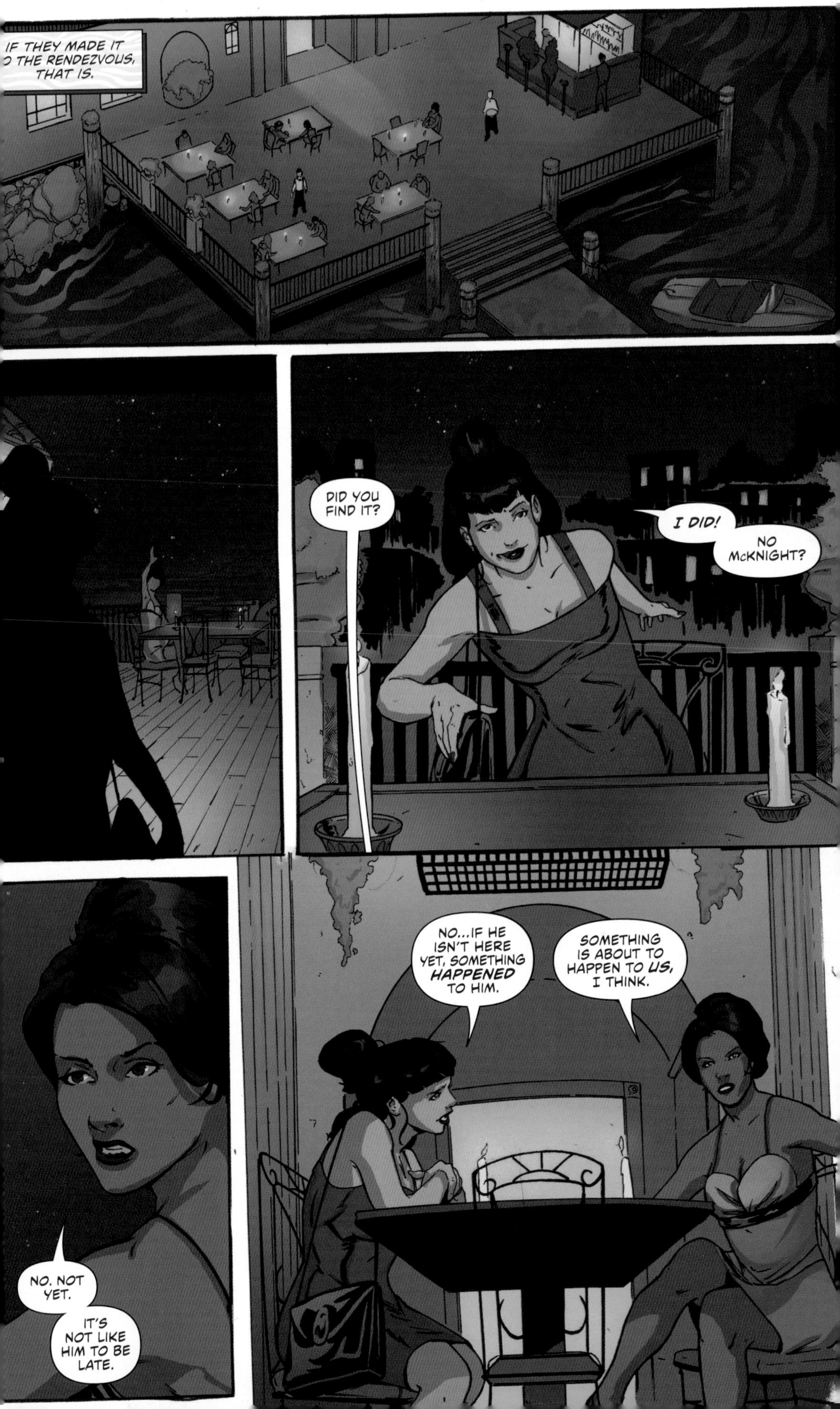
IF THEY MADE IT TO THE RENDEZVOUS, THAT IS.
DID YOU FIND IT?
I DID!
NO McKNIGHT?
NO. NOT YET.
IT'S NOT LIKE HIM TO BE LATE.
NO...IF HE ISN'T HERE YET, SOMETHING HAPPENED TO HIM.
SOMETHING IS ABOUT TO HAPPEN TO US, I THINK.

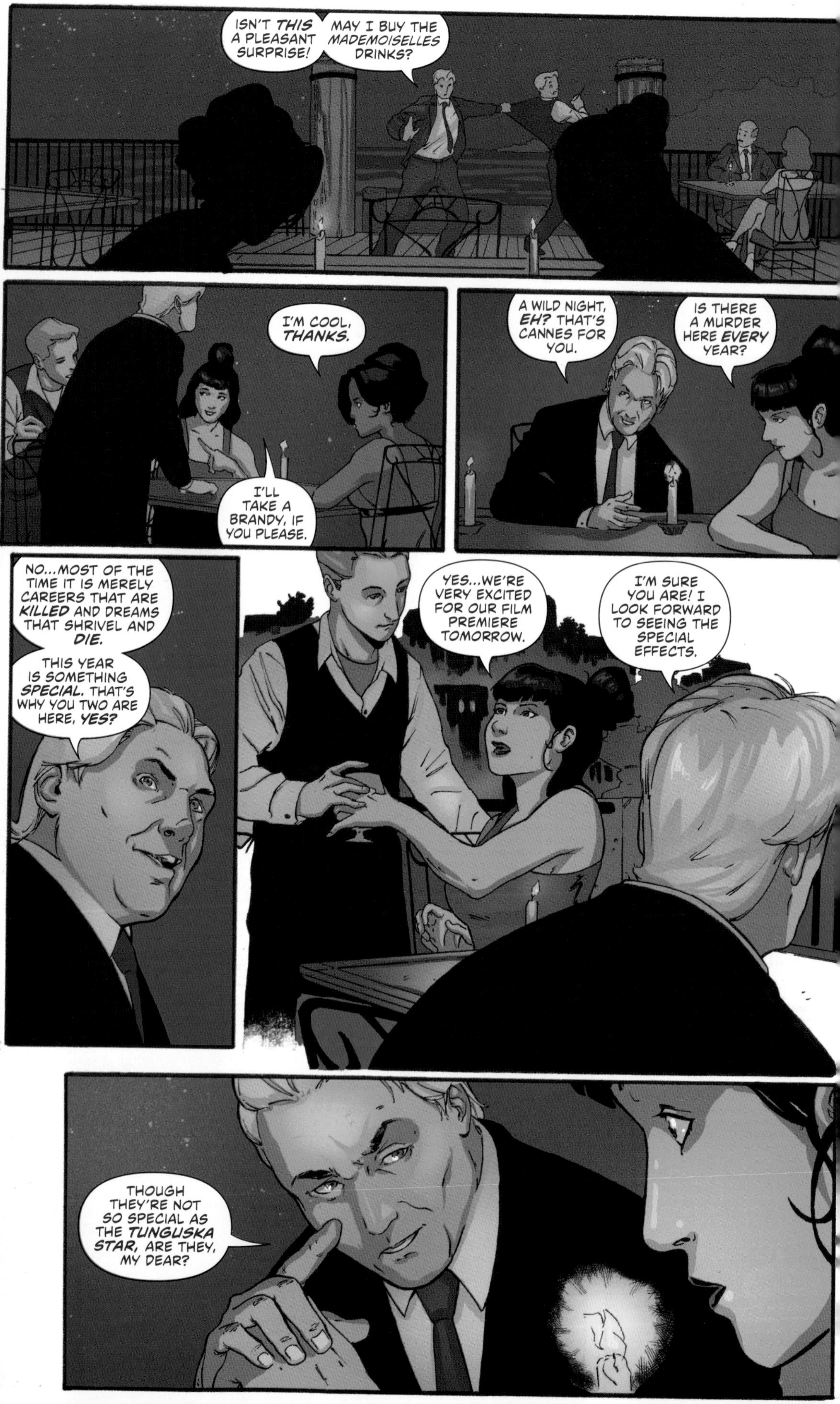
ISN'T THIS A PLEASANT SURPRISE!
MAY I BUY THE MADEMOISELLES DRINKS?
I'M COOL, THANKS.
I'LL TAKE A BRANDY, IF YOU PLEASE.
A WILD NIGHT, EH? THAT'S CANNES FOR YOU.
IS THERE A MURDER HERE EVERY YEAR?
NO...MOST OF THE TIME IT IS MERELY CAREERS THAT ARE KILLED AND DREAMS THAT SHRIVEL AND DIE.
THIS YEAR IS SOMETHING SPECIAL. THAT'S WHY YOU TWO ARE HERE, YES?
YES...WE'RE VERY EXCITED FOR OUR FILM PREMIERE TOMORROW.
I'M SURE YOU ARE! I LOOK FORWARD TO SEEING THE SPECIAL EFFECTS.
THOUGH THEY'RE NOT SO SPECIAL AS THE TUNGUSKA STAR, ARE THEY, MY DEAR?

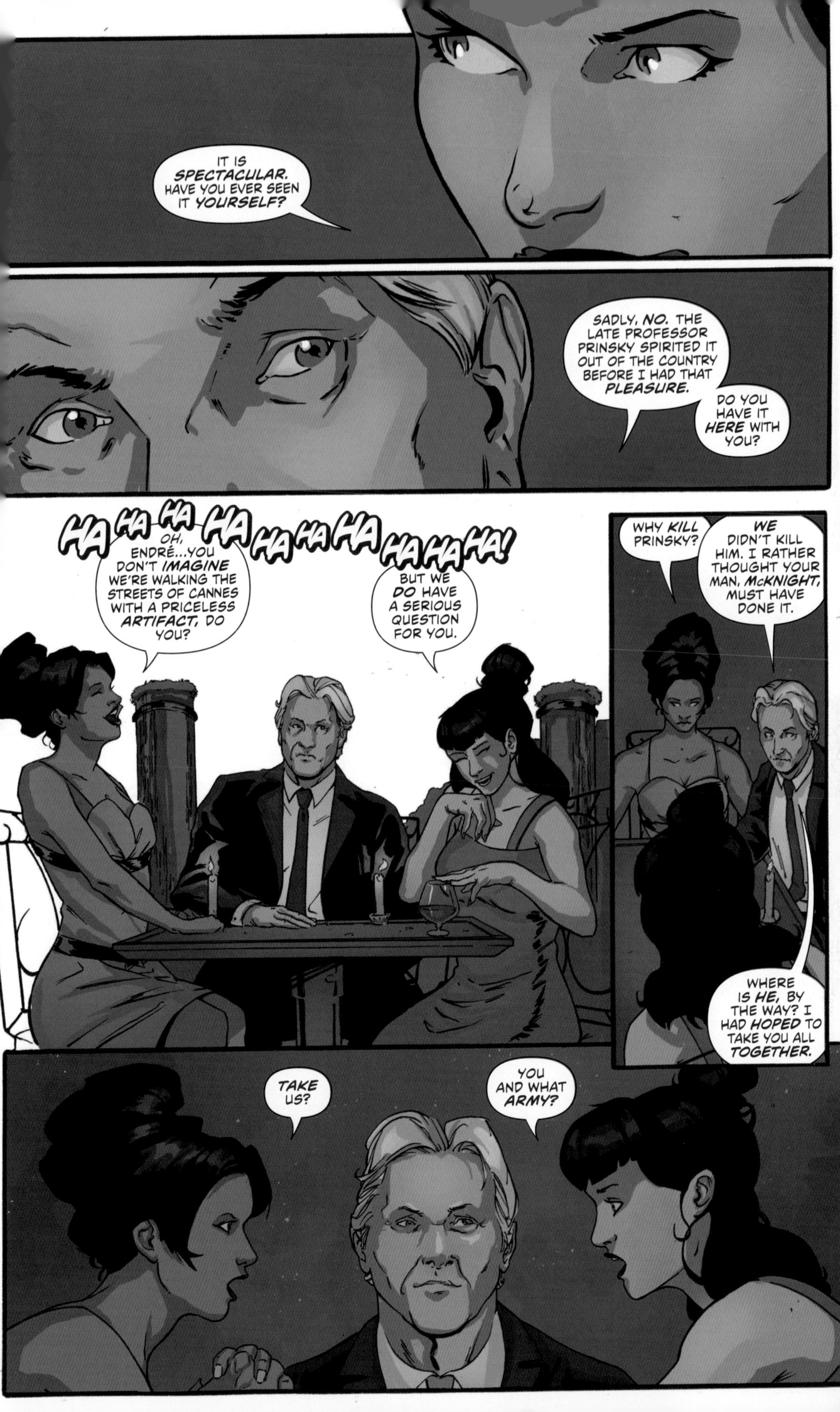
IT IS SPECTACULAR. HAVE YOU EVER SEEN IT YOURSELF?
SADLY, NO. THE LATE PROFESSOR PRINSKY SPIRITED IT OUT OF THE COUNTRY BEFORE I HAD THAT PLEASURE.
DO YOU HAVE IT HERE WITH YOU?
HA HA HA HA HA HA HA HA HA HA HA!
OH, ENDRÉ...YOU DON'T IMAGINE WE'RE WALKING THE STREETS OF CANNES WITH A PRICELESS ARTIFACT, DO YOU?
BUT WE DO HAVE A SERIOUS QUESTION FOR YOU.
WHY KILL PRINSKY?
WE DIDN'T KILL HIM. I RATHER THOUGHT YOUR MAN, McKNIGHT, MUST HAVE DONE IT.
WHERE IS HE, BY THE WAY? I HAD HOPED TO TAKE YOU ALL TOGETHER.
TAKE US?
YOU AND WHAT ARMY?

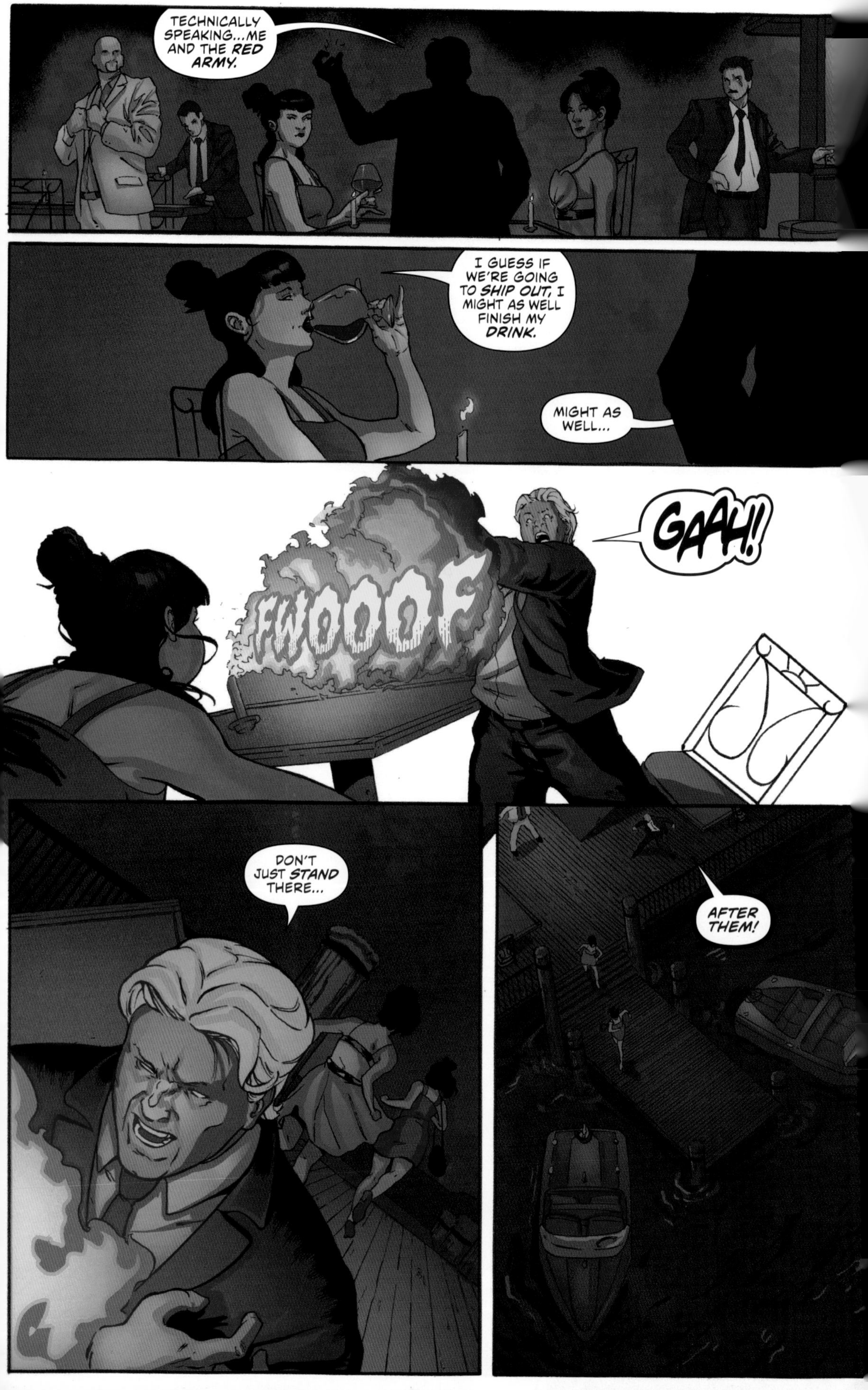
TECHNICALLY SPEAKING...ME AND THE RED ARMY.
I GUESS IF WE'RE GOING TO SHIP OUT, I MIGHT AS WELL FINISH MY DRINK.
MIGHT AS WELL...
FWOOOF
GAAH!
DON'T JUST STAND THERE...
AFTER THEM!

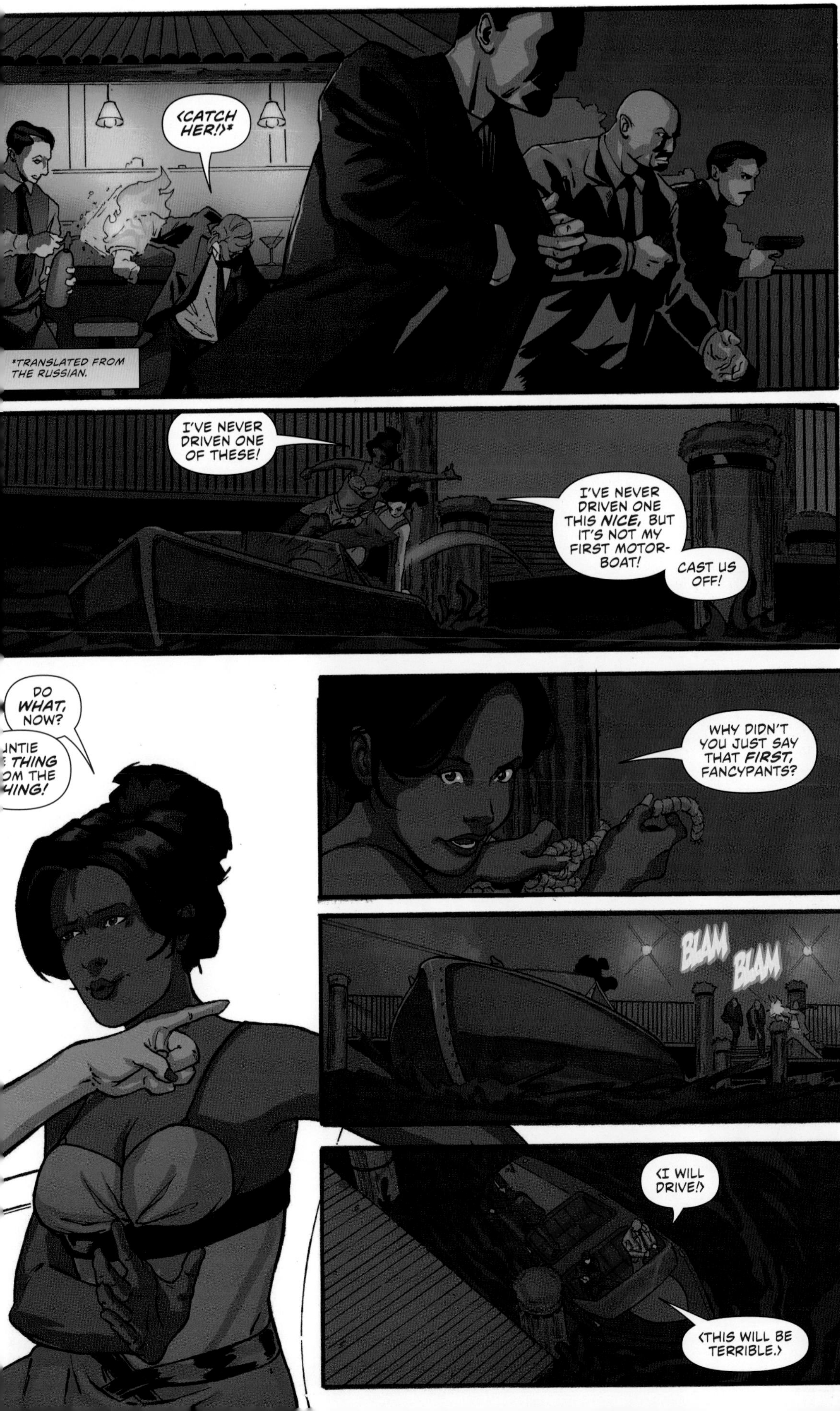

<CATCH HER!>*
*TRANSLATED FROM THE RUSSIAN.
I'VE NEVER DRIVEN ONE OF THESE!
I'VE NEVER DRIVEN ONE THIS NICE, BUT IT'S NOT MY FIRST MOTOR-BOAT!
CAST US OFF!
DO WHAT, NOW?
WHY DIDN'T YOU JUST SAY THAT FIRST, FANCYPANTS?
BLAM
BLAM
<I WILL DRIVE!>
<THIS WILL BE TERRIBLE.>

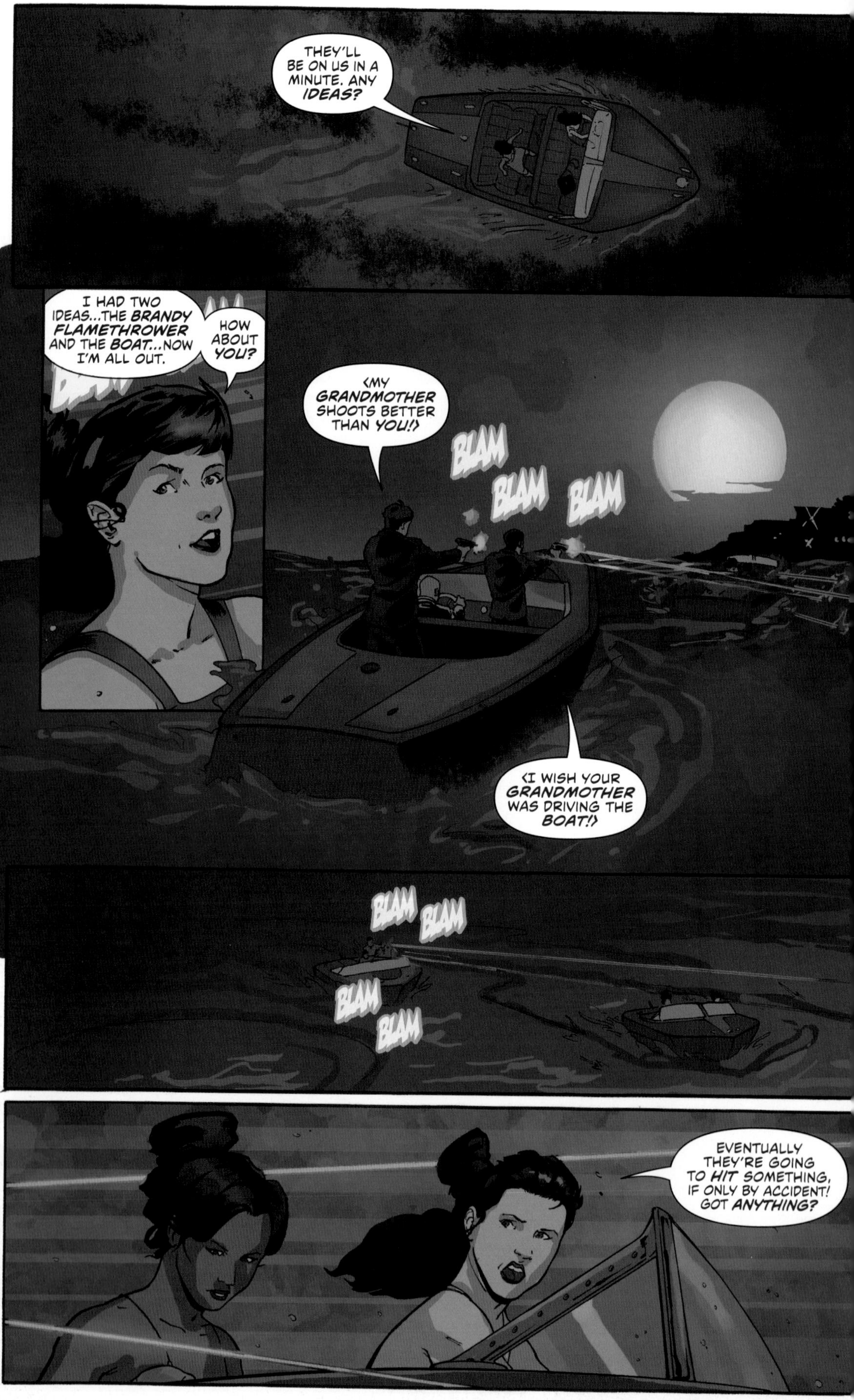
THEY'LL BE ON US IN A MINUTE. ANY IDEAS?
I HAD TWO IDEAS...THE BRANDY FLAMETHROWER AND THE BOAT...NOW I'M ALL OUT.
HOW ABOUT YOU?
‹MY GRANDMOTHER SHOOTS BETTER THAN YOU!›
BLAM
BLAM
BLAM
‹I WISH YOUR GRANDMOTHER WAS DRIVING THE BOAT!›
BLAM
BLAM
BLAM
BLAM
EVENTUALLY THEY'RE GOING TO HIT SOMETHING, IF ONLY BY ACCIDENT! GOT ANYTHING?

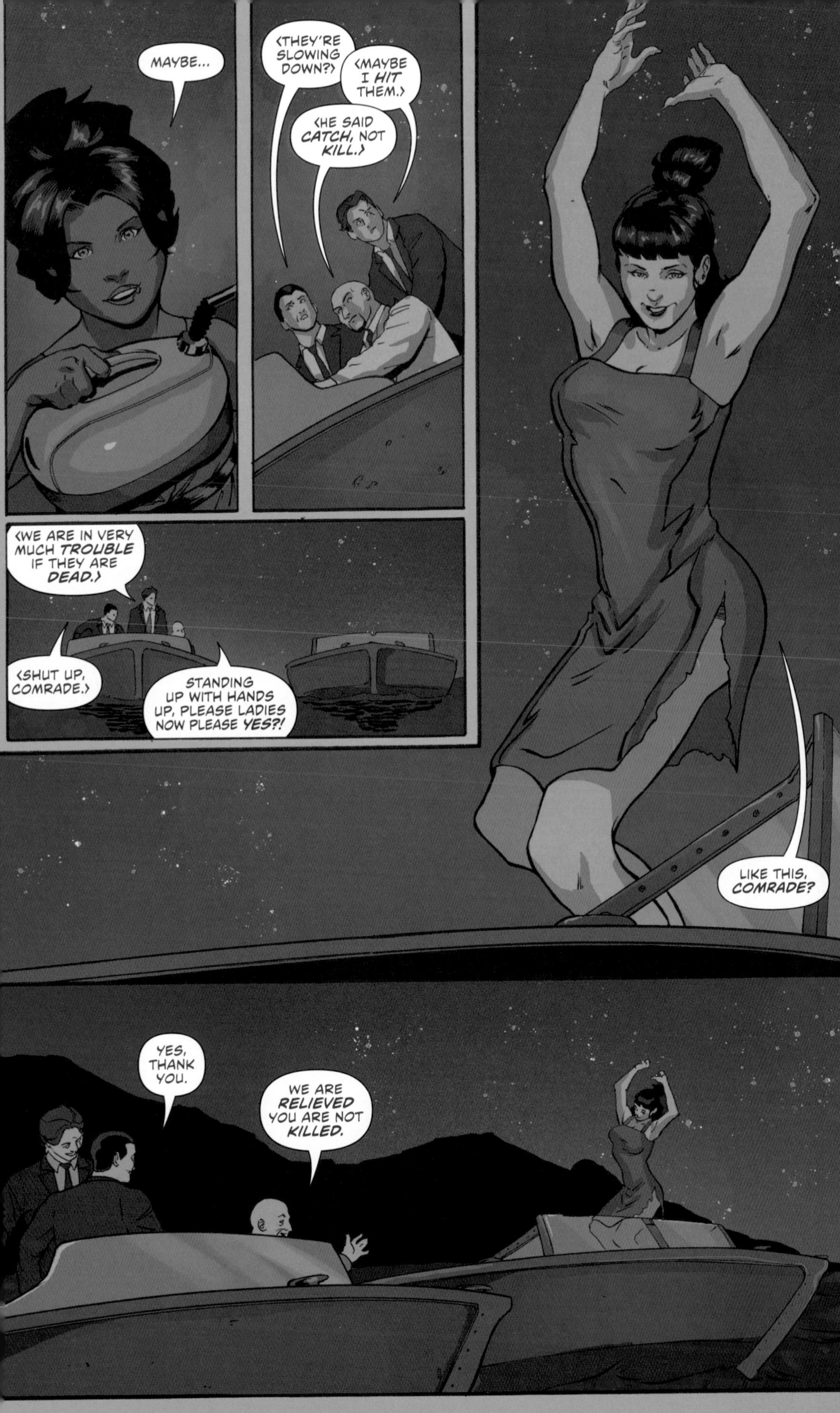
MAYBE...
‹THEY'RE SLOWING DOWN?›
‹MAYBE I HIT THEM.›
‹HE SAID CATCH, NOT KILL.›
‹WE ARE IN VERY MUCH TROUBLE IF THEY ARE DEAD.›
‹SHUT UP, COMRADE.›
STANDING UP WITH HANDS UP, PLEASE LADIES NOW PLEASE YES?!
LIKE THIS, COMRADE?
YES, THANK YOU.
WE ARE RELIEVED YOU ARE NOT KILLED.

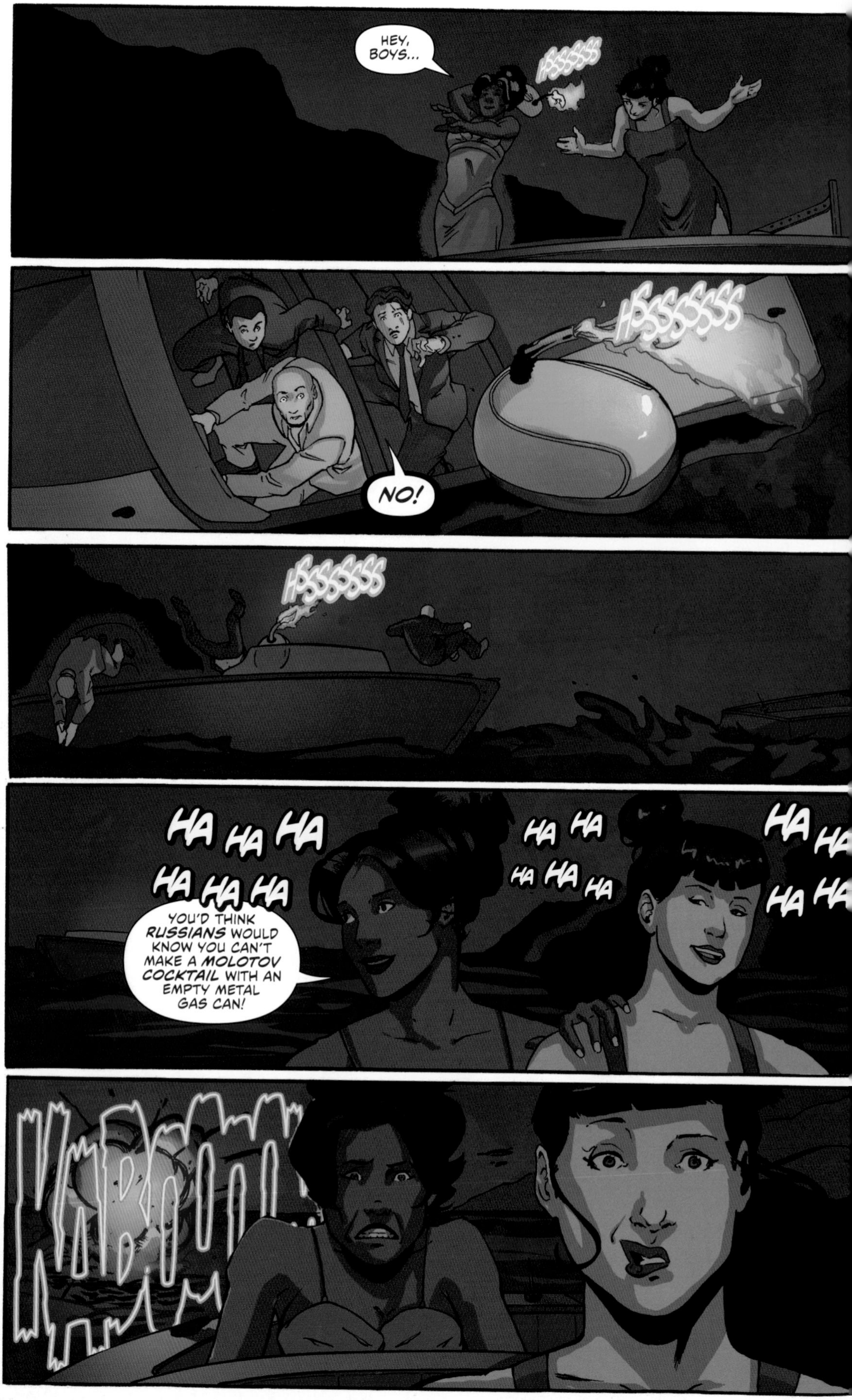

HEY, BOYS...
HSSSSSS
HSSSSSSS
NO!
HSSSSSSS
HA HA HA
HA HA HA
HA HA
HA HA HA
HA HA
HA HA
YOU'D THINK RUSSIANS WOULD KNOW YOU CAN'T MAKE A MOLOTOV COCKTAIL WITH AN EMPTY METAL GAS CAN!

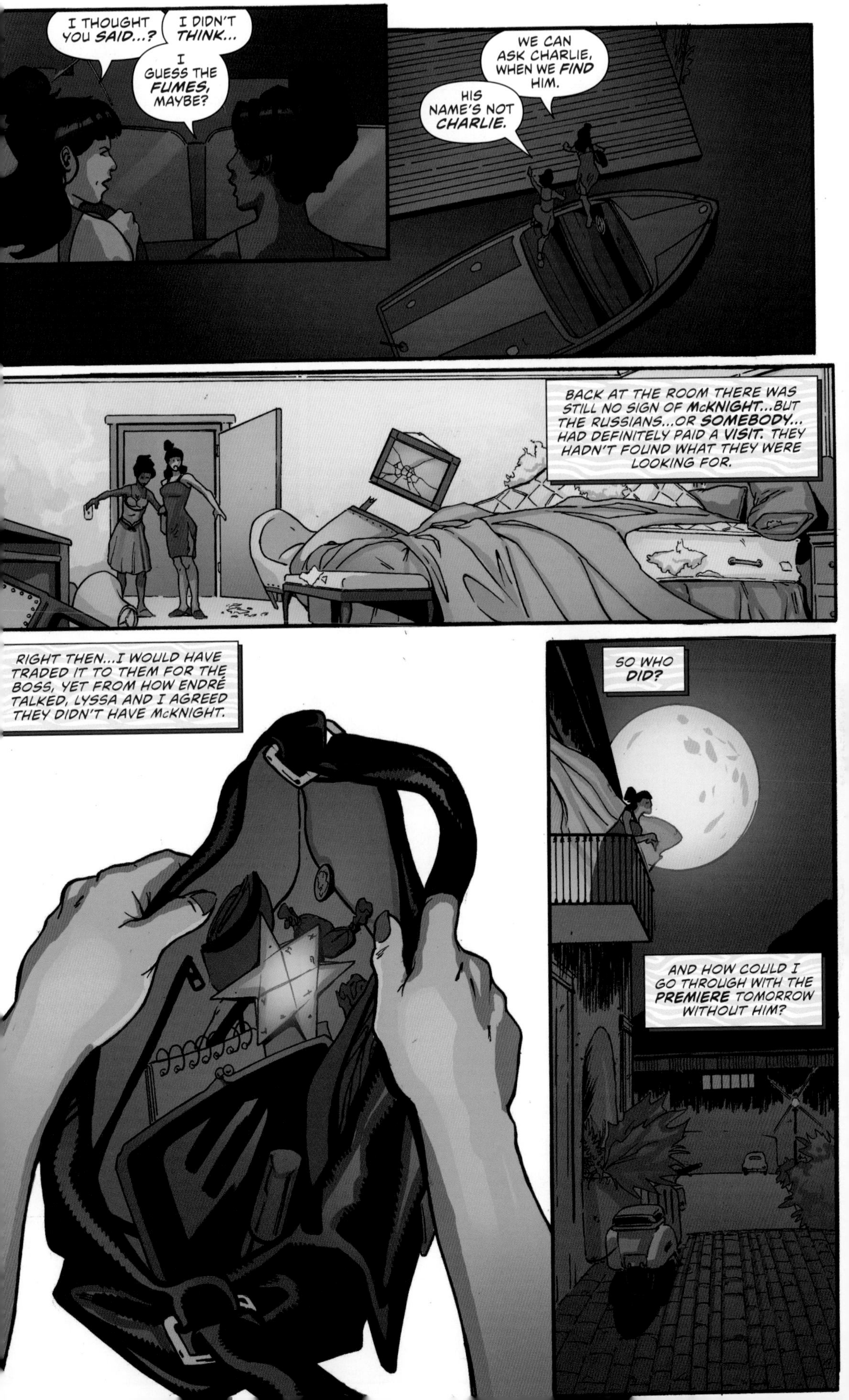
I THOUGHT YOU SAID...?
I DIDN'T THINK...
I GUESS THE FUMES, MAYBE?
WE CAN ASK CHARLIE, WHEN WE FIND HIM.
HIS NAME'S NOT CHARLIE.
BACK AT THE ROOM THERE WAS STILL NO SIGN OF McKNIGHT...BUT THE RUSSIANS...OR SOMEBODY... HAD DEFINITELY PAID A VISIT. THEY HADN'T FOUND WHAT THEY WERE LOOKING FOR.
RIGHT THEN...I WOULD HAVE TRADED IT TO THEM FOR THE BOSS, YET FROM HOW ENDRÉ TALKED, LYSSA AND I AGREED THEY DIDN'T HAVE McKNIGHT.
SO WHO DID?
AND HOW COULD I GO THROUGH WITH THE PREMIERE TOMORROW WITHOUT HIM?

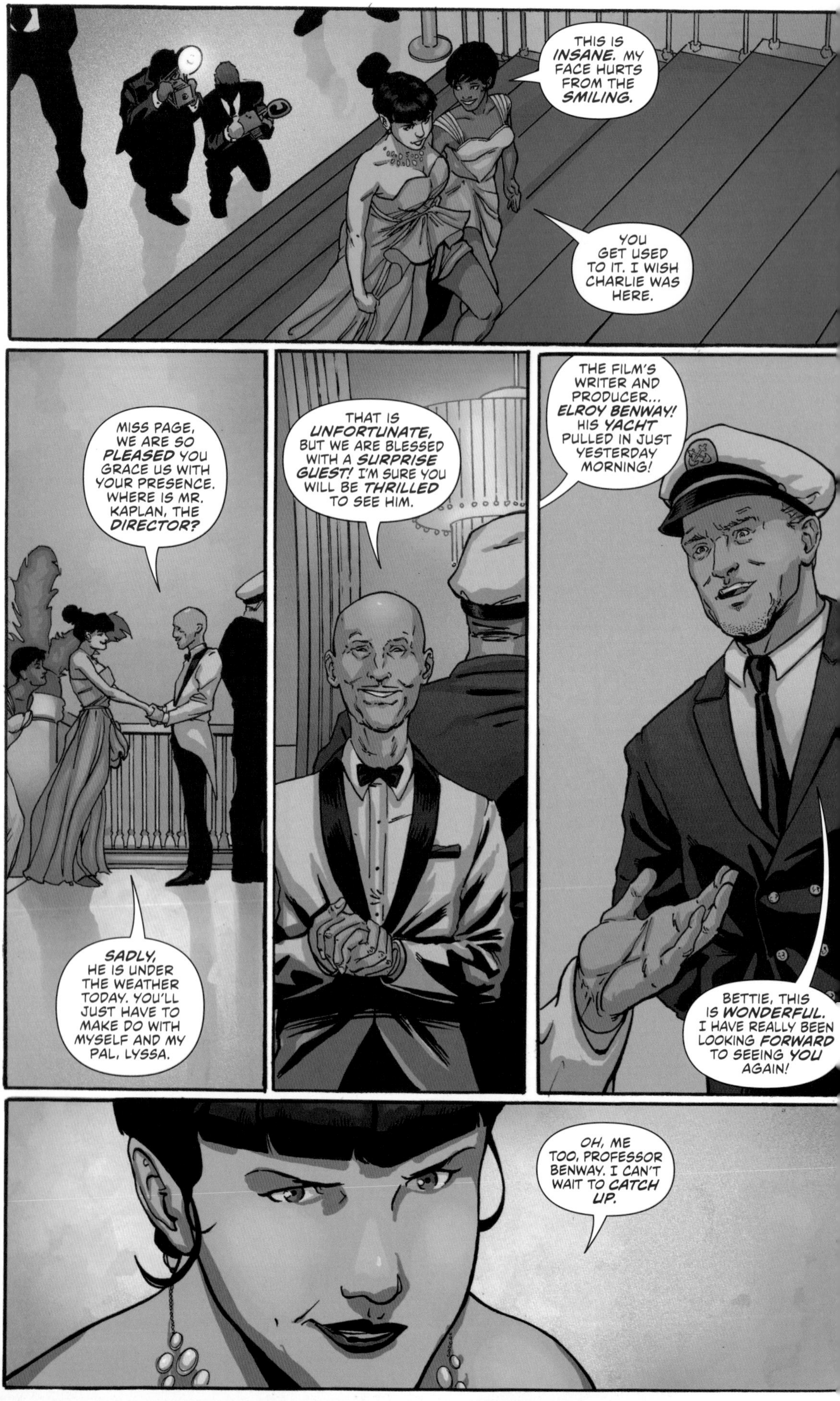
THIS IS INSANE. MY FACE HURTS FROM THE SMILING.
YOU GET USED TO IT. I WISH CHARLIE WAS HERE.
MISS PAGE, WE ARE SO PLEASED YOU GRACE US WITH YOUR PRESENCE. WHERE IS MR. KAPLAN, THE DIRECTOR?
SADLY, HE IS UNDER THE WEATHER TODAY. YOU'LL JUST HAVE TO MAKE DO WITH MYSELF AND MY PAL, LYSSA.
THAT IS UNFORTUNATE, BUT WE ARE BLESSED WITH A SURPRISE GUEST! I'M SURE YOU WILL BE THRILLED TO SEE HIM.
THE FILM'S WRITER AND PRODUCER... ELROY BENWAY! HIS YACHT PULLED IN JUST YESTERDAY MORNING!
BETTIE, THIS IS WONDERFUL. I HAVE REALLY BEEN LOOKING FORWARD TO SEEING YOU AGAIN!
OH, ME TOO, PROFESSOR BENWAY. I CAN'T WAIT TO CATCH UP.

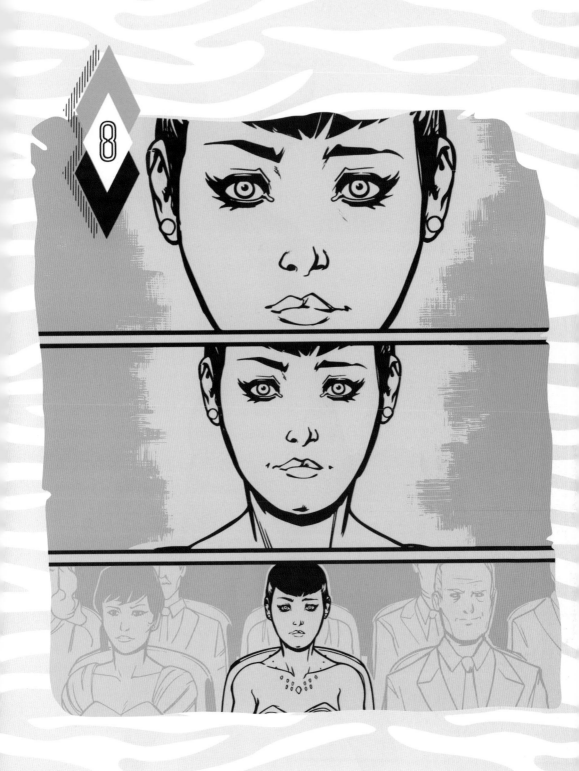

ART: JOSEPH MICHAEL LINSNER

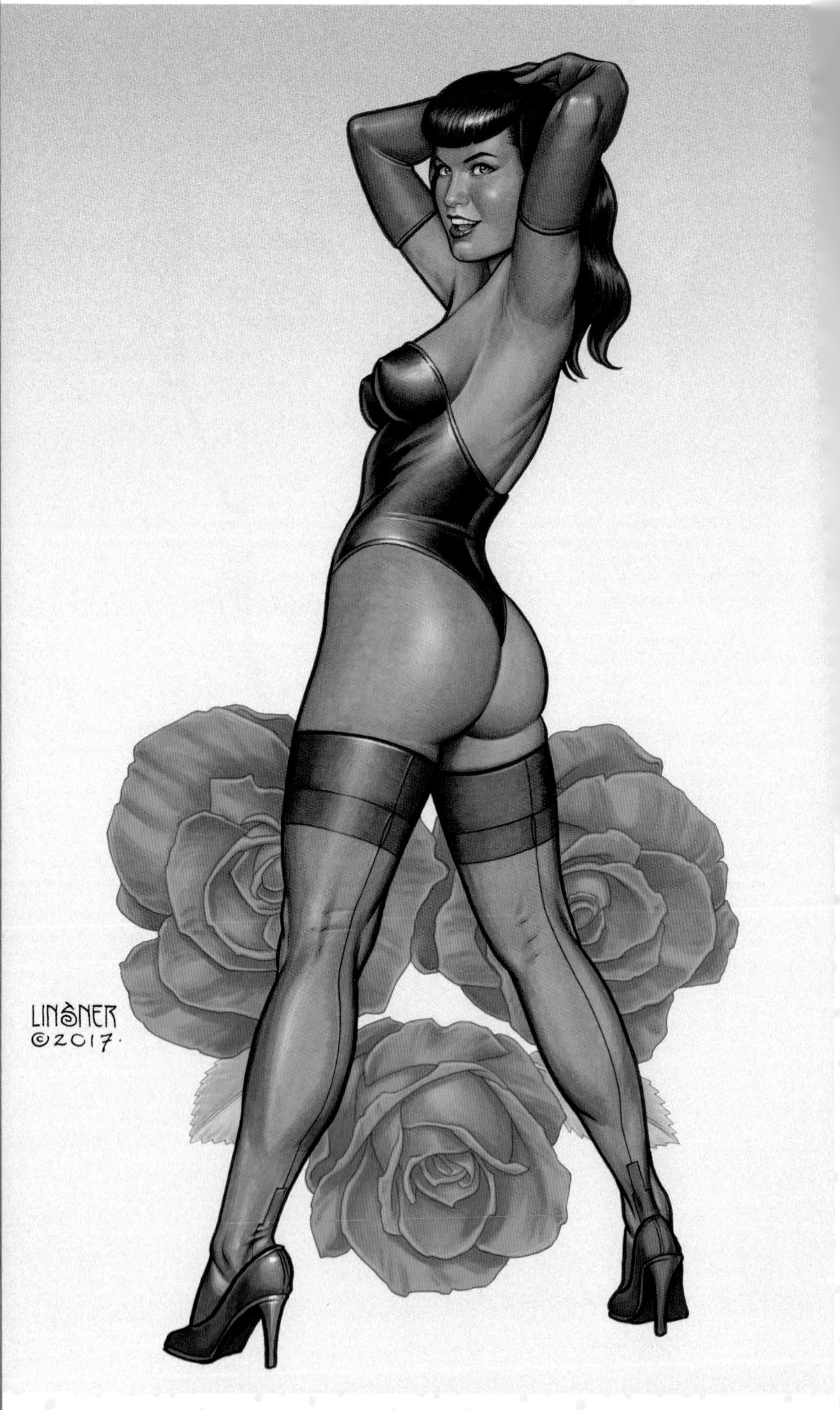
LINSNER
©2017.

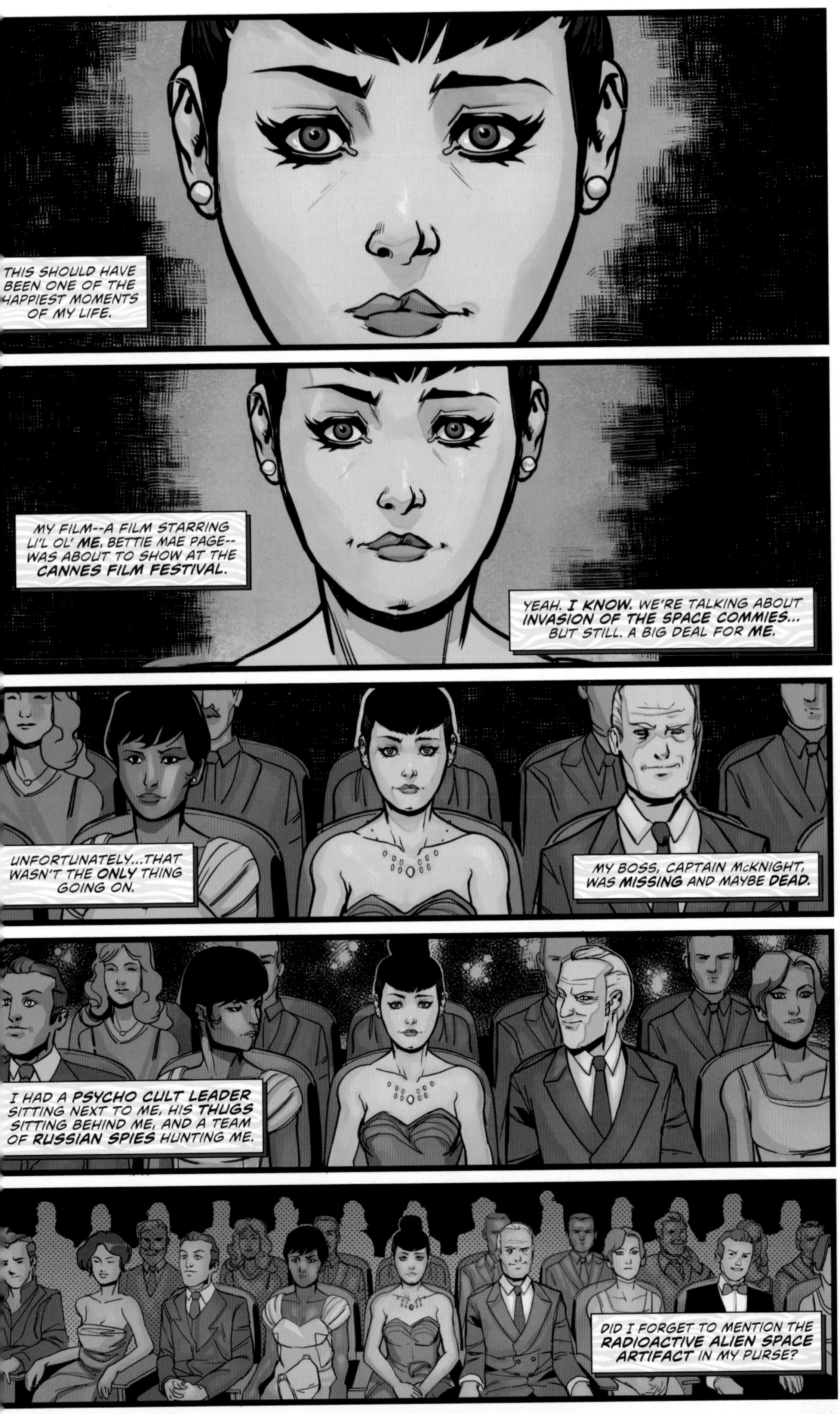
THIS SHOULD HAVE BEEN ONE OF THE HAPPIEST MOMENTS OF MY LIFE.
MY FILM--A FILM STARRING LI'L OL' ME, BETTIE MAE PAGE--WAS ABOUT TO SHOW AT THE CANNES FILM FESTIVAL.
YEAH. I KNOW. WE'RE TALKING ABOUT INVASION OF THE SPACE COMMIES... BUT STILL. A BIG DEAL FOR ME.
UNFORTUNATELY...THAT WASN'T THE ONLY THING GOING ON.
MY BOSS, CAPTAIN McKNIGHT, WAS MISSING AND MAYBE DEAD.
I HAD A PSYCHO CULT LEADER SITTING NEXT TO ME, HIS THUGS SITTING BEHIND ME, AND A TEAM OF RUSSIAN SPIES HUNTING ME.
DID I FORGET TO MENTION THE RADIOACTIVE ALIEN SPACE ARTIFACT IN MY PURSE?

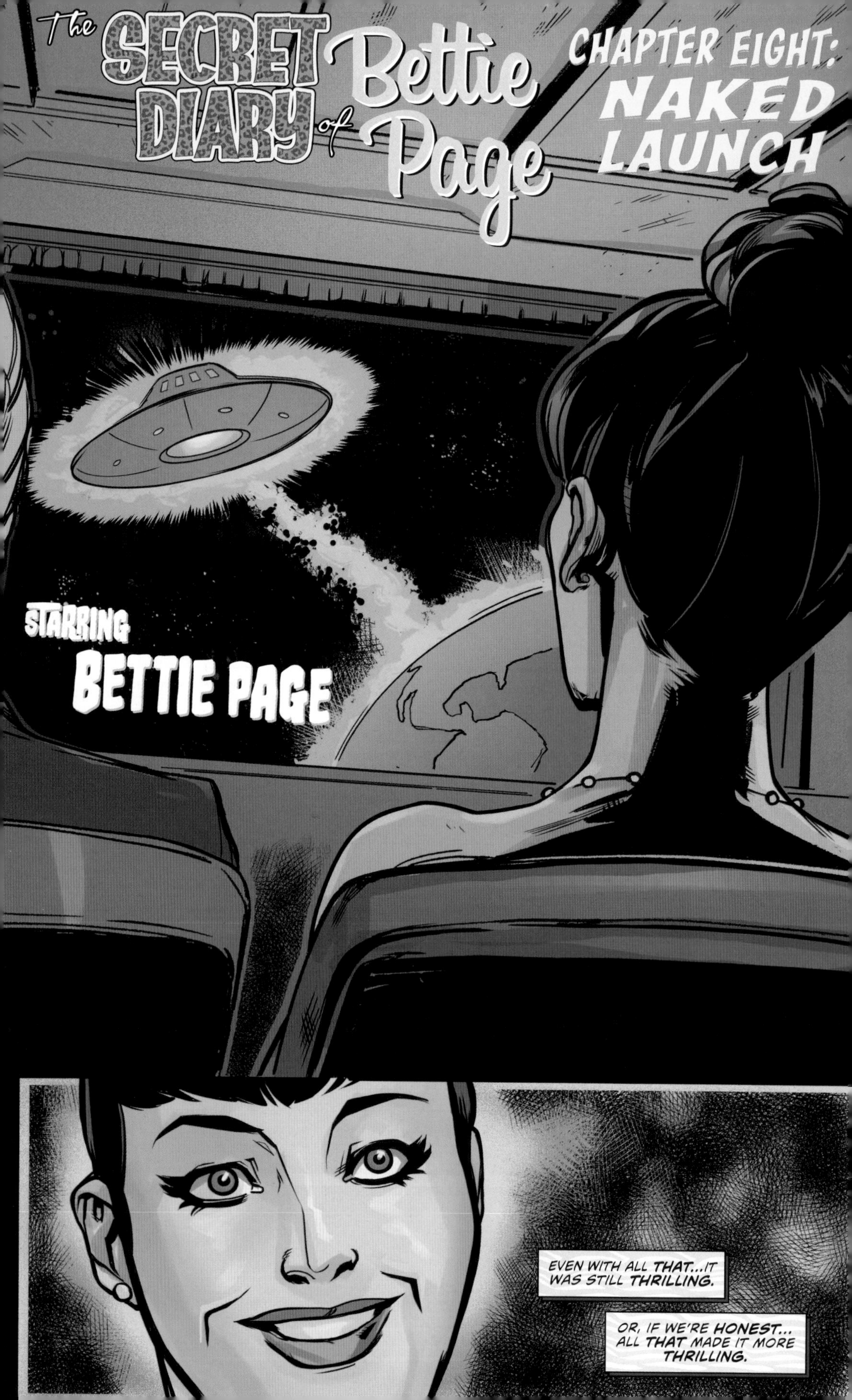
The SECRET DIARY of Bettie Page
CHAPTER EIGHT: NAKED LAUNCH
STARRING
BETTIE PAGE
EVEN WITH ALL THAT...IT WAS STILL THRILLING.
OR, IF WE'RE HONEST... ALL THAT MADE IT MORE THRILLING.

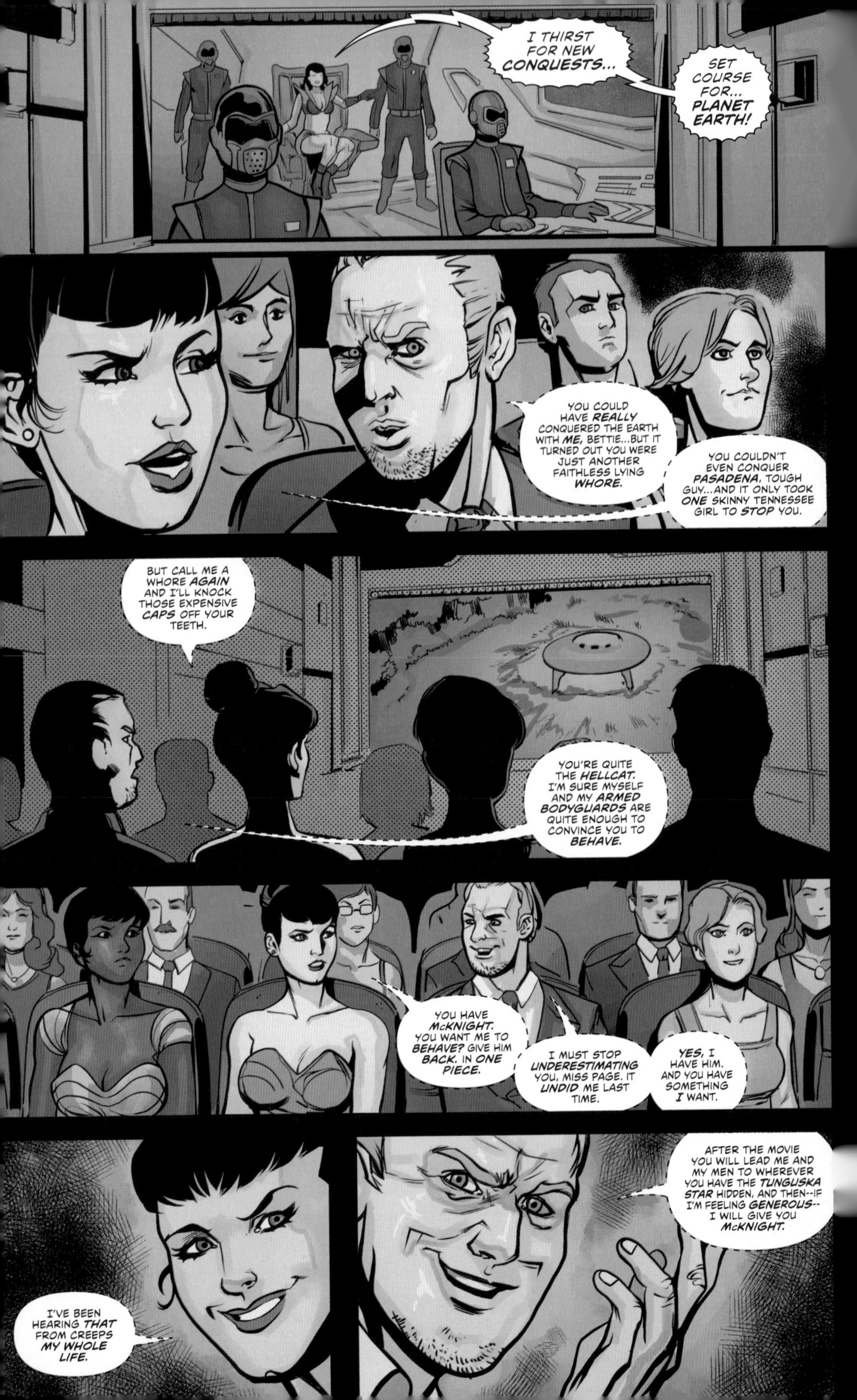
I THIRST FOR NEW CONQUESTS...
SET COURSE FOR... PLANET EARTH!
YOU COULD HAVE REALLY CONQUERED THE EARTH WITH ME, BETTIE...BUT IT TURNED OUT YOU WERE JUST ANOTHER FAITHLESS LYING WHORE.
YOU COULDN'T EVEN CONQUER PASADENA, TOUGH GUY...AND IT ONLY TOOK ONE SKINNY TENNESSEE GIRL TO STOP YOU.
BUT CALL ME A WHORE AGAIN AND I'LL KNOCK THOSE EXPENSIVE CAPS OFF YOUR TEETH.
YOU'RE QUITE THE HELLCAT. I'M SURE MYSELF AND MY ARMED BODYGUARDS ARE QUITE ENOUGH TO CONVINCE YOU TO BEHAVE.
YOU HAVE McKNIGHT. YOU WANT ME TO BEHAVE? GIVE HIM BACK. IN ONE PIECE.
I MUST STOP UNDERESTIMATING YOU, MISS PAGE. IT UNDID ME LAST TIME.
YES, I HAVE HIM. AND YOU HAVE SOMETHING I WANT.
AFTER THE MOVIE YOU WILL LEAD ME AND MY MEN TO WHEREVER YOU HAVE THE TUNGUSKA STAR HIDDEN, AND THEN--IF I'M FEELING GENEROUS--I WILL GIVE YOU McKNIGHT.
I'VE BEEN HEARING THAT FROM CREEPS MY WHOLE LIFE.

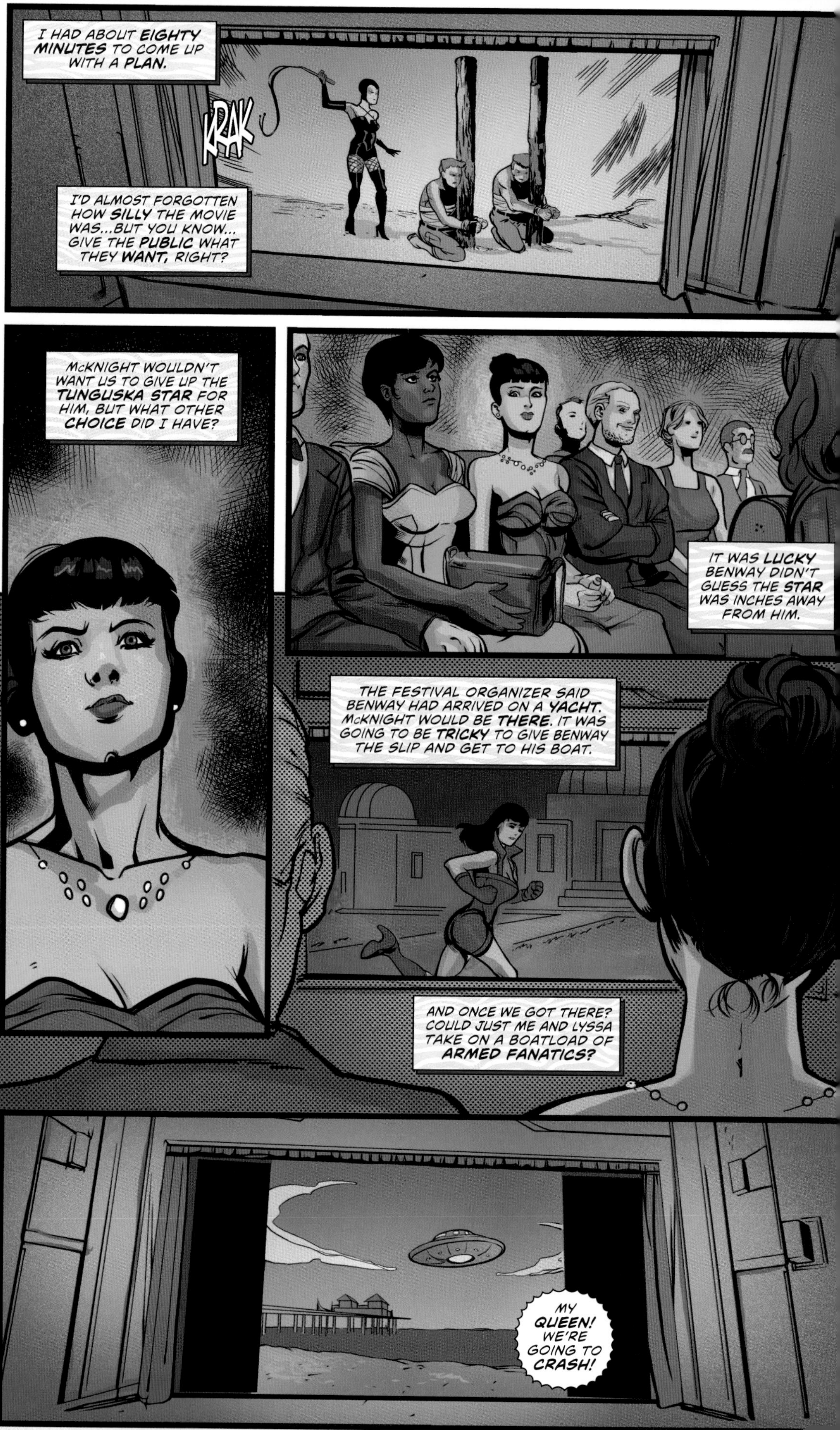
I HAD ABOUT EIGHTY MINUTES TO COME UP WITH A PLAN.
KRAK
I'D ALMOST FORGOTTEN HOW SILLY THE MOVIE WAS...BUT YOU KNOW... GIVE THE PUBLIC WHAT THEY WANT, RIGHT?
McKNIGHT WOULDN'T WANT US TO GIVE UP THE TUNGUSKA STAR FOR HIM, BUT WHAT OTHER CHOICE DID I HAVE?
IT WAS LUCKY BENWAY DIDN'T GUESS THE STAR WAS INCHES AWAY FROM HIM.
THE FESTIVAL ORGANIZER SAID BENWAY HAD ARRIVED ON A YACHT. McKNIGHT WOULD BE THERE. IT WAS GOING TO BE TRICKY TO GIVE BENWAY THE SLIP AND GET TO HIS BOAT.
AND ONCE WE GOT THERE? COULD JUST ME AND LYSSA TAKE ON A BOATLOAD OF ARMED FANATICS?
MY QUEEN! WE'RE GOING TO CRASH!

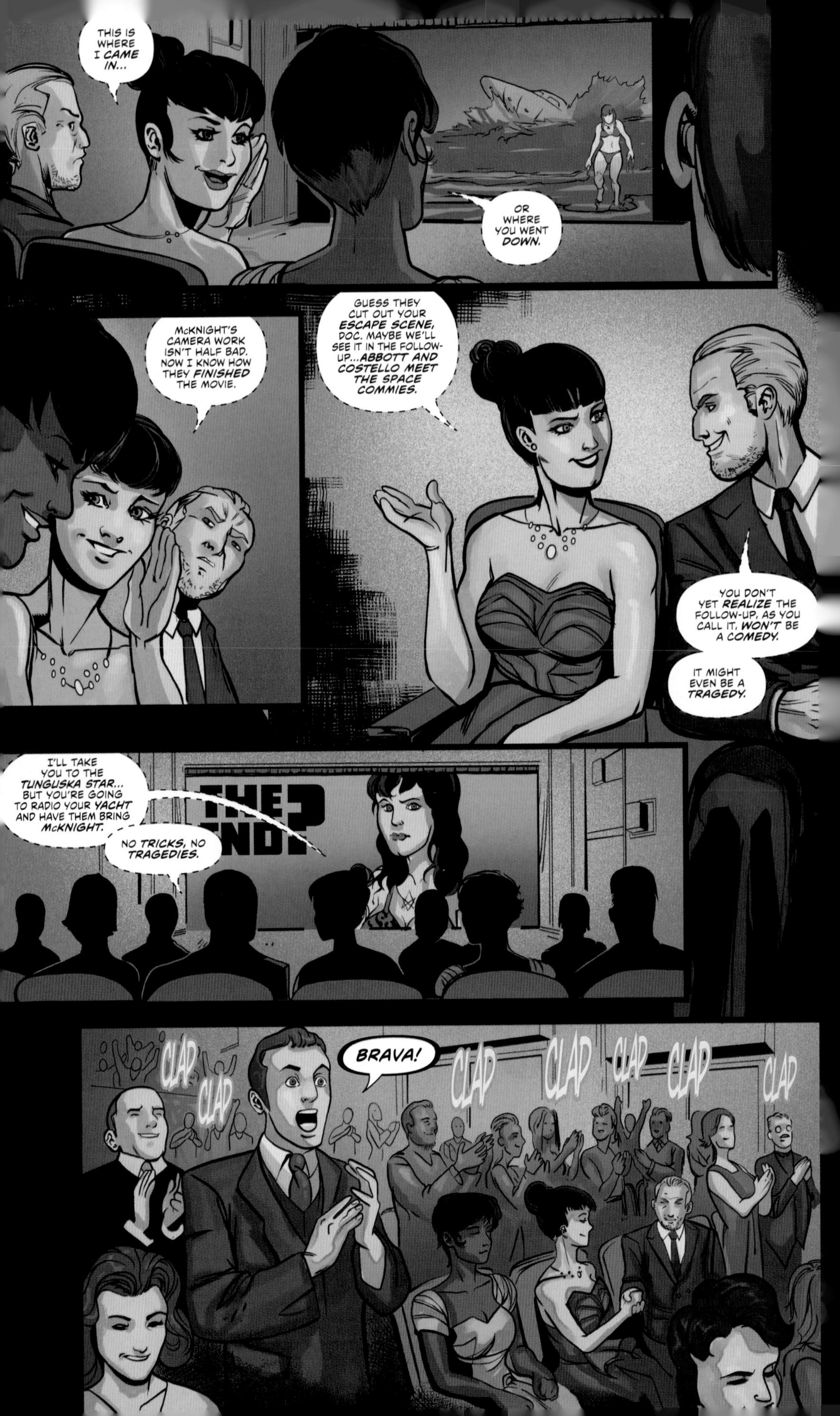
THIS IS WHERE I CAME IN...
OR WHERE YOU WENT DOWN.
McKNIGHT'S CAMERA WORK ISN'T HALF BAD. NOW I KNOW HOW THEY FINISHED THE MOVIE.
GUESS THEY CUT OUT YOUR ESCAPE SCENE, DOC. MAYBE WE'LL SEE IT IN THE FOLLOW-UP...ABBOTT AND COSTELLO MEET THE SPACE COMMIES.
YOU DON'T YET REALIZE THE FOLLOW-UP, AS YOU CALL IT, WON'T BE A COMEDY.
IT MIGHT EVEN BE A TRAGEDY.
I'LL TAKE YOU TO THE TUNGUSKA STAR... BUT YOU'RE GOING TO RADIO YOUR YACHT AND HAVE THEM BRING McKNIGHT.
NO TRICKS, NO TRAGEDIES.
THE END?
CLAP
CLAP
BRAVA!
CLAP
CLAP
CLAP
CLAP
CLAP

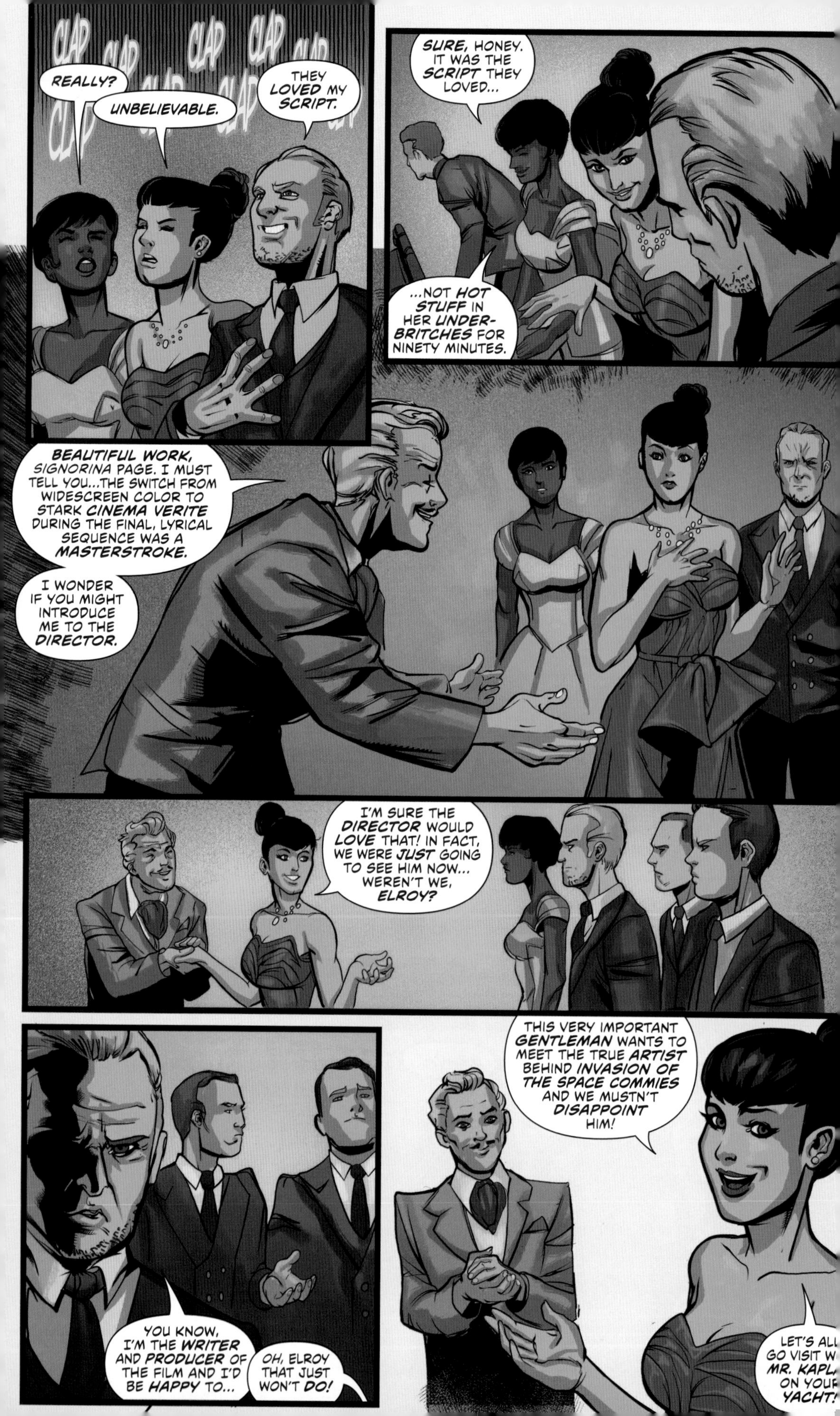
CLAP CLAP CLAP CLAP CLAP CLAP CLAP CLAP CLAP
REALLY?
UNBELIEVABLE.
THEY LOVED MY SCRIPT.
SURE, HONEY. IT WAS THE SCRIPT THEY LOVED...
...NOT HOT STUFF IN HER UNDER-BRITCHES FOR NINETY MINUTES.
BEAUTIFUL WORK, SIGNORINA PAGE. I MUST TELL YOU...THE SWITCH FROM WIDESCREEN COLOR TO STARK CINEMA VERITE DURING THE FINAL, LYRICAL SEQUENCE WAS A MASTERSTROKE.
I WONDER IF YOU MIGHT INTRODUCE ME TO THE DIRECTOR.
I'M SURE THE DIRECTOR WOULD LOVE THAT! IN FACT, WE WERE JUST GOING TO SEE HIM NOW... WEREN'T WE, ELROY?
YOU KNOW, I'M THE WRITER AND PRODUCER OF THE FILM AND I'D BE HAPPY TO...
OH, ELROY THAT JUST WON'T DO!
THIS VERY IMPORTANT GENTLEMAN WANTS TO MEET THE TRUE ARTIST BEHIND INVASION OF THE SPACE COMMIES AND WE MUSTN'T DISAPPOINT HIM!

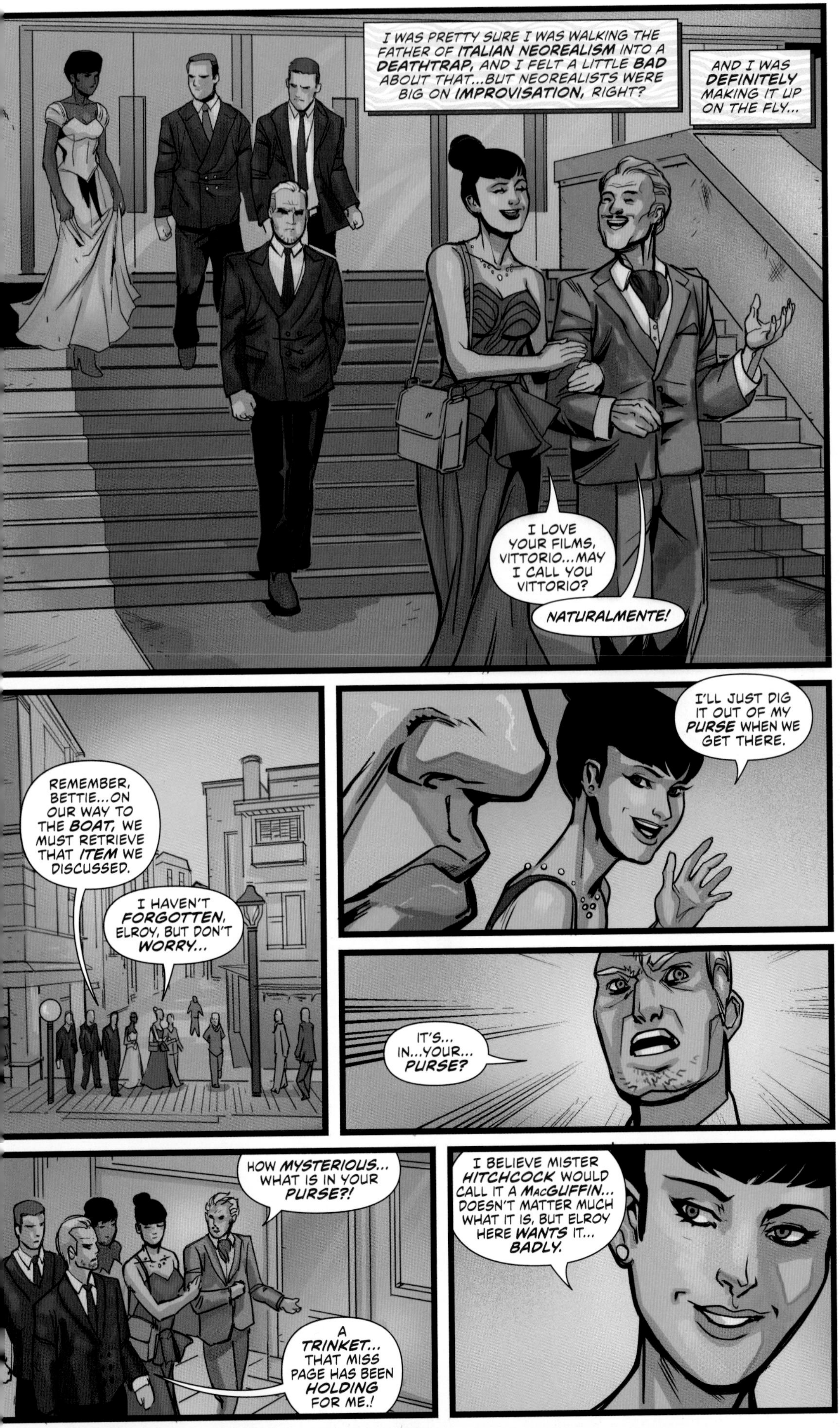
I WAS PRETTY SURE I WAS WALKING THE FATHER OF ITALIAN NEOREALISM INTO A DEATHTRAP, AND I FELT A LITTLE BAD ABOUT THAT...BUT NEOREALISTS WERE BIG ON IMPROVISATION, RIGHT?
AND I WAS DEFINITELY MAKING IT UP ON THE FLY...
I LOVE YOUR FILMS, VITTORIO...MAY I CALL YOU VITTORIO?
NATURALMENTE!
REMEMBER, BETTIE...ON OUR WAY TO THE BOAT, WE MUST RETRIEVE THAT ITEM WE DISCUSSED.
I HAVEN'T FORGOTTEN, ELROY, BUT DON'T WORRY...
I'LL JUST DIG IT OUT OF MY PURSE WHEN WE GET THERE.
IT'S... IN...YOUR... PURSE?
HOW MYSTERIOUS... WHAT IS IN YOUR PURSE?!
A TRINKET... THAT MISS PAGE HAS BEEN HOLDING FOR ME.!
I BELIEVE MISTER HITCHCOCK WOULD CALL IT A MacGUFFIN... DOESN'T MATTER MUCH WHAT IT IS, BUT ELROY HERE WANTS IT... BADLY.

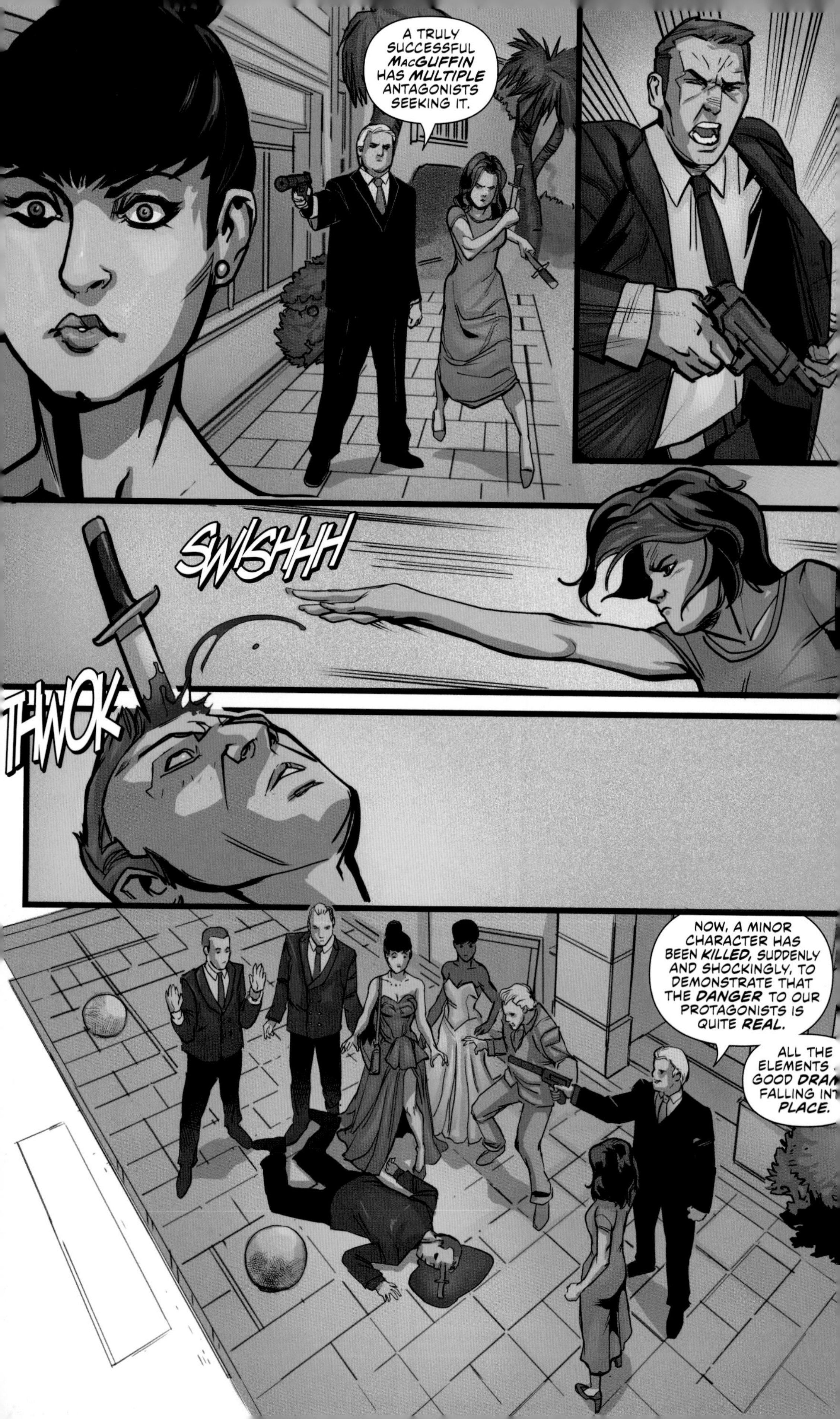
A TRULY SUCCESSFUL MacGUFFIN HAS MULTIPLE ANTAGONISTS SEEKING IT.
SWISHHH
THWOK
NOW, A MINOR CHARACTER HAS BEEN KILLED, SUDDENLY AND SHOCKINGLY, TO DEMONSTRATE THAT THE DANGER TO OUR PROTAGONISTS IS QUITE REAL.
ALL THE ELEMENTS GOOD DRAM FALLING INT PLACE.

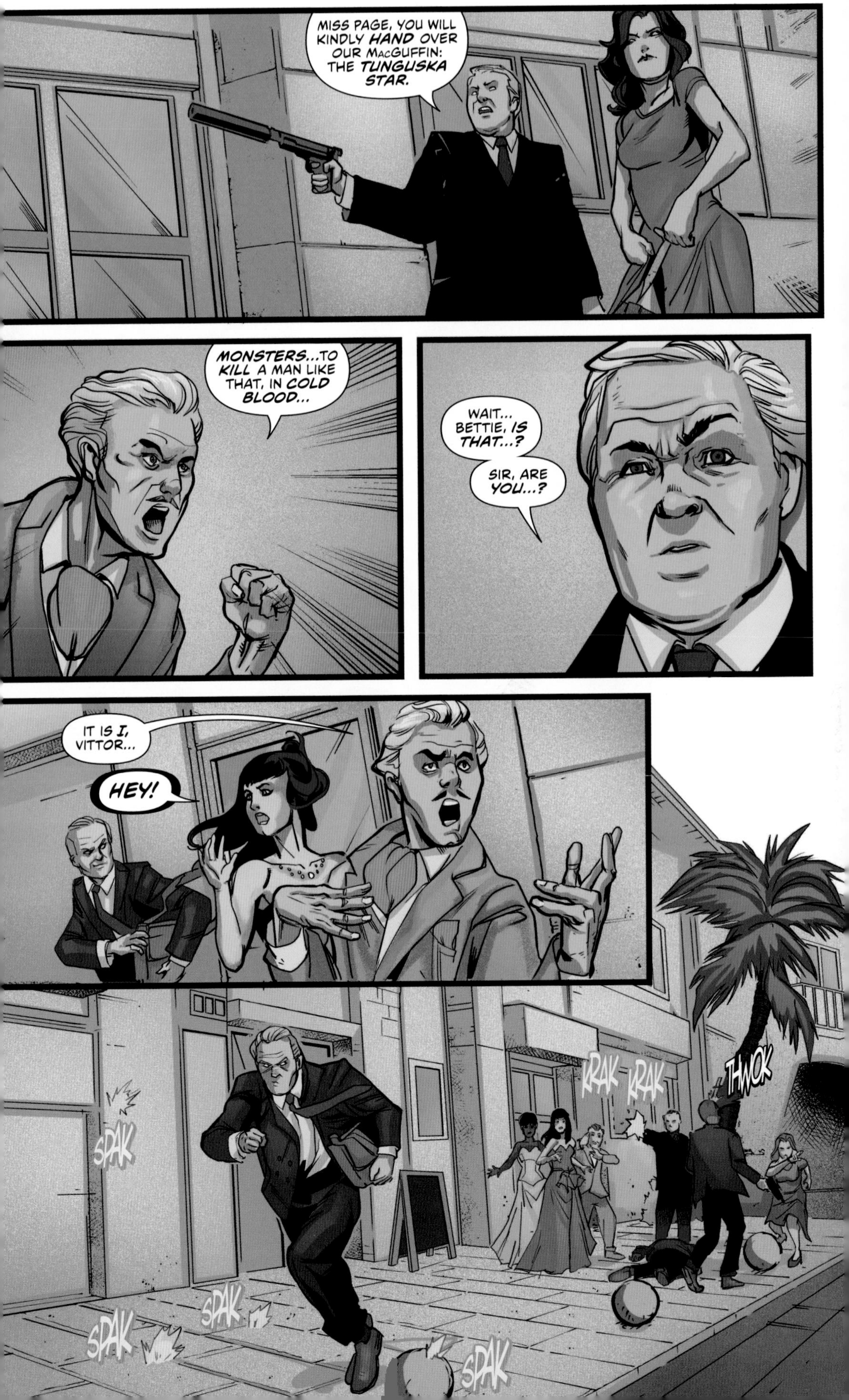

MISS PAGE, YOU WILL KINDLY HAND OVER OUR MACGUFFIN: THE TUNGUSKA STAR.
MONSTERS...TO KILL A MAN LIKE THAT, IN COLD BLOOD...
WAIT... BETTIE, IS THAT...?
SIR, ARE YOU...?
IT IS I, VITTOR...
HEY!
SPAK
KRAK KRAK
THWOK
SPAK
SPAK
SPAK

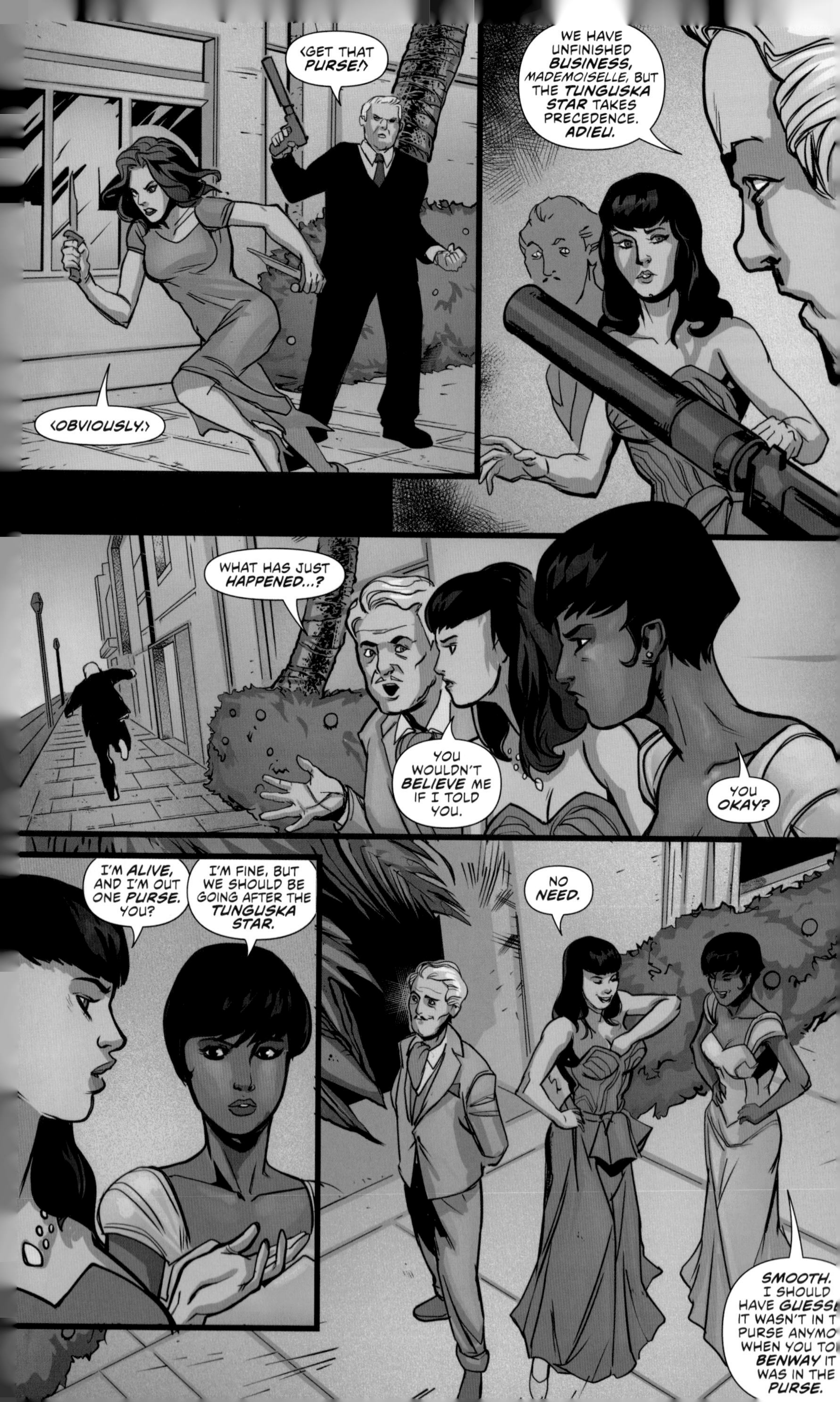

<GET THAT PURSE!>
<OBVIOUSLY.>
WE HAVE UNFINISHED BUSINESS, MADEMOISELLE, BUT THE TUNGUSKA STAR TAKES PRECEDENCE. ADIEU.
WHAT HAS JUST HAPPENED...?
YOU WOULDN'T BELIEVE ME IF I TOLD YOU.
YOU OKAY?
I'M ALIVE, AND I'M OUT ONE PURSE. YOU?
I'M FINE, BUT WE SHOULD BE GOING AFTER THE TUNGUSKA STAR.
NO NEED.
SMOOTH. I SHOULD HAVE GUESS IT WASN'T IN T PURSE ANYMO WHEN YOU TO BENWAY IT WAS IN THE PURSE.

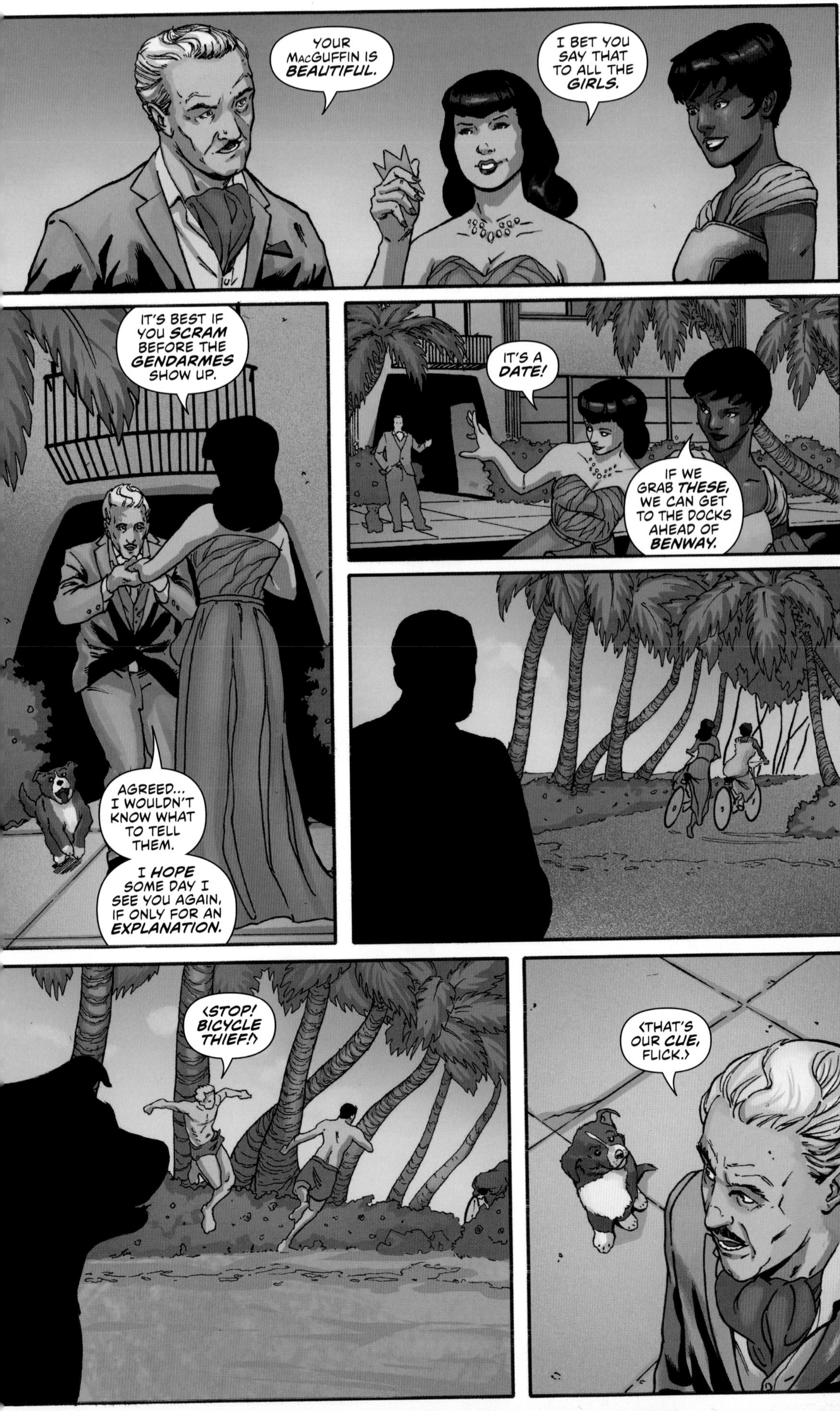
YOUR MacGUFFIN IS BEAUTIFUL.
I BET YOU SAY THAT TO ALL THE GIRLS.
IT'S BEST IF YOU SCRAM BEFORE THE GENDARMES SHOW UP.
AGREED... I WOULDN'T KNOW WHAT TO TELL THEM.
I HOPE SOME DAY I SEE YOU AGAIN, IF ONLY FOR AN EXPLANATION.
IT'S A DATE!
IF WE GRAB THESE, WE CAN GET TO THE DOCKS AHEAD OF BENWAY.
‹STOP! BICYCLE THIEF!›
‹THAT'S OUR CUE, FLICK.›

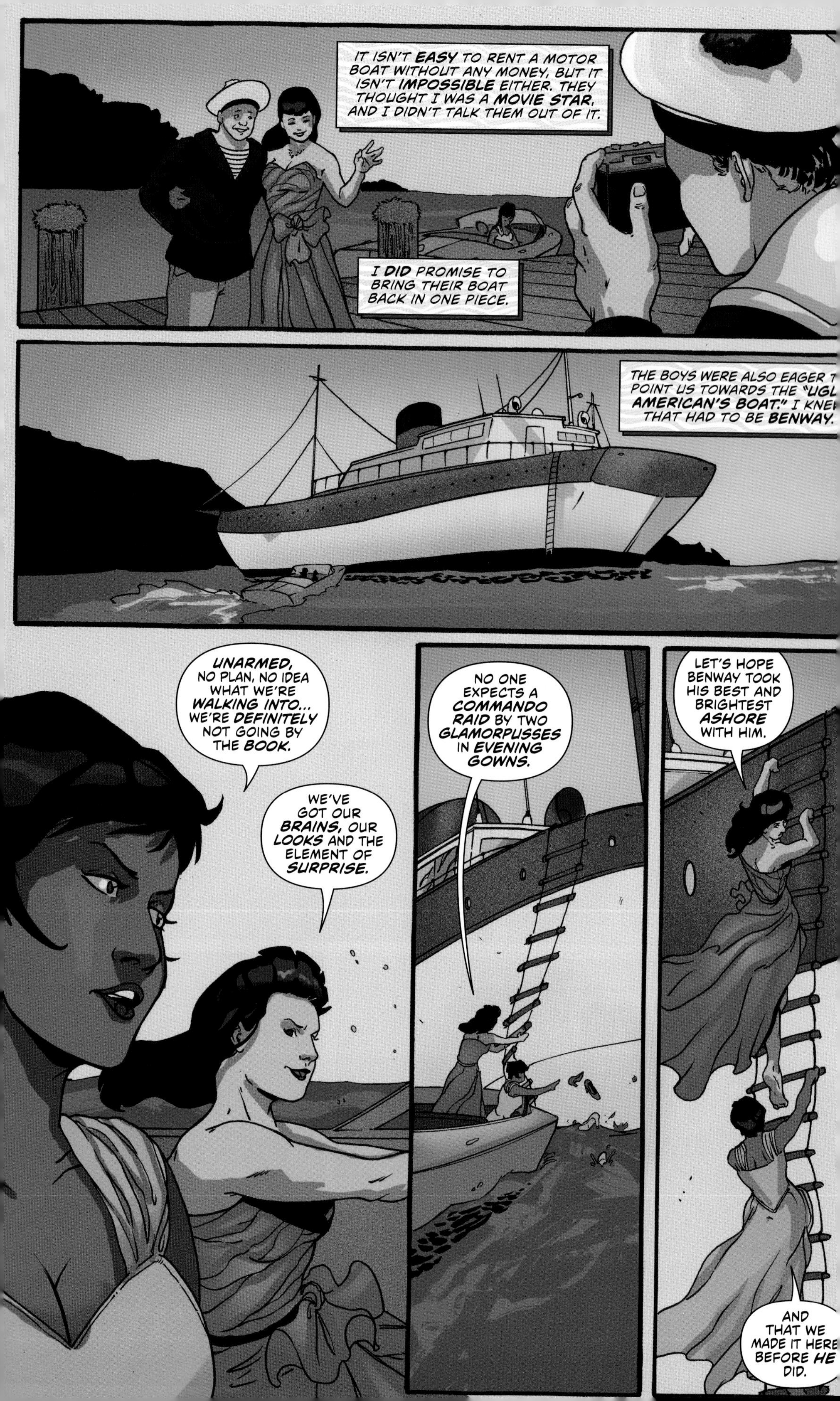

IT ISN'T EASY TO RENT A MOTOR BOAT WITHOUT ANY MONEY, BUT IT ISN'T IMPOSSIBLE EITHER. THEY THOUGHT I WAS A MOVIE STAR, AND I DIDN'T TALK THEM OUT OF IT.
I DID PROMISE TO BRING THEIR BOAT BACK IN ONE PIECE.
THE BOYS WERE ALSO EAGER T POINT US TOWARDS THE "UGL AMERICAN'S BOAT." I KNE THAT HAD TO BE BENWAY.
UNARMED, NO PLAN, NO IDEA WHAT WE'RE WALKING INTO... WE'RE DEFINITELY NOT GOING BY THE BOOK.
WE'VE GOT OUR BRAINS, OUR LOOKS AND THE ELEMENT OF SURPRISE.
NO ONE EXPECTS A COMMANDO RAID BY TWO GLAMORPUSSES IN EVENING GOWNS.
LET'S HOPE BENWAY TOOK HIS BEST AND BRIGHTEST ASHORE WITH HIM.
AND THAT WE MADE IT HERE BEFORE HE DID.

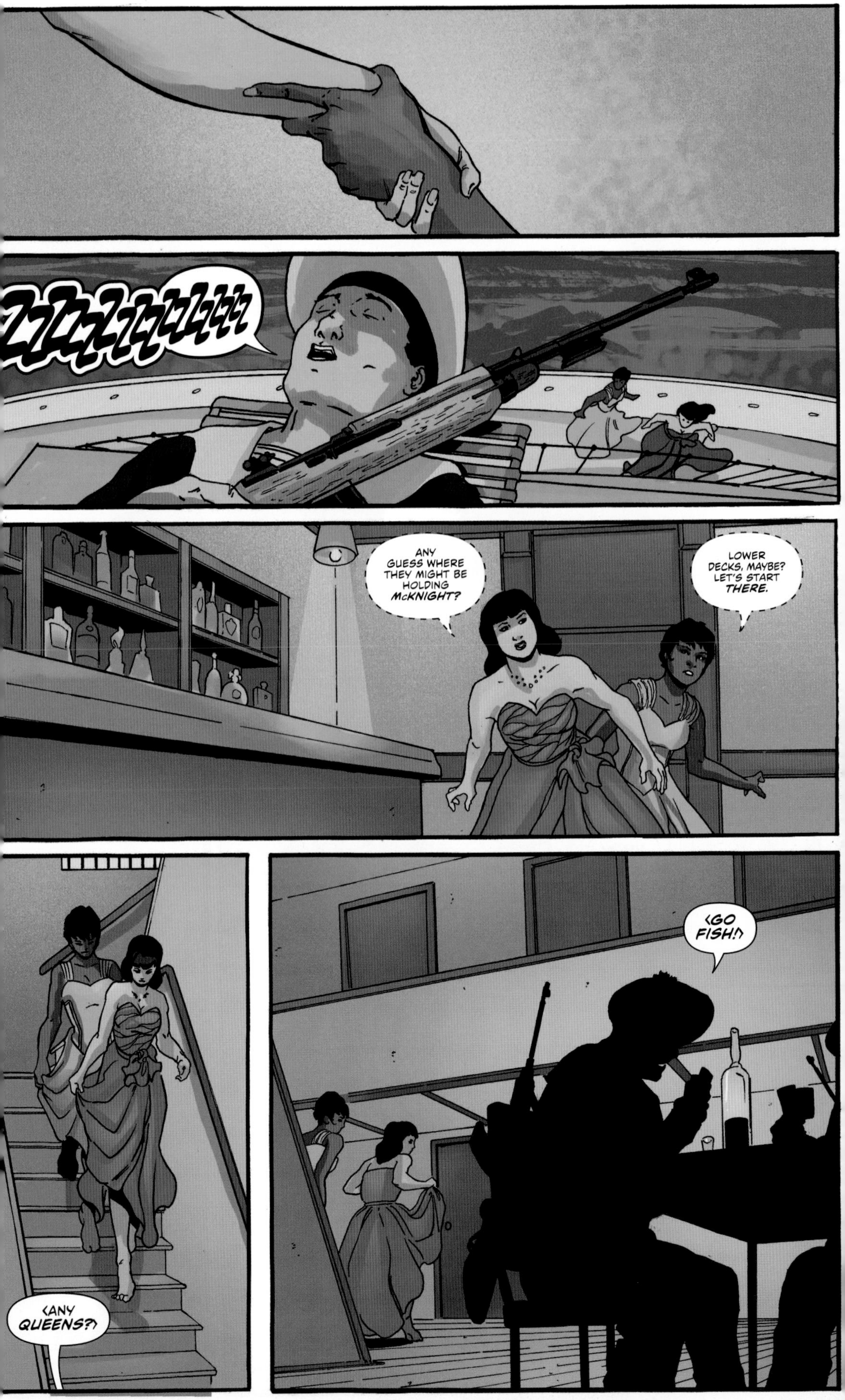
ZZZZZZZZZZZZZZZ
ANY GUESS WHERE THEY MIGHT BE HOLDING McKNIGHT?
LOWER DECKS, MAYBE? LET'S START THERE.
‹ANY QUEENS?›
‹GO FISH!›

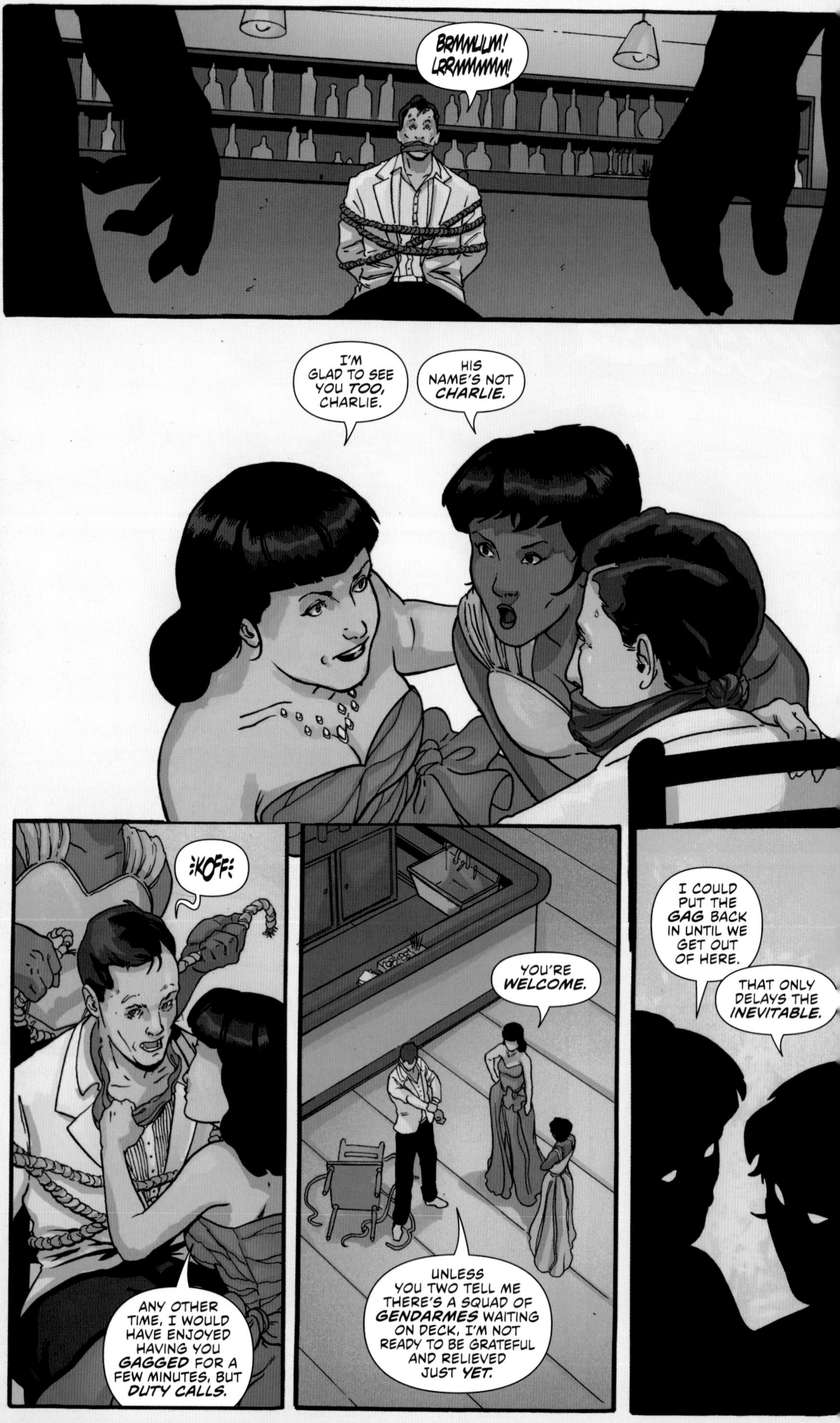
BRMMULUM! LRRMMMMM!
I'M GLAD TO SEE YOU TOO, CHARLIE.
HIS NAME'S NOT CHARLIE.
KOFF
ANY OTHER TIME, I WOULD HAVE ENJOYED HAVING YOU GAGGED FOR A FEW MINUTES, BUT DUTY CALLS.
YOU'RE WELCOME.
UNLESS YOU TWO TELL ME THERE'S A SQUAD OF GENDARMES WAITING ON DECK, I'M NOT READY TO BE GRATEFUL AND RELIEVED JUST YET.
I COULD PUT THE GAG BACK IN UNTIL WE GET OUT OF HERE.
THAT ONLY DELAYS THE INEVITABLE.

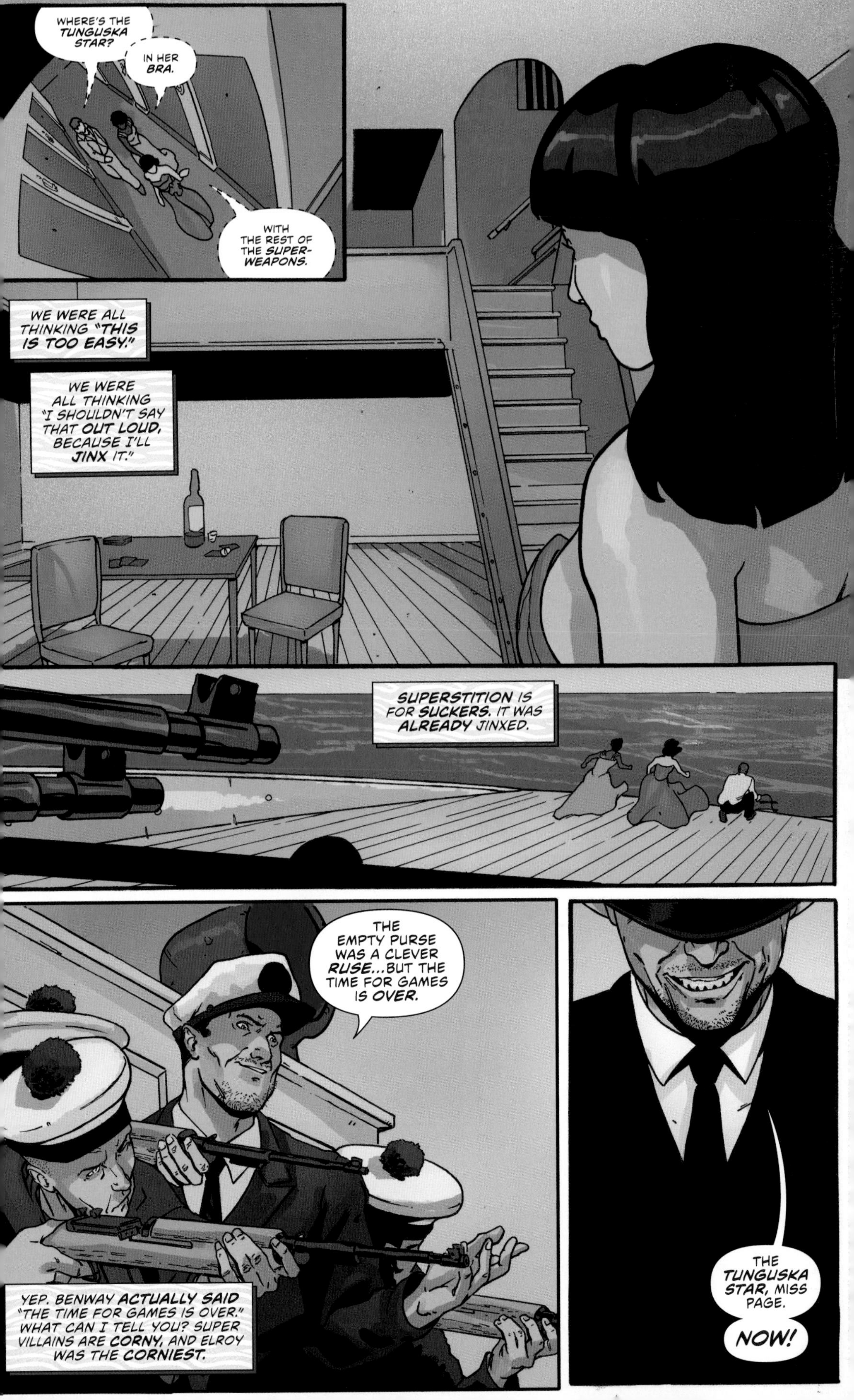

WHERE'S THE TUNGUSKA STAR?
IN HER BRA.
WITH THE REST OF THE SUPER-WEAPONS.
WE WERE ALL THINKING "THIS IS TOO EASY."
WE WERE ALL THINKING "I SHOULDN'T SAY THAT OUT LOUD, BECAUSE I'LL JINX IT."
SUPERSTITION IS FOR SUCKERS. IT WAS ALREADY JINXED.
THE EMPTY PURSE WAS A CLEVER RUSE...BUT THE TIME FOR GAMES IS OVER.
YEP. BENWAY ACTUALLY SAID "THE TIME FOR GAMES IS OVER." WHAT CAN I TELL YOU? SUPER VILLAINS ARE CORNY, AND ELROY WAS THE CORNIEST.
THE TUNGUSKA STAR, MISS PAGE.
NOW!

THE *STAR* WILL MAKE UP FOR ALL THE *TROUBLES* YOU'VE CAUSED ME SO FAR.

NO ONE WILL BE ABLE TO STOP M[...]

KEEP YOUR *PANTS ON,* ELROY. I'VE *GOT* IT.

IT'S *MAGNIFICENT.* NOW...

BLAM

BLAM

BLAM

...KILL THEM ALL.

NO!

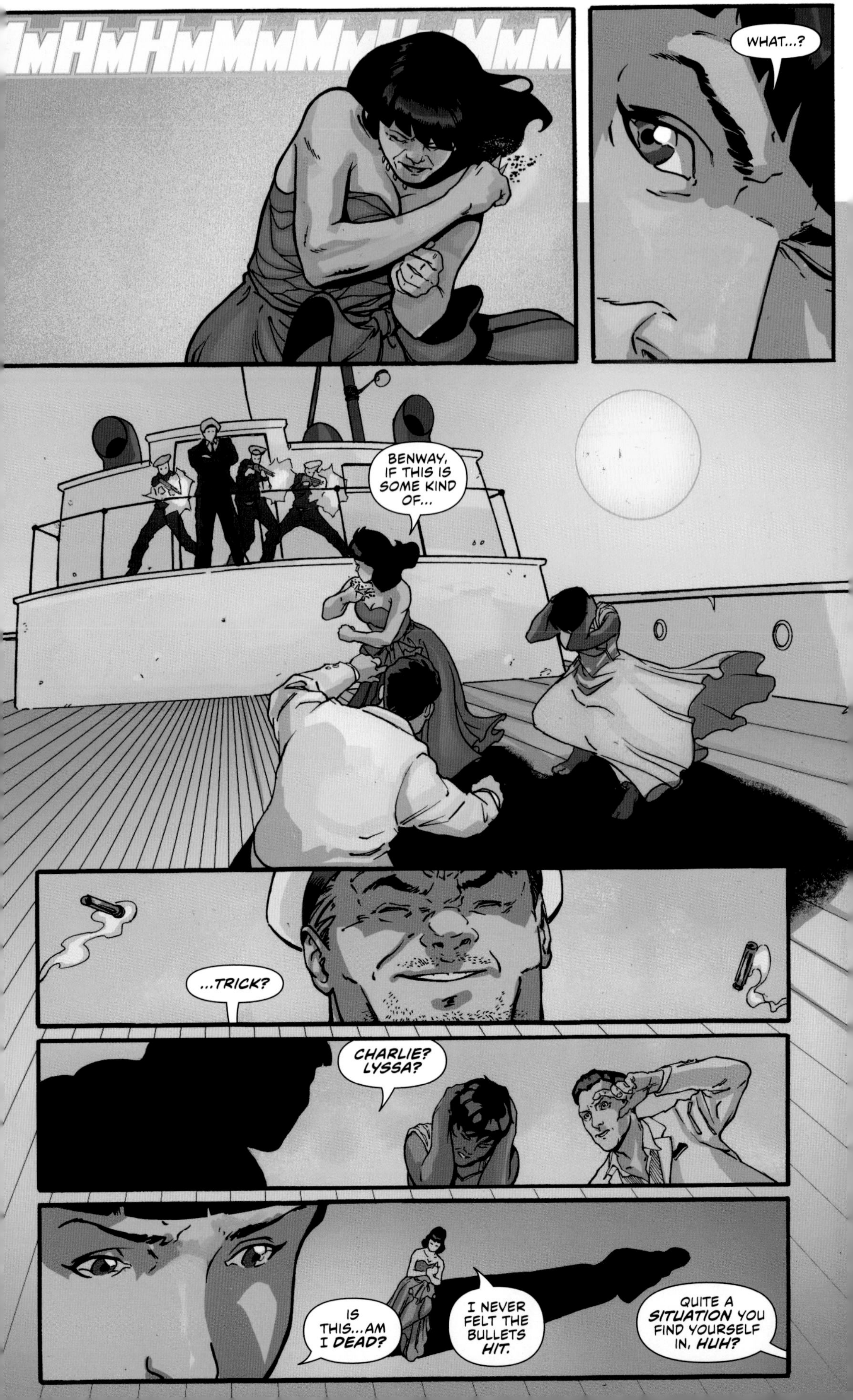

MMHMHMMMMMNHMMMM
WHAT...?
BENWAY, IF THIS IS SOME KIND OF...
...TRICK?
CHARLIE? LYSSA?
IS THIS...AM I DEAD?
I NEVER FELT THE BULLETS HIT.
QUITE A SITUATION YOU FIND YOURSELF IN, HUH?

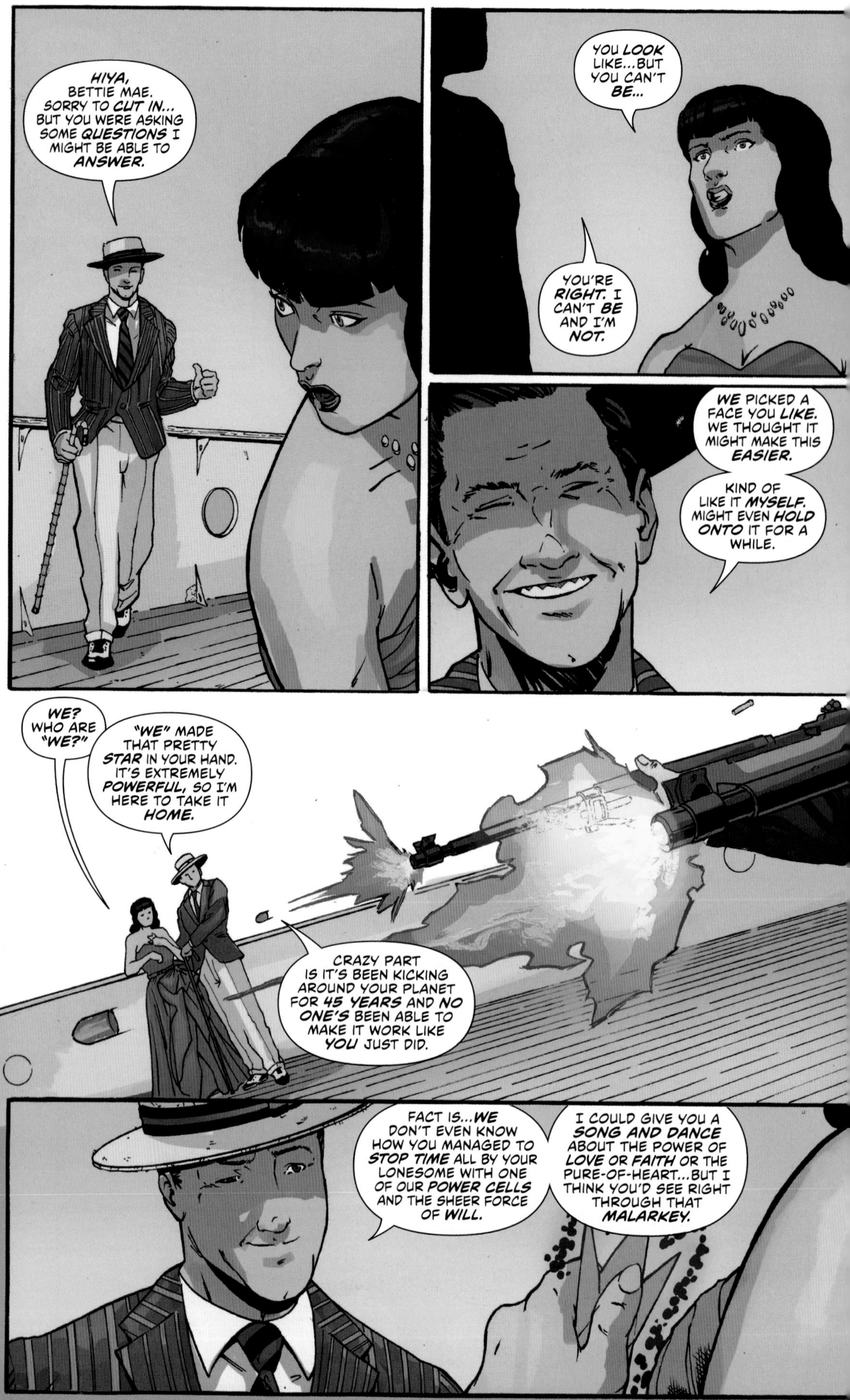
HIYA, BETTIE MAE. SORRY TO CUT IN... BUT YOU WERE ASKING SOME QUESTIONS I MIGHT BE ABLE TO ANSWER.
YOU LOOK LIKE...BUT YOU CAN'T BE...
YOU'RE RIGHT. I CAN'T BE AND I'M NOT.
WE PICKED A FACE YOU LIKE. WE THOUGHT IT MIGHT MAKE THIS EASIER.
KIND OF LIKE IT MYSELF. MIGHT EVEN HOLD ONTO IT FOR A WHILE.
WE? WHO ARE "WE?"
"WE" MADE THAT PRETTY STAR IN YOUR HAND. IT'S EXTREMELY POWERFUL, SO I'M HERE TO TAKE IT HOME.
CRAZY PART IS IT'S BEEN KICKING AROUND YOUR PLANET FOR 45 YEARS AND NO ONE'S BEEN ABLE TO MAKE IT WORK LIKE YOU JUST DID.
FACT IS...WE DON'T EVEN KNOW HOW YOU MANAGED TO STOP TIME ALL BY YOUR LONESOME WITH ONE OF OUR POWER CELLS AND THE SHEER FORCE OF WILL.
I COULD GIVE YOU A SONG AND DANCE ABOUT THE POWER OF LOVE OR FAITH OR THE PURE-OF-HEART...BUT I THINK YOU'D SEE RIGHT THROUGH THAT MALARKEY.

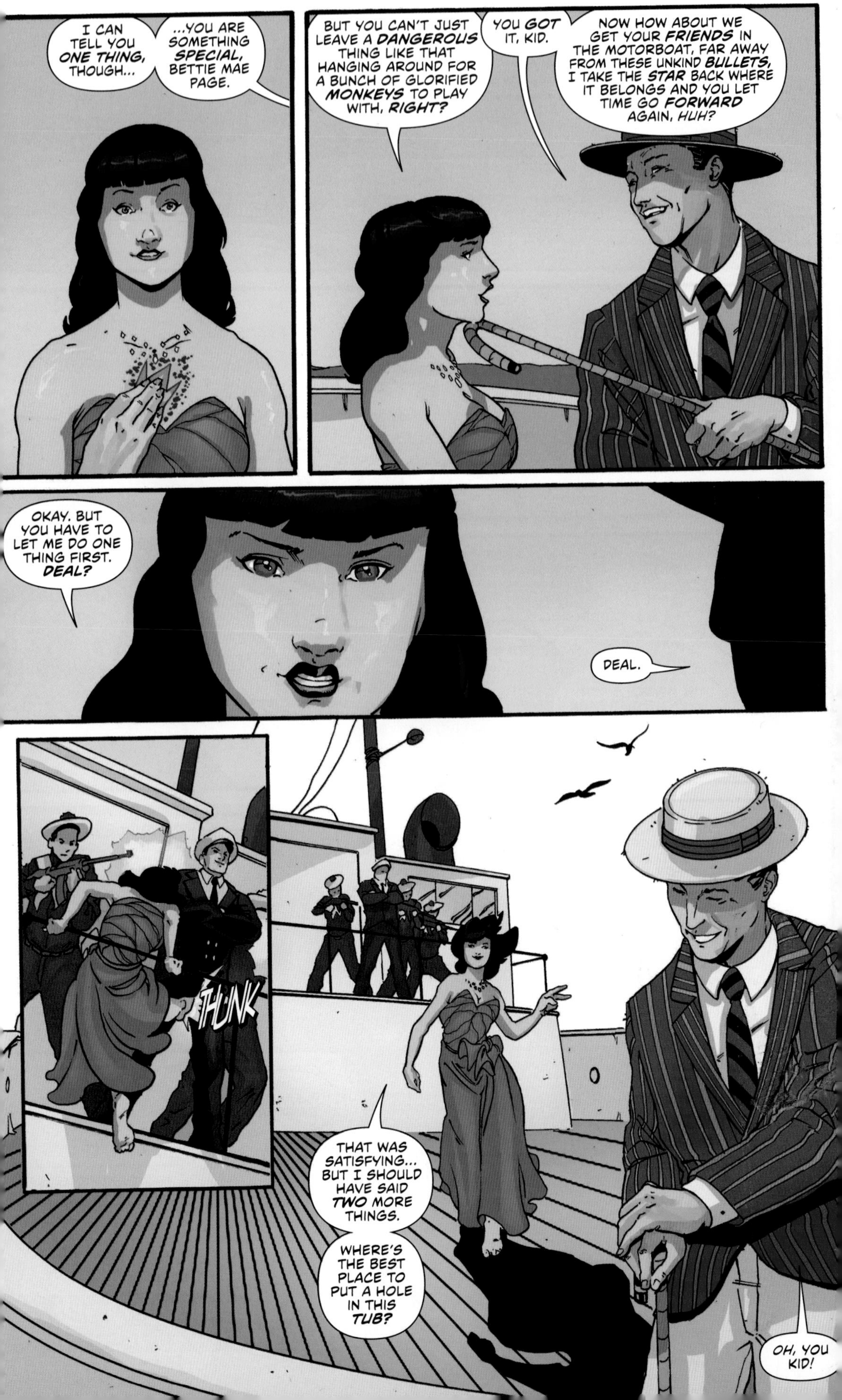

I CAN TELL YOU ONE THING, THOUGH...
...YOU ARE SOMETHING SPECIAL, BETTIE MAE PAGE.
BUT YOU CAN'T JUST LEAVE A DANGEROUS THING LIKE THAT HANGING AROUND FOR A BUNCH OF GLORIFIED MONKEYS TO PLAY WITH, RIGHT?
YOU GOT IT, KID.
NOW HOW ABOUT WE GET YOUR FRIENDS IN THE MOTORBOAT, FAR AWAY FROM THESE UNKIND BULLETS, I TAKE THE STAR BACK WHERE IT BELONGS AND YOU LET TIME GO FORWARD AGAIN, HUH?
OKAY. BUT YOU HAVE TO LET ME DO ONE THING FIRST. DEAL?
DEAL.
THUNK
THAT WAS SATISFYING... BUT I SHOULD HAVE SAID TWO MORE THINGS.
WHERE'S THE BEST PLACE TO PUT A HOLE IN THIS TUB?
OH, YOU KID!

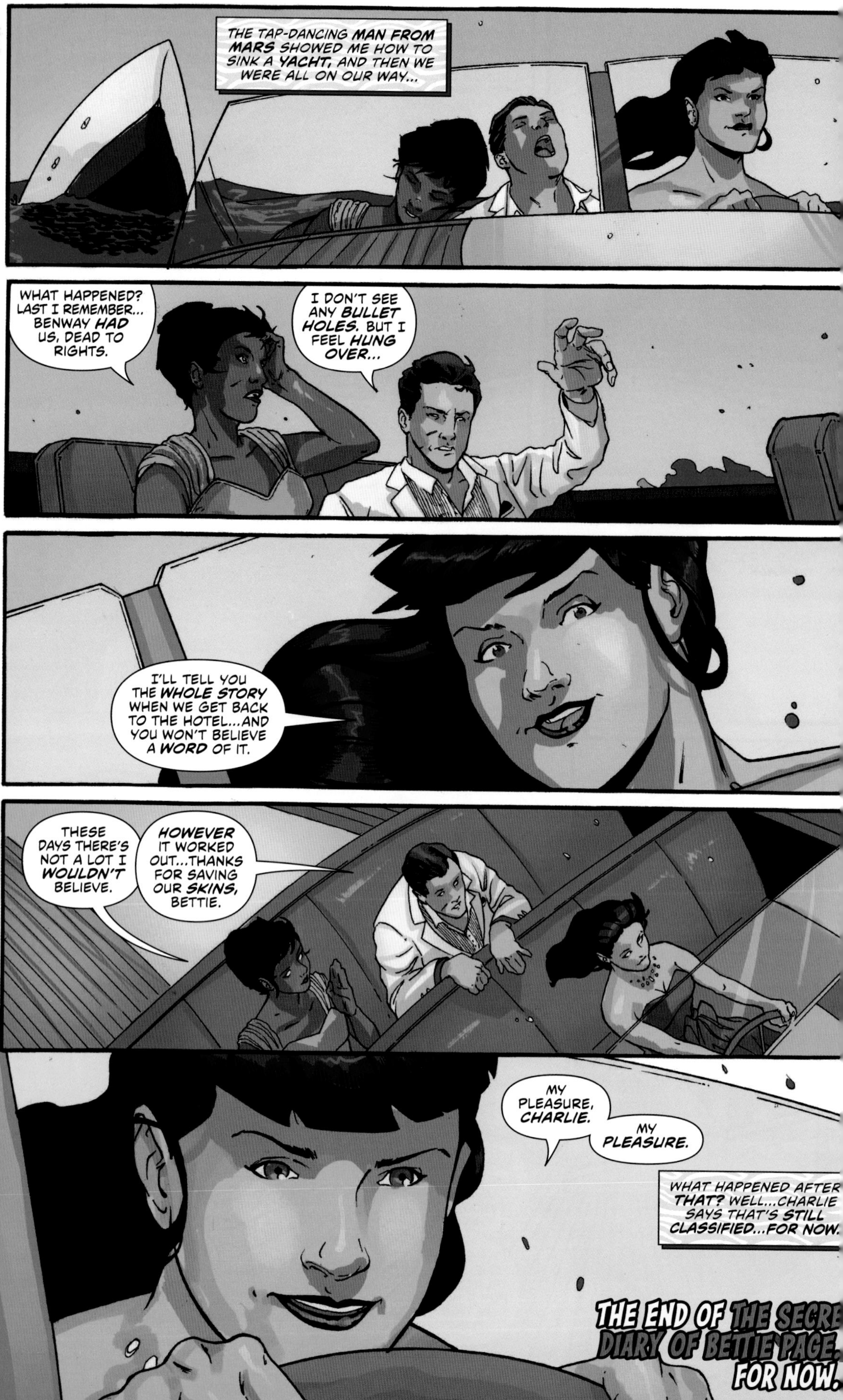
THE TAP-DANCING MAN FROM MARS SHOWED ME HOW TO SINK A YACHT, AND THEN WE WERE ALL ON OUR WAY...
WHAT HAPPENED? LAST I REMEMBER... BENWAY HAD US, DEAD TO RIGHTS.
I DON'T SEE ANY BULLET HOLES. BUT I FEEL HUNG OVER...
I'LL TELL YOU THE WHOLE STORY WHEN WE GET BACK TO THE HOTEL...AND YOU WON'T BELIEVE A WORD OF IT.
THESE DAYS THERE'S NOT A LOT I WOULDN'T BELIEVE.
HOWEVER IT WORKED OUT...THANKS FOR SAVING OUR SKINS, BETTIE.
MY PLEASURE, CHARLIE.
MY PLEASURE.
WHAT HAPPENED AFTER THAT? WELL...CHARLIE SAYS THAT'S STILL CLASSIFIED...FOR NOW.
THE END OF THE SECRE
DIARY OF BETTIE PAGE
FOR NOW.

COVERS

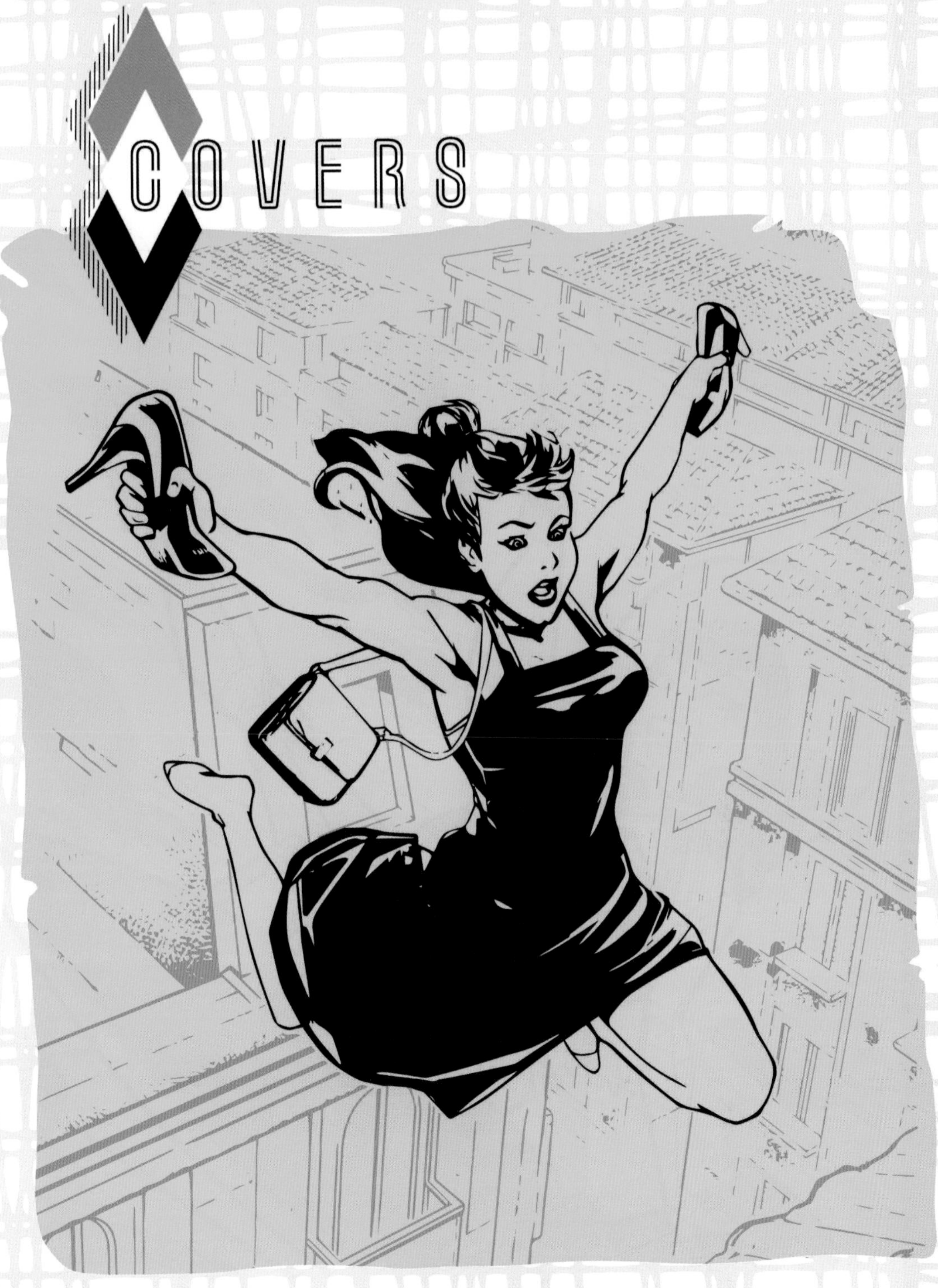

ART: J. BONE

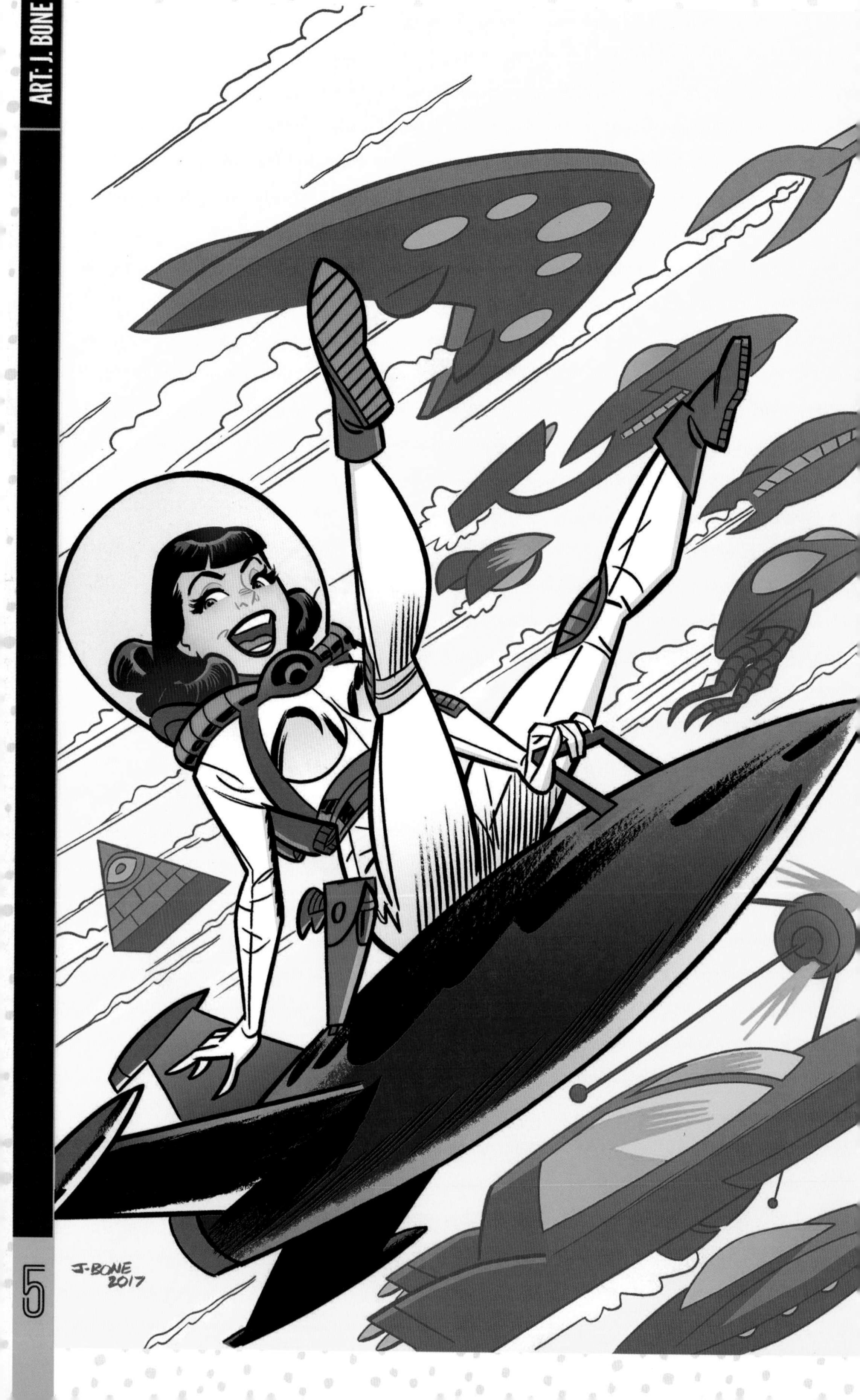
J-BONE
2017

5

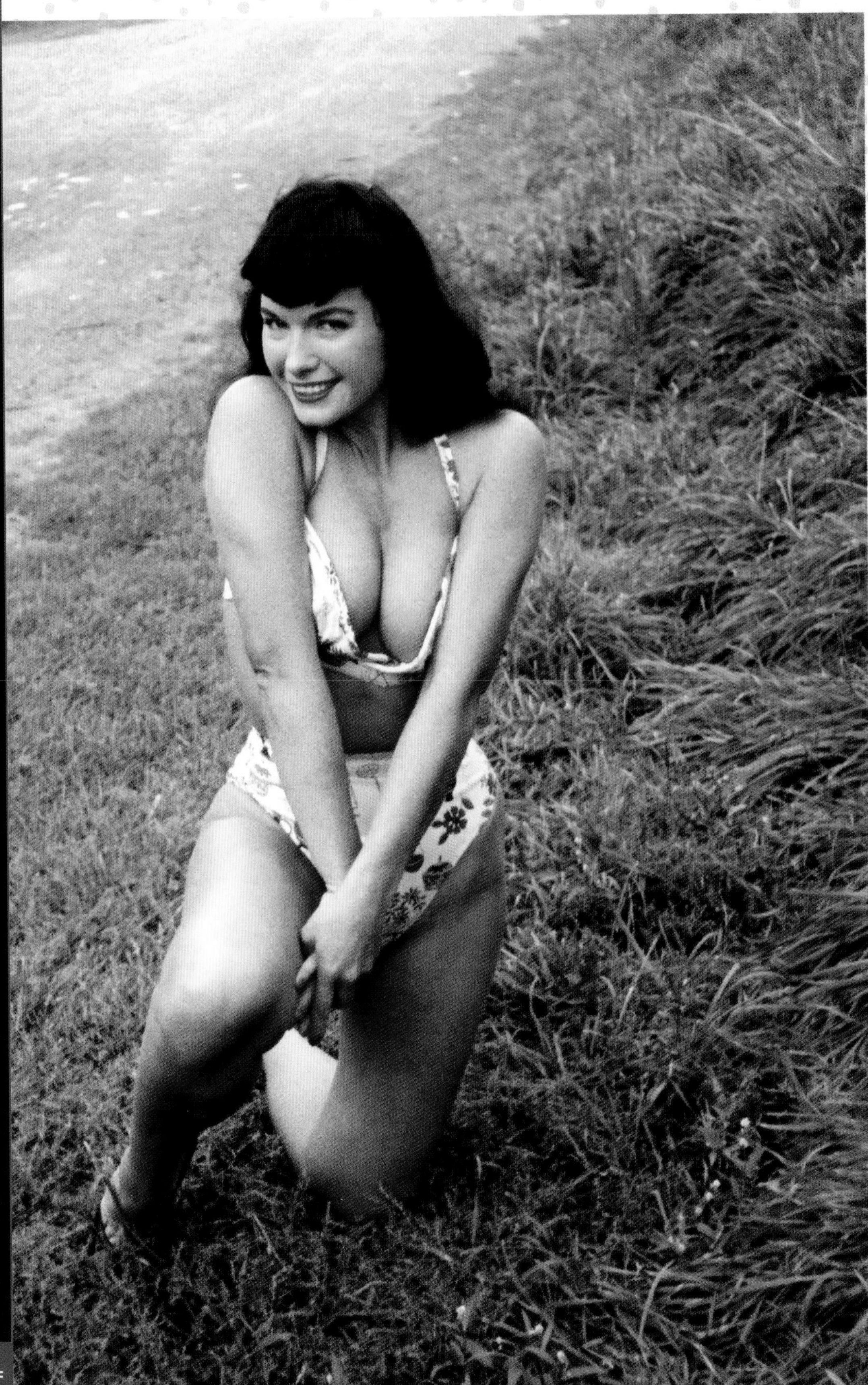

ART: SCOTT CHANTLER

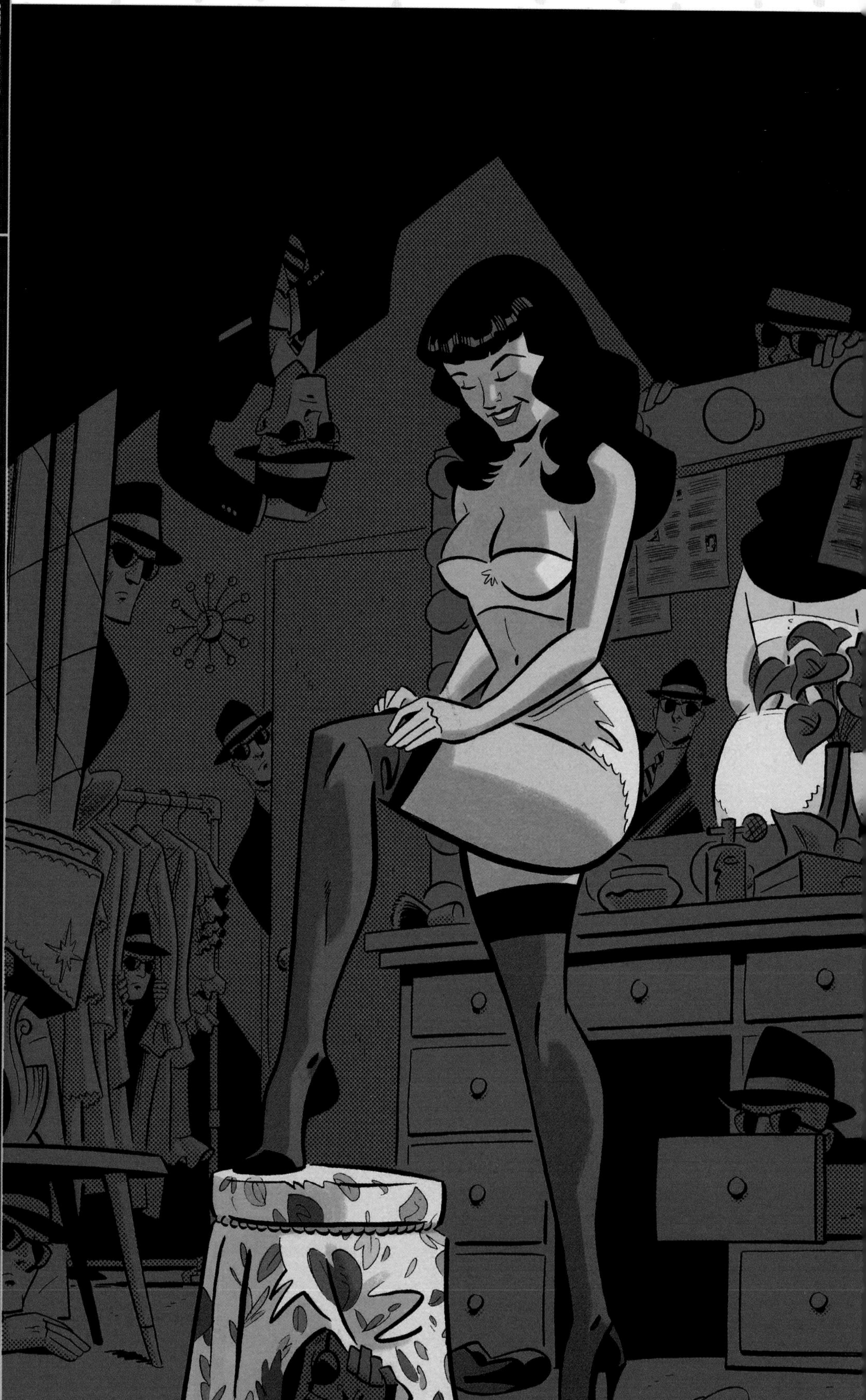

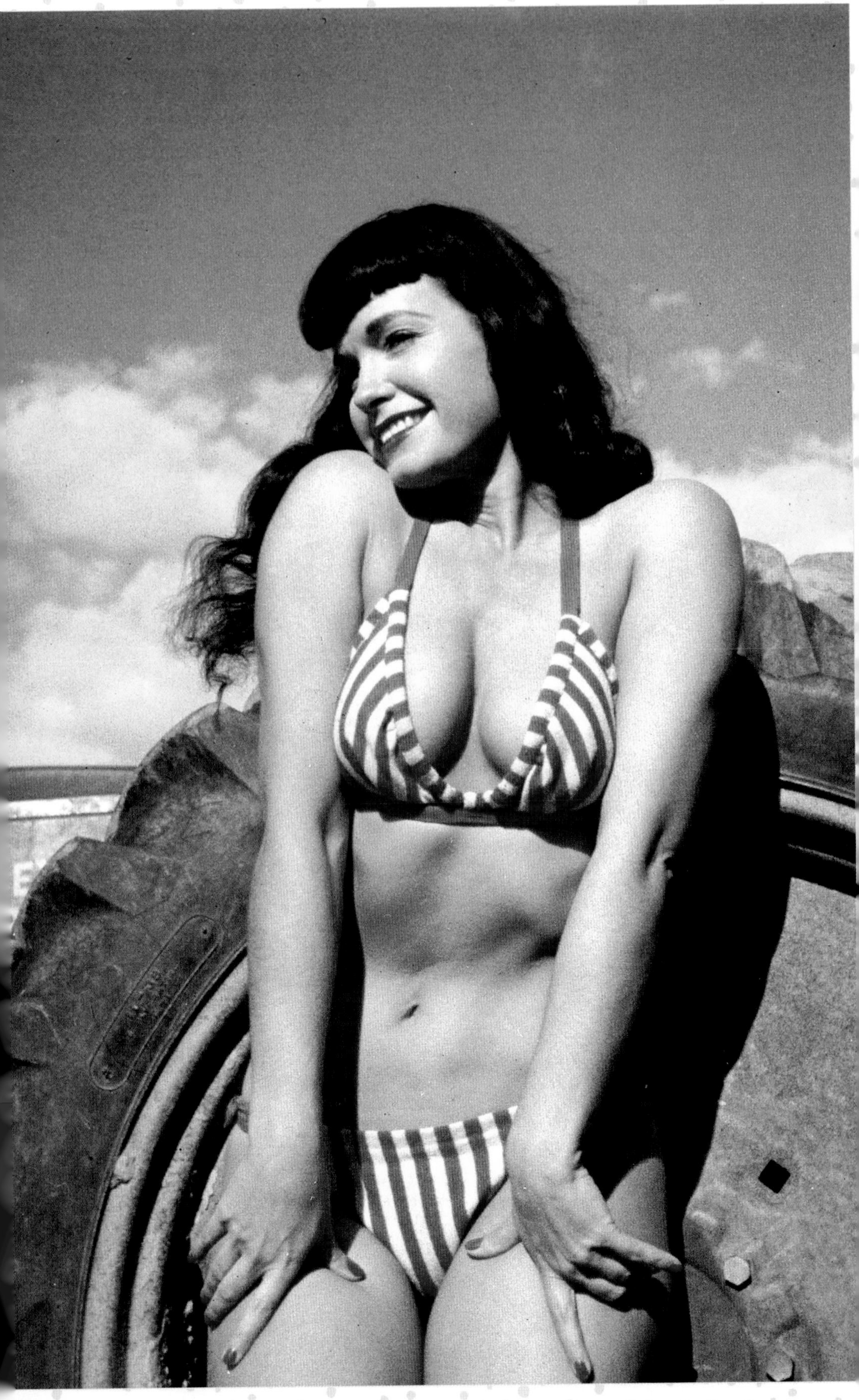

ART: SCOTT CHANTLER

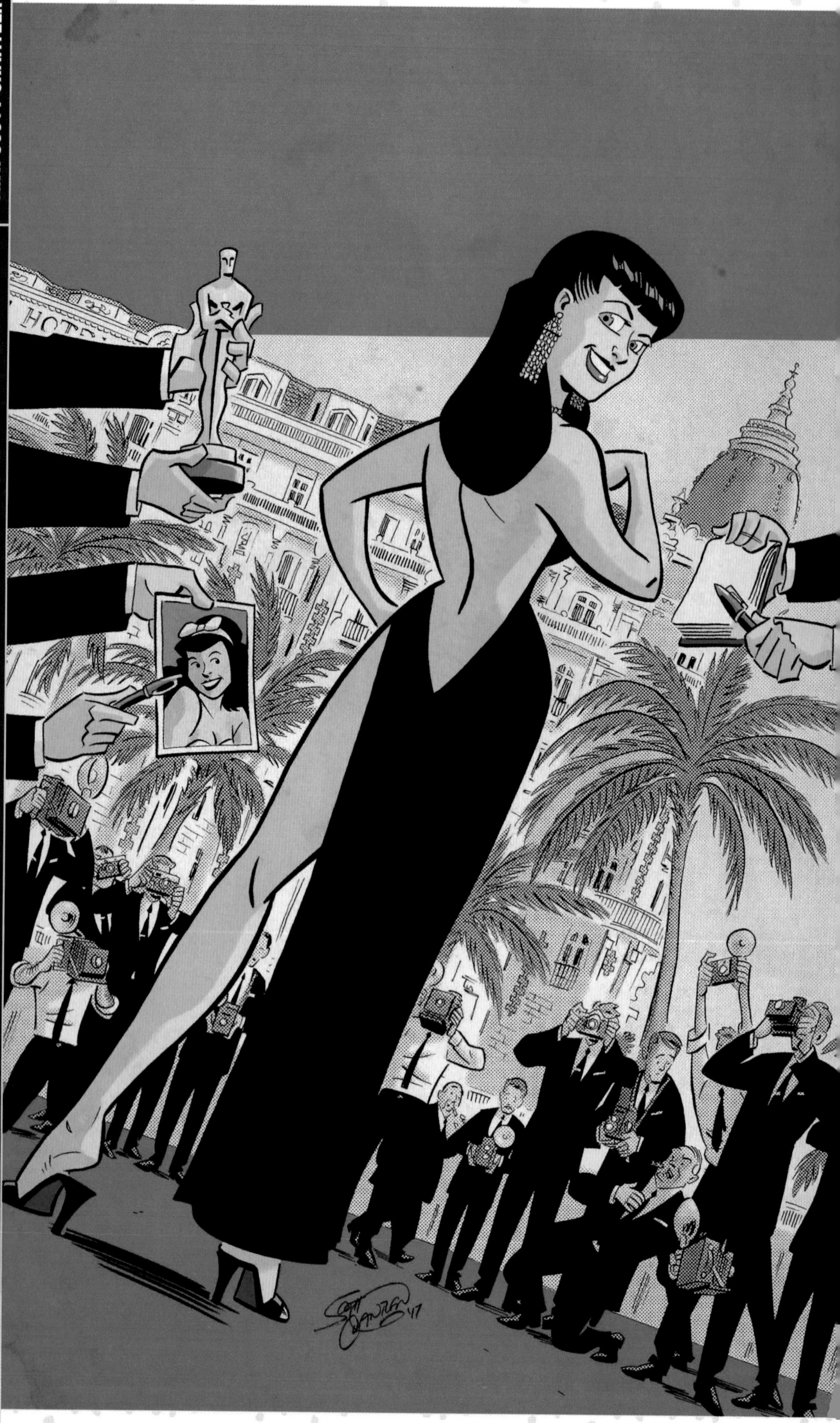

7

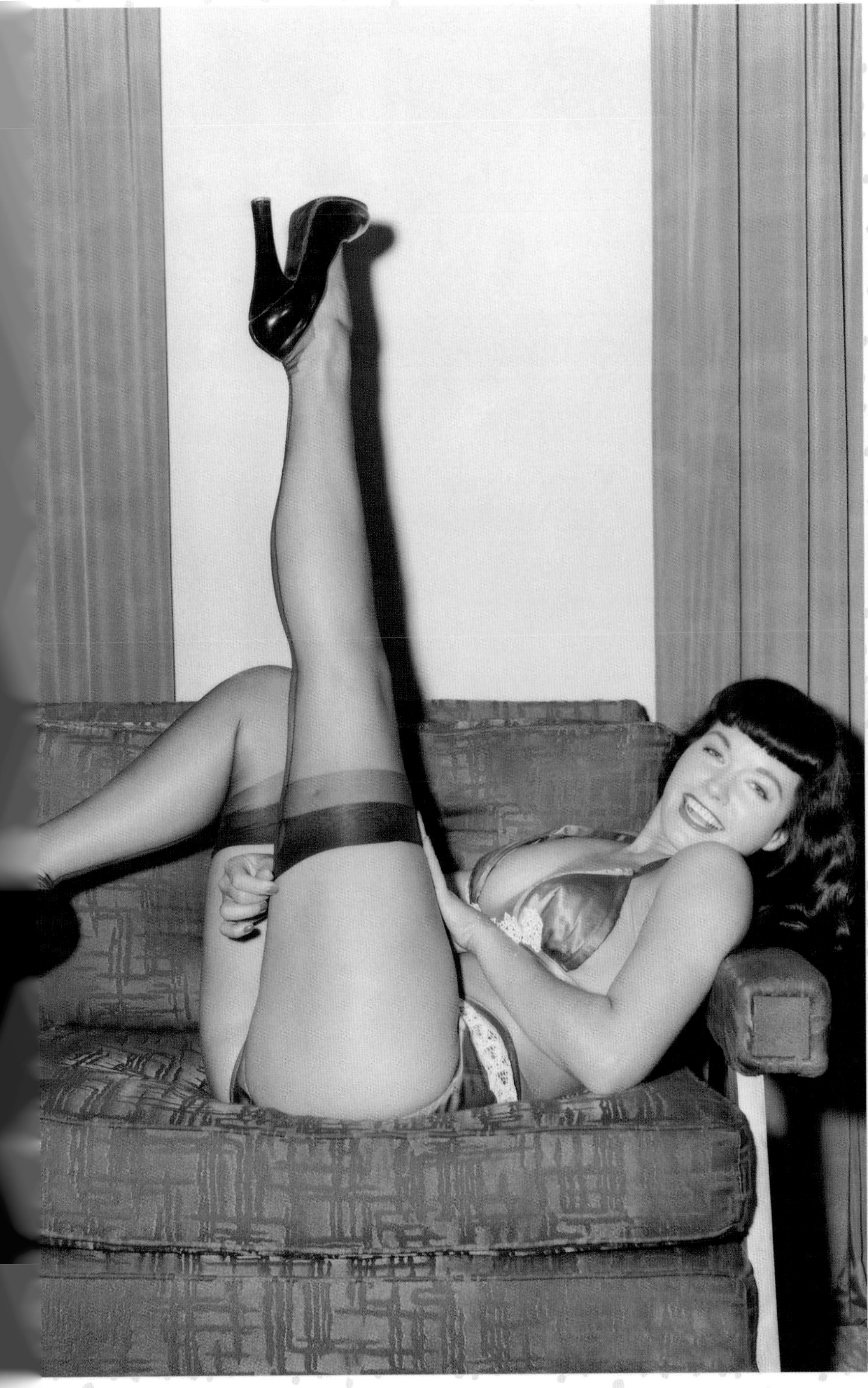

ART: SCOTT CHANTLER

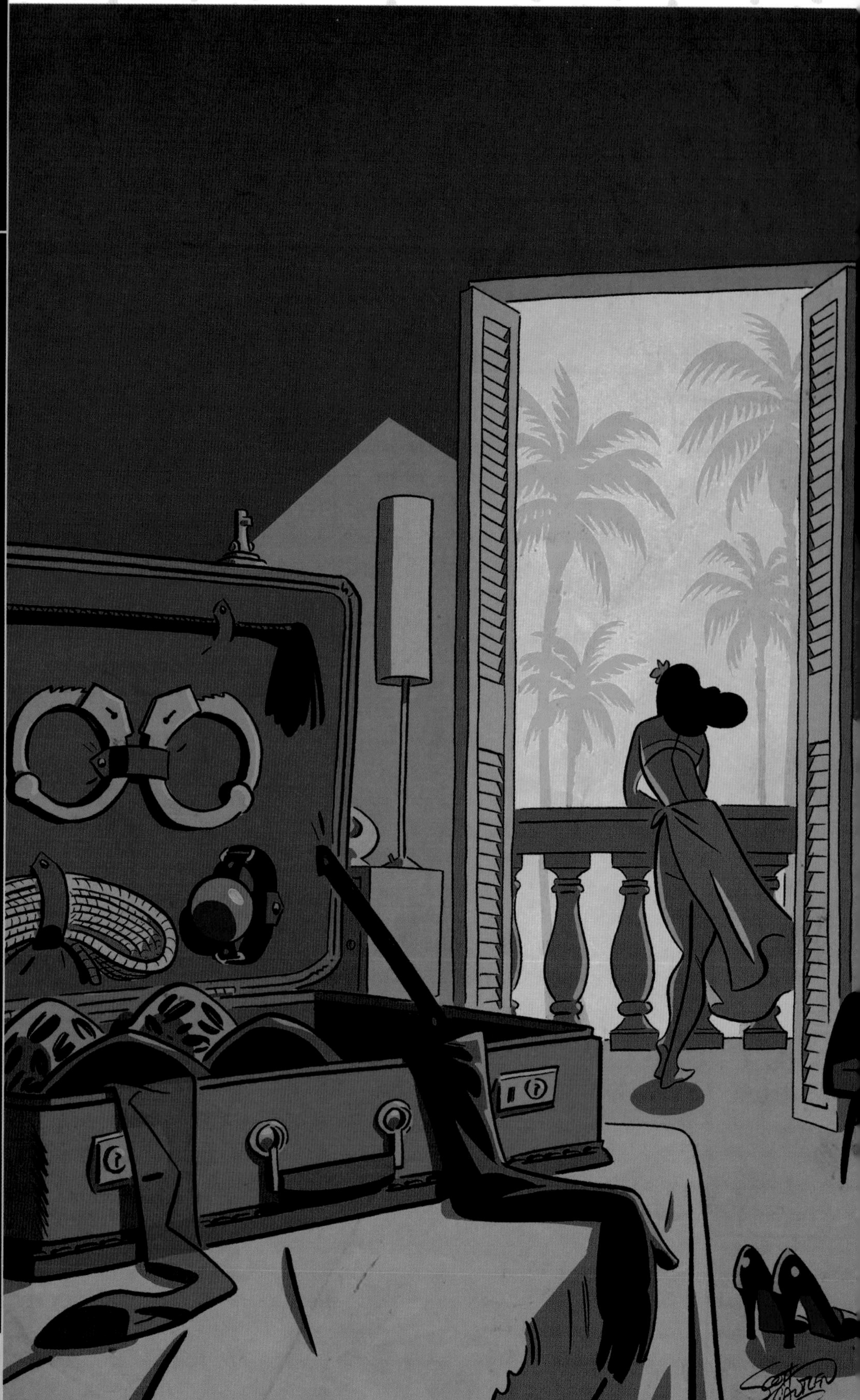

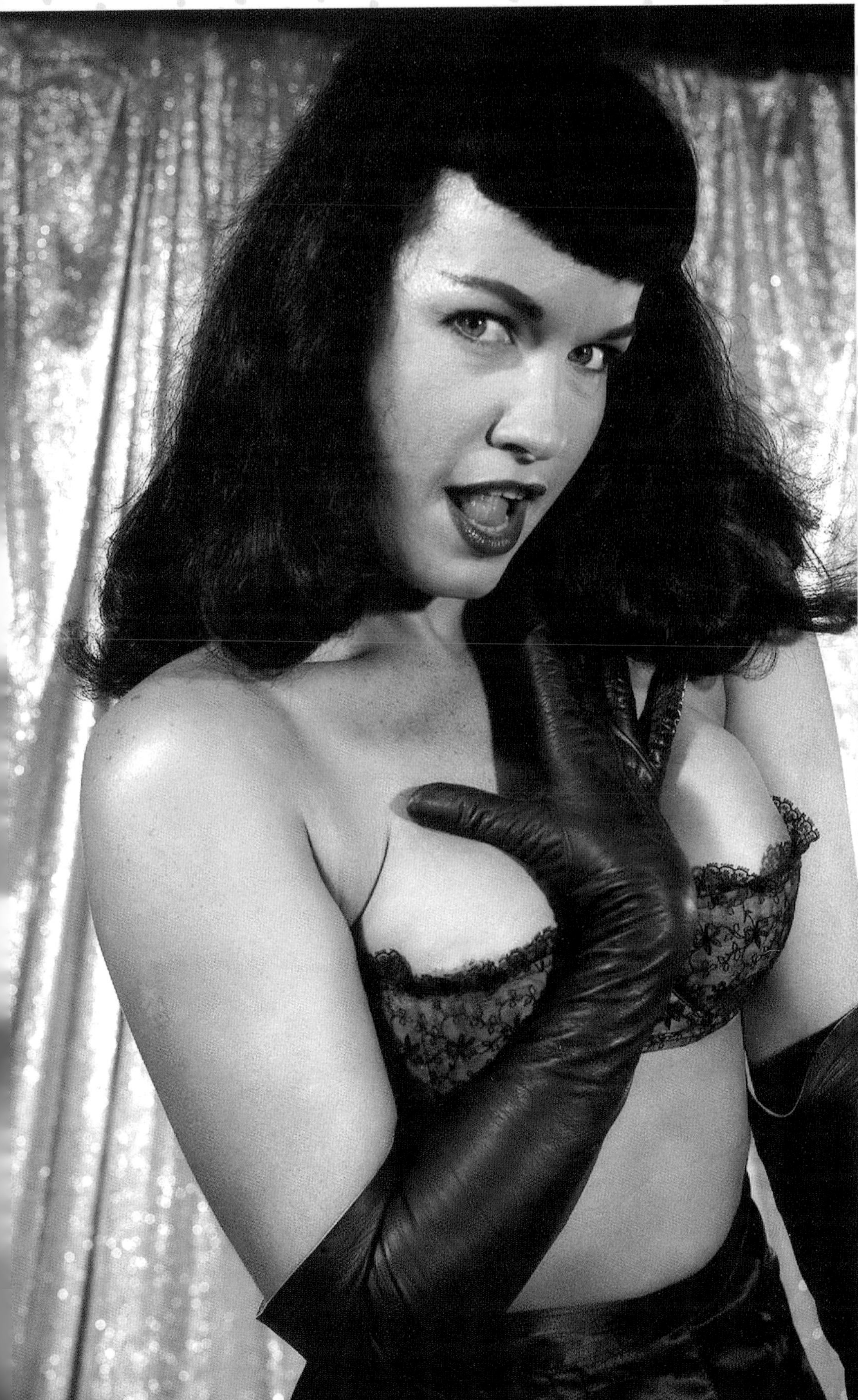

THE ORIGINAL QUEEN OF THE PIN-UPS IS BACK IN ACTION!

Bettie Page

AVALLONE | WORLEY

BETTIE IN HOLLYWOOD

1

LINSNER ©2017.

DYNAMITE.

PLUS AN EXCLUSIVE SHORT STORY BY AVALLONE & JOSEPH MICHAEL LINSNER ORIGINALLY PUBLISHED IN PLAYBOY!

Collecting issues 1-4 of the hit series by David Avallone, Colton Worley & more!

AVAILABLE IN PRINT AND DIGITALLY

ISBN13: 978-1-5241-0644-7

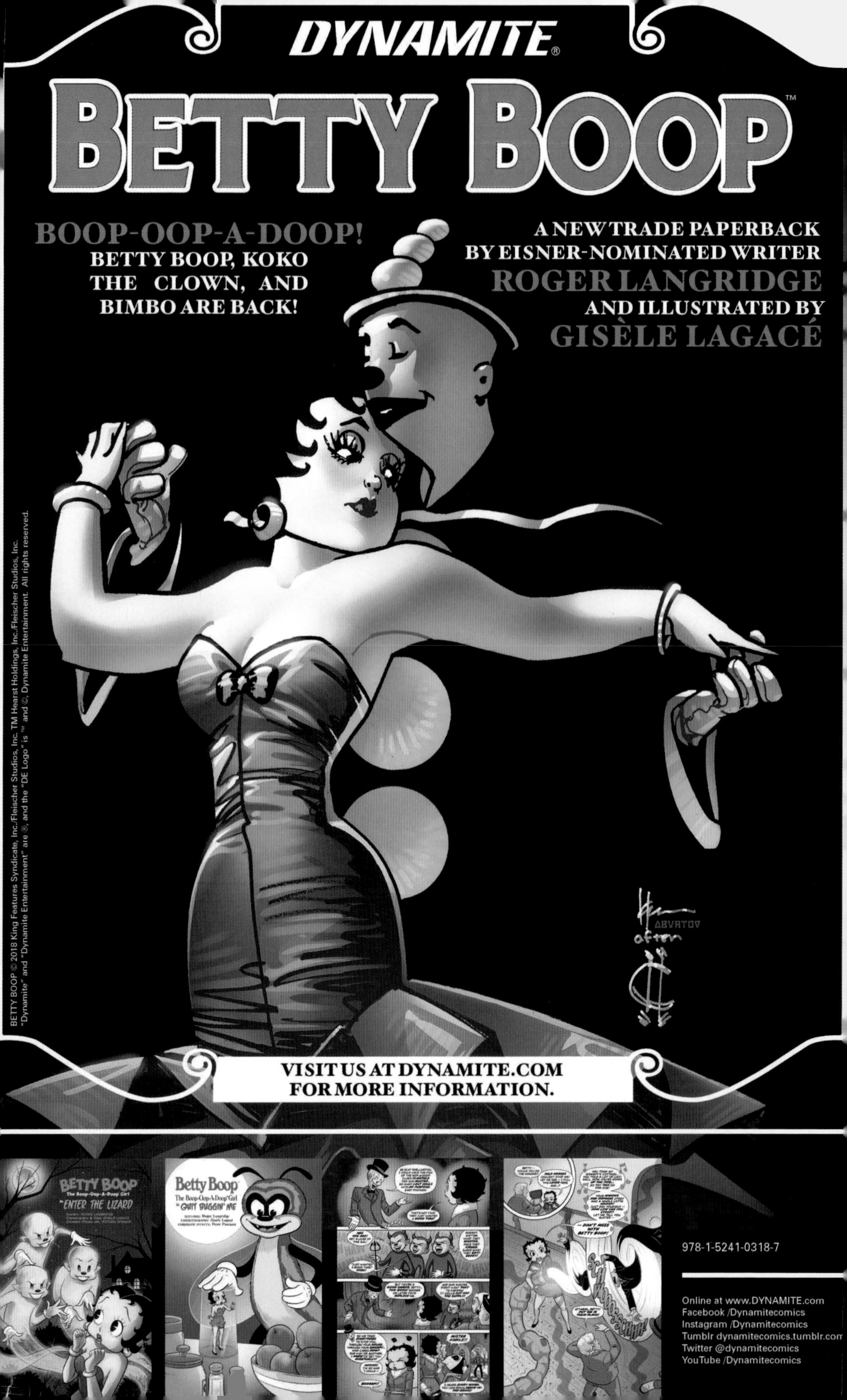
DYNAMITE®
BETTY BOOP™
BOOP-OOP-A-DOOP!
BETTY BOOP, KOKO THE CLOWN, AND BIMBO ARE BACK!
A NEW TRADE PAPERBACK BY EISNER-NOMINATED WRITER
ROGER LANGRIDGE
AND ILLUSTRATED BY
GISÈLE LAGACÉ
VISIT US AT DYNAMITE.COM FOR MORE INFORMATION.
BETTY BOOP
The Boop-Oop-A-Doop Girl
in "ENTER THE LIZARD
Betty Boop
The Boop-Oop-A-Doop Girl
in "QUIT BUGGIN' ME
978-1-5241-0318-7
Online at www.DYNAMITE.com
Facebook /Dynamitecomics
Instagram /Dynamitecomics
Tumblr dynamitecomics.tumblr.com
Twitter @dynamitecomics
YouTube /Dynamitecomics

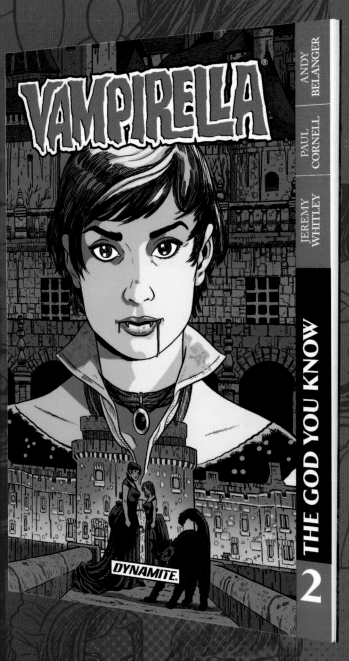
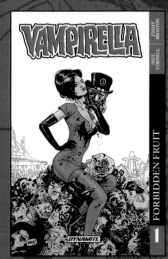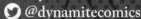